TWICE AN ANGEL

Living and Dying with Lyme Disease

The Jenny Umphress Story

For Jeanne & Russ
for LOVE of FAMILY
Marilyn Nelson
April 2012

by

Susan Umphress

and

Marilyn Nelson

Published in the United States.

ISBN 1-890050-39-3

- Some scripture quotations are taken from *The Living Bible* copyright © 1971. Used by permission of Tyndale House Publishers, Inc., Wheaton, IL, 60189. All rights reserved.

- *Climb Till Your Dream Comes True* used with permission of The Helen Steiner Rice Foundation, Atrium Two, 221 E. Fourth St., Cincinnati, OH 45202.

- *The Dance* by Tony Arata; publishers—Morgan Music Group, Nashville, TN.

- Josh Loth Liebman's *Treasure each other* verse from *Just Between Friends* DayBrightener TM by Garborgs, Bloomington, MN.

Book cover background photograph by Eric V. Nelson. Photograph on divider pages by Eric V. Nelson.

Book cover designed by and book printed at

Carlisle Printing

WALNUT CREEK

Sugarcreek, OH 44681

DEDICATION

This book is dedicated with love and encouragement
to Jenny's special friend, Amy Poe, and to all
who gallantly fight Lyme—especially patients
and their loved ones.

A REASONABLE THOUGHT

"Mom, it is bad enough to be sick and have Lyme
disease. But it is worse to have to keep proving
it over and over again."

Jenny

ILLUSTRATIONS

Pages 149 – 154
Pages 269 – 276

CONTENTS

PART ONE
NO MORE WONDERLAND FOR JENNY

PART TWO
REMISSION REVOKED

PART THREE
THE FINAL JOURNEY

ACKNOWLEDGMENTS

When Jenny Umphress told her mother, Sue, she wanted to write a book about her life with Lyme disease, her mother said no. Sue could not conceive of reliving Jenny's painful, traumatic struggles with Lyme. After Jenny died, Sue said, "It is the only time I ever told Jenny no. This book must be written. Jenny wanted to help others through her story."

Twice An Angel is a kaleidoscope of information gleaned from many sources: conversations and interviews with Jenny's family, friends, teachers, therapists and nurses, and selections from medical records. Jenny's diaries and other personal papers are imprinted with her vibrancy for life, her intense internal pain and confusion, her deep desire to just be normal, and her great love for people and her God. In school papers and professional correspondence, Jenny was careful about spelling. In her personal writing, she concentrated only on her subject. This book contains her "original" spelling.

Anecdotes and dialogue have been recorded as accurately as possible to preserve the richness and generosity of the pattern of her life. The names of some people, hospitals and places have been changed.

We are indebted to Lyme patients and their families we have met, and the stories of others shared through Lyme support group newsletters and books, including Polly Murray's *The Widening Circle: A Lyme Disease Pioneer Tells Her Story.* Scientific papers provided a better understanding of the complexity and many faces of Lyme disease.

The heartfelt thoughts in the Foreward were written by the first doctor who diagnosed and treated Jenny for Lyme—we extend her our sincere appreciation. We are also indebted to Dr. Joseph T. Joseph for his sensitive message in the Afterward, and to Rodney P. Anderson, Ph.D., for his advice. The spirited support and expertise of Claude C. Smith, D.A., whose brother was diagnosed with Lyme disease after this manuscript was completed, has been invaluable. And we thank friends who reviewed all or parts of the manuscript: Pastor Dave Thompson, Sandy Waggoner, Cathy Nelson, Pat Parteleno and Fran Dean.

Jenny's mother has relived Jenny's journey with Lyme—many times over. Sue wrote the initial pages upon which this book is based, provided invaluable details along the way, and reviewed the manuscript. Without Sue's love for and belief in her daughter, Jenny's story would have remained in the memories of those who knew her.

Lastly, I am grateful to my life partner, my husband, Eric V. Nelson, Ph.D., for his love and encouragement. In addition to critiquing and formatting the manuscript, he faithfully kept both me and our computers "in program" during the research and writing of Jenny's book.

Marilyn Nelson
Celina, Ohio

FOREWARD

Twice An Angel is the extraordinary story of a very remarkable young girl who died in 1994 after living with and suffering through many years of chronic Lyme disease with relapses and remissions.

I had the privilege of caring for Jenny during a few of those years and seeing the courage and patience that she had to endure not only the symptoms of her illness but the ordeal of treatment. In spite of all she went through, Jenny made every effort to live as full a life of a teenager as possible.

Not only was she an inspiration to her family and friends, but she was very much an inspiration to the physicians and other medical personnel who had the privilege of caring for her during these difficult years.

Jenny's mother has done an outstanding job of presenting the inspirational story of her daughter's journey through not only this illness but through life.

Reading *Twice An Angel* is an inspiration not just for Lyme patients and their families, but also for those in the medical profession entrusted with their care.

The reader can see how aggressively Jenny fought to live and appreciate how precious she believed life to be. Would that all young people could have such respect for life and for the years allowed them on this earth.

Shared by *Dr. Paige,* the first doctor to
diagnose and treat Jenny for Lyme disease

INTRODUCTION

In the summer of 1988, Jenny Umphress, 15, was unknowingly bitten by a tick. During a checkup that fall for Jenny's acne, her mother had the dermatologist look at a rash that was all over Jenny's body. "I have never seen anything quite like it," he puzzled. Jenny also had two tiny bites that seemed to be infected. One on her wrist and the other on her thigh.

That Thanksgiving, Jenny became sick. When she did not get better and tests did not provide a medical diagnosis, doctors concluded her physical symptoms were due to psychiatric problems, a common catch-all for Lyme disease patients.

Repeatedly hospitalized from December 1988 through May 1989, Jenny lost her memory and physically deteriorated. She could not walk, talk or eat. After months of frustration and anguish, a nursing friend "diagnosed" Jenny from *Newsweek's* May 22, 1989, cover story, "Tiny Tick, Big Worry."

Medical crises took Jenny and Sue from Ohio to New Jersey twice by air ambulance where Jenny spent 70 days in intensive care. She was the most serious Lyme case her specialists in New Jersey, had ever seen and her story was carried nationwide on the AP news service. Jenny's medical combat was fought on the home front, in emergency rooms, and in intensive care units in three states. After many bitter experiences, her mother was forged into Jenny's patient advocate and one of her primary caretakers.

Enduring the cruel stages of Lyme, Jenny slowly made determined steps forward. The family celebrated "a cure" in 1991. On a local Christian television segment called "Learning By Heart" Jenny was chatty, reflective, sincere, tender, loving and funny. Jenny learned to drive a car and volunteered at a hospital. But after a relapse that fall, the family had to come face to face with the fact—Jenny was not cured.

Jenny's struggle with Lyme lasted almost six years. As she battled the disease known as the Great Masquerader, Jenny spoke of thankfulness, anger, impatience with God, of a stronger faith in God and of greater love for people. "I'm going to make the most of what I have," she said at a difficult time.

She graduated from high school with honors in 1994. That summer, this bright, right-to-my-life young lady roller-bladed through her hometown, Ada, Ohio. For a very short time, life was golden. She died that August. She was 21.

The April before she died, Jenny went to the Gospel Music Association Convention and Dove Awards in Nashville, Tennessee, with hometown musicians. Jenny became excited about sharing her story to encourage Lyme patients to persistently seek out medical institutions and doctors knowledgeable about Lyme. There is no 100 % accurate test for Lyme, and no single dependable treatment. Jenny knew this frustration and didn't want others to suffer abuse and humiliation of misdiagnosis.

The Centers for Disease Control and Prevention cited almost 16,000 cases of Lyme *reported* thus far for 1998. The CDC believes Lyme is *under* diagnosed and *under* reported, and *the real number could be six to ten times that reported.* A doctor who has treated over 3,000 Lyme patients believes Lyme is the second fastest growing infectious disease in the U.S. It is the fastest growing vector-borne disease.

The Lyme vaccine recently made available is a hopeful first step, but not infallible or approved for everyone, according to a Lyme expert. Increased research funds, and the dissemination of facts to the general public and to medical communities will change Lyme disease statistics and suffering.

As managing editor of Jenny's hometown newspaper, I featured her successes. I wrote, "Much of her recent history is recorded on hospital charts and prescription labels. But, as in all great stories, the dearest lessons are written deeply upon the hearts of people..." This is Jenny's story, as told by her mother.

Marilyn Nelson

PART ONE

NO MORE
WONDERLAND
FOR JENNY

1. A Wilted Birthday Cake

We had never had a real vacation. Our great adventure came along in 1988, when my youngest brother, Scott, moved his family to Georgia from our hometown of Ada, Ohio. I promised our kids, Jenny, almost 15, and Tommy, 11, that if there was any way we could possibly pay for it, we would visit their three cousins and Uncle Scott and Aunt Connie. Scott and his family were homesick and we missed them too. Our families had always been close.

After brain storming and scrimping, we managed to finance the trip with the help, as Tommy remembers, of having a garage sale. When my husband, Jon, decided he would stay home and work, it was just the Three Musketeers to get ready for the road.

The kids were thrilled. Tommy and Jenny were tight as skin for a brother and sister, so I wasn't worried about how they would get along on a trip. In all their growing up years, I couldn't remember them having a real fight, and their spankings could be counted on one hand. As little tykes, if one did happen to get a spanking, it was predictable that the other one would cry too.

The previous summer, when Jenny was asked what she wanted for her 14th birthday, she had requested an evening of World Federation Wrestling. Jon, Tommy and Jenny were into it, so we made an overnight trip to Dayton.

The jam-packed arena and sweaty fans made me so miserable I would have paid $5 for a soft drink. Sitting on a straight chair with my long legs crammed almost clear to my chin, I thought, "Jenny, I hope you are really enjoying this birthday."

When Junk Yard Dog picked Tommy to go up into the big ring, Jenny rooted and carried on like the little old ladies who weren't looking any too prim and proper. Jenny's interest in wrestling was contrary to her "have to have everything just so-

so" femininity. Intense about all her interests, our sweet Jenny subscribed to wrestling magazines, and posters of wrestlers decorated her bedroom walls that year.

As our Georgia trip approached, Jenny made a list for each of us, detailing clothing, personal items and other things she was sure we would need for our vacation. Organization was Jenny's middle name. Tommy said this was a "super dumb" idea and proceeded to just throw things into his suitcase. To this day, those Georgia travel lists are tucked away with Jenny's things.

Arrangements were made to travel by bus. Plans included celebrating Jenny's 15th birthday on July 16, and celebrating Connie's birthday on July 17. "If you had waited six more minutes to be born, we would have shared a birthday," Connie always teased Jenny.

There was a terrible drought that summer. The grass was so brown you couldn't walk barefoot without cutting your feet, water was limited, and the crops looked terrible. But, the buses were running and our travel plans remained firm.

Grandma Epley took us to the station. As we boarded the bus, Jenny sat beside a black, middle-aged military man who had no idea what was ahead of him. Jenny loved to talk and he was about to get at least one leg talked off.

Tommy and I sat smashed together in a seat with a heavy-set lady, while Jenny enjoyed her new friend. It seemed like a long, long trip. Through dusty bus windows, we saw dry, dying grass trailing the roadsides all along the way. At certain stops, new drivers took over the route. The kids took delight in each little thing.

The cousins went wild when they saw each other, and Connie was anxious to show us their home where she had a beautiful double-layer birthday cake waiting. Just as planned, we arrived on Jenny's birthday. But, by the time we got to the house, the heat and humidity had taken a toll on Jenny's cake. The frosting was melting and the whole cake drooped sadly to one side of the plate. Wilted cake or not, Jenny blew out her candles and we celebrated her birthday in style.

It was as wild as a Mardi Gras when our two families were together. First, the kids fussed over their new puppies. Then Tommy and Eric played soldiers of fortune by shooting each other in the bottom with BB guns, much to the distress of parents. Scott got the video camera as close as possible for a picture of the peach fuzz appearing on Tommy's chin. "It's man stuff!" Tommy told his Uncle Scott.

Trying to make up for lost time, we were constantly on the go. We ate peaches, peaches and more peaches, and rode hang gliders and raced cars and visited monuments and amusement parks. And then we spent an idyllic day at Lookout Mountain, Tennessee. Little did we know, our lives would change forever from that outing.

Jenny and her youngest cousin, Gail, decided to tramp off on their own. After searching for some time, we finally found them. Overflowing with giggles, the girls thought it was funny that we had formed a mini-search party for them.

"You were lost, not us," they laughed. In the photo album from that trip there is a picture of Jenny, Tommy and me standing next to their cousins on Lookout Mountain with four states in view over our shoulders. I don't need the picture to vividly remember the scene.

In no time our week visit was swiftly gone. As we organized to return home, it was decided Tommy would stay with Eric in Georgia and cousin Sharon would use Tom's ticket. Scott's family planned to travel north the following week so we "swapped kids." The ride home could not match the excitement of the trip south. Even Sharon was bored.

Gracie

Life returned to normal when we got back home where Jenny easily entertained herself in her room if others were busy. She loved music and spent a lot of time making tapes and singing to tapes. Before singing a solo at church, she would practice the music over and over. Other times her room was a beehive of cleaning and "decorating." She arranged, rearranged and organized everything she touched.

With a natural love for people and a delight in doing things for others, Jenny had many friends, but one friend was special, another Jenny. The two girls had shared the silliness of youth and the grief of great loss. Jenny Young had lost her mother to cancer and a few years later her father to a heart problem.

Through the good times and the bad the girls were there for each other. I always told our Jenny, "If you are lucky enough to have one special friend in your lifetime, you are a very fortunate person." A regular in our household, bright, brunette, button-sized Jenny Y. seemed just like another daughter.

During that summer, our Jenny sold ads house to house for the school yearbook staff. She also baby-sat, and did odd jobs to make money so she could go shopping. Jenny loved to shop. When she found a perfect something, especially a gift for someone else, it always made her day. She also enjoyed playing the piano, a refined interest compared to her love of wrestling.

Both kids were homebodies. As youngsters they had friends over for camping in the backyard, parties, putting on original plays which Jenny made up and directed, playing school and Barbies (girls only), and discovering the joy of cooking—along with just plain foolin' around. Other times, Jenny raced around town on her bike or on roller skates. When I heard a roaring thunder, I knew kids would soon be rolling right into the house.

Jenny loved to tell friends, "Oh, I have this hole in my leg because my mom never took care of me when I fell on my roller skates. She was too cheap—she never got me stitches. That's why I have that hole in my knee." After she became sick with Lyme, she had no memory of the incident except when told stories from her childhood.

A smiling Jenny would frequently pop in the back door at my folks' house, usually with little friends in tow. Both Grandma and Grandpa Epley received warm hugs. If they weren't feeling well, she would make sure to check up on them.

Even as a youngster there didn't seem to be enough time for all she wanted to do. Clumsy and hurried in everything she did, she earned the family nickname "Gracie."

Most of the people Jenny came in contact with were special to her, and she took the time to visit and write personal notes.

She had a warmth, a way of making them close to her, and when she smiled, she radiated the serenity of a sunset. People felt good just being around her. At other times, she was wonderfully goofy. I was constantly aware of how much I loved her.

One day, when she was around 12 or so, Jenny shocked me to my toes. She had just come back from visiting an elderly friend.

"Mom, did you know Mrs. Hermanne has boobs that hang clear down to her belly button?"

Apparently, Mrs. Hermanne had been dressed in an ill-fitting nightgown. I paused for a breath before responding. "Jenny, why are you saying that stuff?"

"Mom, I never seen such long things in my life. Did you know they hung clear down there, Mom? Did you?" She was as honest and as innocent as a newborn babe.

Ninth Grade

Toward the end of summer, we bought school clothes and school supplies. It remained hot and dry and the kids dreaded going back to school where the classrooms would be stifling with the heat.

Several people asked me, "What bit Jenny?" when they noticed two tiny bites on her. It seemed like she had the marks for a long time, but I thought they were nothing more than infected mosquito bites. Each bite had a large red area around it.

Except for the heat, nothing slowed her down. In the fall, she went off to school with her brother and some of the kids I baby-sat. As a ninth grader, Jenny loved school. She earned good grades and got along with everyone. Mature for her age, she was blunt without being rude. If she didn't agree with something, she would say so. Teachers liked her and her circle of friends knew no end.

Jenny didn't require a lot of attention. She wasn't loud. Years later, when her senior class voted her "the shyest," she was embarrassed. "Mom, the shyest—now isn't that a compliment? The shyest. Why would they vote *me* the shyest?" I had told her, "It could have been worse. You could have been voted the ugliest. Now *that* would be embarrassing."

In October, a schoolmate asked her to go to the homecoming dance. He was Jenny Y.'s cousin, so the two Jennys decided to double date. On the eve of homecoming, her first date, I wrote Jenny a letter:

> ...my thoughts are on you right now. I am so fortunate to have a girl like you. I thought this weekend would take forever to come, but these last 15 years have flown by so quickly. I can't believe my little girl is going on her first date and to her first high school dance.
>
> Sometimes it scares me that this time is going so fast. But I know in the back of my mind, even though you are growing up, you are not growing AWAY from me, because we will always be close...
>
> I know we will always share, feel, love and care for each other...I wish I could protect you from all the tough times, but I wouldn't be letting you have a normal life. Life has ups and downs. You just have to ride the hilly roads. But believe me the ups definitely outweigh the downs. And after you go through the downs, it makes you appreciate the ups so much more. I'm so proud of you, and all your achievements so far in your

life. You have to be the most caring, loving child a person could have. I know you will always stay the same and also please bear with me, because moms have ups and downs too!

I LOVE YOU and will always be there.

Love, Mom

We hunted everywhere to find the *right* dress. After we found the right dress, we needed the *right* scarf to go with it. Then we needed bright red shoes to match. Jenny begged me to give her a permanent because her hair had no curl whatsoever. I took a chance. Rather, Jenny took a chance. It was the first permanent I ever gave and it took me three hours just to roll it. Surprisingly, it took and the curly style with bangs looked great on her.

Jenny beamed with confidence in her cream dress with red scarf and shoes. Her date gave her a red wrist corsage. She was one excited freshman by the time she left for her first high school dance. Both Jennys and their dates looked all grown up. Memories of this special evening would one day seem disconnected to the years which followed.

Later that fall, everything seemed okay, except Jenny wasn't as energetic as usual. She tired easily and started taking little catnaps. Other than that, all was normal. Jenny still had a little mark on her wrist, but nothing else seemed out of the ordinary.

Thanksgiving

In November, we were delighted when Scott's family announced they were coming home from Georgia for Thanksgiving. Letters never made up for visits. Jenny asked if she could plan the Thanksgiving menu and make the meal. I told her I would buy what she needed and help her if she wanted help.

As Thanksgiving approached, Jenny seemed tired and not up to par, but she showed me her Thanksgiving menu and we bought the groceries for her special dinner. The day before Thanksgiving I asked her if she wanted me to help.

"I don't feel good. I don't think I have the energy to cook," she responded.

Jenny always gave a task her best. I couldn't understand what was wrong. It wasn't like her to give up the honor of being the chef for something like a Thanksgiving feast.

She thought maybe she had the flu, and asked me to make the meal she had planned. It was odd, but we had a full house of company and I needed to get the Thanksgiving dinner made. Jenny rested. She obviously didn't feel good.

Our double family enjoyed the dinner except for Jenny, who had little appetite. It just wasn't our lively, go-getter Jenny who had been so excited to make plans for the visit with Scott's family. Along with her holiday food list, she had made a list of things to do, including a night of family bowling.

Friday night came and Jenny still didn't feel good, but she wanted to go along with the family. At the bowling alley, she seemed confused and weak. She rubbed her head as if it was really hurting, but she never complained.

"What's wrong with Jenny?" Aunt Connie asked. Observant as an eagle, Connie never missed anything. While we enjoyed pizza, Jenny sipped on pop. Finally, it became obvious Jenny was very sick and we needed to leave. When we got home, she went straight to bed.

Jenny slept all through Saturday until Sunday noon. We had plans to go out for dinner around three in the afternoon, since some of the other kids had also slept in. Jenny got up and forced herself to get ready.

When I checked on a loud thump in the bathroom, I found her passed out on the floor. After arousing her, I helped her change her clothes and put her to bed

"What's wrong?" I asked. She simply said, "I don't feel good." Her symptoms were a headache, weakness, and "just being sick." She was also nauseated.

The next day, I made an appointment with Dr. Porter, our family doctor. His casual appearance contrasted with his direct approach in diagnosing. He said she had the flu and I should take her home, give her an over-the-counter pain medicine, bed rest and liquids. Nothing helped.

When I took her back to the doctor, he determined she had a really bad case of the flu that was probably going to take a while to get over. I continued treating her as instructed, but she was getting weaker by the day. I had never seen a flu like this. When she said her muscles and joints hurt, I decided that was from being in bed so much.

Pale, with no strength, Jenny had to drop out of the jazz and gymnastic lessons she had recently started. On our third trip to Dr. Porter, he drew blood for a mononucleosis test. It proved to be negative. Jenny had not been this sick when she did have a case of mono the previous April. Worrying and visits to our family doctor weren't making her better. Something else had to be done.

2. The Nightmare Begins

By early December 1988, Jenny looked terrible. She tried to eat, but continued to be nauseated and weak. "Are you hungry for anything?" I would ask. Biscuits and gravy from a local restaurant or a milk shake were the only things she desired. When she lost 15 pounds in two weeks and began to complain of abdominal pain, I called our family doctor again.

When I discovered he was out of town, it gave me the boost I needed to make an appointment with another doctor. Jenny was so sick I had a hard time getting her to the office, but I thought—maybe by going to another doctor, maybe Jenny would get better. Unfortunately, the reverse was true, and the next office visit proved to be the first scene of a long nightmare.

On this first visit to Dr. Adder, Jenny was diagnosed with a possible urinary tract infection and he put her on an antibiotic. When Jenny didn't get any better, I took her back and Dr. Adder re-examined her. Heavy-set and balding, his examination appeared precise but his diagnosis was inconclusive. Realizing she was worse, he admitted her to the hospital for examination by a pediatrician for a possible pelvic infection.

It was December 7, 1988, when Jenny was admitted to Miseracordia Hospital in the northwest Ohio community of Lamont, with a diagnosis of abdominal pains of unknown etiology and a second diagnosis of carbohydrate intolerance with persistent hypoglycemia. We had no way of knowing this hospital visit would stretch to almost six years of rushing by private car, in rescue squads, air ambulances and life flight to emergency rooms, to long-term intensive care admissions, and for endless surgeries, medications and therapy sessions.

On her medical record of that first hospital physical, the pediatrician, Dr. Masser, wrote, "She is a very happy looking child who does not resist any suggestions at all and goes along with everything that is explained and told to her."

On December 9, they brought in a gynecologist who felt a diagnostic laparoscopy was needed. Surgery went well and no problems were found. Coming back from surgery, Jenny was alert. When the pediatrician came into the room, Jenny suddenly became lethargic and pale.

The five hour glucose ordered by the doctor showed abnormal results. The next day, Jenny began having dry heaves and was put on IV fluids since she couldn't eat. An ultrasound of her pancreas tested negative.

On December 12, Jenny was put on an 1800 calorie diabetic diet and the IVs were discontinued. Dr. Masser wrote on her chart, "In spite of significant encouragement and significant amounts of try on the patient's part, we would not get more than 200 - 400 calories per day and blood sugars ranged below 60."

Before Jenny got sick, she carried 160 pounds on her 5' 7" frame. Upon discharge from this first hospitalization she weighed 136 pounds. The pediatrician ordered a NG (nasogastric) tube because Jenny was continuing to go downhill. On December 13, a NG feeding tube was inserted down Jenny's nose.

More Punishment than Treatment

I felt so bad for Jenny. She was trying hard to eat and gain weight, but she wasn't improving. The doctor made Jenny feel like the NG tube was a punishment, since her weight wasn't going up. It broke my heart to see her in such pain and discomfort. At times, all I could do was leave her hospital room so Jenny wouldn't see me cry.

One day when I returned to her room, she held my hand and said, "It's okay." She told me I shouldn't feel bad. That was Jenny's mode of operation. Always more worried about how others felt than about how she was doing. Dr. Masser told us to put the nose tube in and take it out everyday. It was difficult to think about doing this to Jenny, considering the pain of having the tube inserted and the discomfort while in place.

The doctor hoped Jenny would not like having the nose tube put in often, so she would begin to eat and gain weight. As far as I was concerned, this was no better than medieval thinking. Jenny was giving all she could, as the doctor had acknowledged in her written report.

Why would a doctor want to make any patient feel they needed to be punished? My constant prayer was that Dr. Masser would start thinking clearer and come through for our girl.

A nurse, a large, large lady, came in to insert the tube. Jenny had a night light on her bedside table, a gift from a friend. The nurse knocked it over, breaking it, and never said a word. While I was upset about the indifferent attitude of the nurse, I had an even harder time accepting Dr. Masser's instruction about daily insertions of the nose tube.

The nurse had a difficult time getting the tube down Jenny's nose. When they showed me how to do the procedure, I knew right then I wasn't about to do that to Jenny all the time. The doctor didn't need to know that tube would just stay in. Jenny didn't need punishment.

When Jenny was discharged from the hospital, her chart read: "Her condition does not show any significant improvement, maybe a little more energy." The gynecologist felt the abdominal pain was from adhesions from an earlier surgery. We were instructed to return to the pediatrician's office in three days. We also had to have a home health nurse, since Jenny had a NG tube.

One good thing came from the nose tube. Arrangements were made with an area pharmacy for Jenny's food supplement, which proved to be a blessing in disguise. We didn't know it, but we were in for a long struggle, and the staff at this pharmacy would become supportive, understanding friends.

The first home health nurse knew instantly something was really wrong with Jenny, and she told us it was ridiculous to put the NG tube in as instructed. "No one deserves that treatment," she said. One time, when the tube came out, even the nurse couldn't get it back in. We called Cathy Nelson, a good friend who is a nurse. Cathy eventually managed to get the tube into Jenny's nose.

Outspoken, determined Cathy always stood up for what she believed was right. Together we decided the doctor didn't need to know the tube was just left in. When we visited her office, we took the tube out, then put it back in when we got home. The home health nurse couldn't have been kinder to Jenny.

Hardly a Christmas

Our house filled up at Christmas time when Scott's family came back to town for the holidays. They were shocked to see how Jenny looked. Even with the tube feedings and her enormous efforts to eat, Jenny was getting weaker and weaker.

On December 26, I took Jenny back to Dr. Masser's office for a checkup. We had been doing blood sugar tests on her regularly, which continued to be low even with tube feedings. Jenny was lethargic by this time. At the office she weighed in two pounds less. The doctor decided to put her back into the hospital to do a pancreatic scan and put her on around the clock tube feedings.

Jenny was admitted on December 27, and discharged on December 28. The diagnosis was hyperinsulinemia with carbohydrate intolerance. We were to keep her on 1800 calorie tube feedings around the clock and take her to Overton, a teaching hospital in Clark, Ohio, an hour plus drive east of home, after the first of the year. Her tube feedings were switched from one brand to another.

When the home health nurse came to check Jenny the next day, she was shocked at her condition. Lethargic, with severe diarrhea, Jenny could no longer walk, so we had her sleeping on a hide-a-bed in the living room. In fact, she was so weak she could hardly raise her head off the pillow. Concerned that our Jenny would become dehydrated, the nurse called the pediatrician and said Jenny needed immediate medical care. It was decided to re-admit her to the hospital.

Only one day after discharge, Jenny was back in Miseracordia with a principal diagnosis of possible viral syndrome and a second diagnosis of carbohydrate intolerance with hyperinsulinemia. She was put on IVs because of dehydration. The doctor thought the diarrhea was caused from changing the type of tube feedings.

Shock Treatment

During her December 29, admission to Miseracordia, Jenny received unbelievably malicious treatment. One day Dr. Masser slapped Jenny across the face right in front of me, saying it would knock some sense into her, since her problems were all psychosomatic.

I was appalled beyond belief and I thought our gentle minister, Pastor Dave, was going to knock the doctor out. With her jet black eyes piercing through us, Dr. Masser also told us Jenny was dumping her tube feeding in an effort to lose weight because of anorexia.

In my whole life I couldn't remember ever disliking someone that much. I never felt I could leave Jenny's side, not knowing what would happen to her next.

"I try and I try, but it's never enough," Jenny told me. "I'm so afraid they will never find out what's wrong with me. I know they think it's all in my head and they want to send me away. I just want to get well."

Psychological cases are often grave and alarming. But a mother knows her child, and there was no doubt in my mind Jenny was physically sick. She had been a happy, well-balanced teenager who loved life, who got along with everyone, and was looking forward to Thanksgiving when she suddenly collapsed. This doctor had to be crazy if she thought Jenny was crazy.

By December 30, Jenny was experiencing tremendous memory loss. Just five days earlier, for Christmas, she had received a gift camera because she so enjoyed her photography class at school. Jenny had no memory of the camera or of Christmas. She had forgotten so much. I couldn't take it in. What was happening to our Jenny?

Her headaches were severe and she was now experiencing photophobia. Any light bothered her terribly. She also continued to be extremely lethargic.

Earlier, when the pediatrician mentioned diabetes, I remembered Jenny having those bites and mentioned them to the doctor, knowing diabetic sores do not heal easily. Our family and friends were also concerned as we tried to make sense of what was happening. Anything seemed more reasonable than what the doctors were suggesting.

Jenny continued to receive appalling treatment from the pediatrician and some of the staff. I could feel a difference in attitude from nurse to nurse. One time, as I returned from the snack shop, I saw Jon at the nursing station and heard sobbing from Jenny's room. When I entered the room, Jenny was propped up in a chair with a pelvic spotlight shining in her face and a food tray pushed up to her. There was a different nurse with Jenny who had told her, "When you eat the meal, the spotlight will be removed." Already desperately sick and suffering with photophobia, she was being tortured by the light.

Mentally, I had had many arguments with the pediatrician's statement that Jenny was dumping her feeding tube at home and that was why she was losing weight. We had made a room for Jenny in the front of the house. She was so weak she couldn't walk. Even if she could have gotten to the bathroom, we were always with her.

My mental argument continued: If this was the case, why did Jenny continue losing weight in the hospital under their care? Jenny was losing weight because she was sick. Something was *really physically wrong.*

When I took in how Jenny was being tortured with the pelvic light beamed at her face, I raced to the nursing station. A nurse who had taken care of Jenny previously jumped up and flew to Jenny's room. She ordered the other nurse to get rid of the food tray, unplugged the light herself and pushed it back, demanding that the nurse, "Get this child back into bed, now!"

To say the least, she was shocked at the other nurse's behavior. When I said I never wanted that nurse allowed in Jenny's room again, I was assured it would be taken care of.

During the New Year's holiday, Jenny's pediatrician, Dr. Masser, went on a trip with her family. Part of me was so upset. She was out having fun with her children, and my daughter was in the hospital. I had to keep in mind that, after the first of the year, Jenny was scheduled for a transfer to Overton Hospital in Clark. Maybe we would find some hope there.

Another pediatrician covered the case while Jenny's pediatrician was gone. After examining Jenny, he felt strongly she had encephalitis because of her symptoms. He wanted Dr. Sommers, a neurologist, to see Jenny.

My girlfriend, Cathy, had been following Jenny's case closely. She was there when the neurologist came. People always knew exactly where they stood with her. She didn't hesitate to say what she believed. Cathy had worked with Dr. Sommers several times and told me, "This doctor tells you right up front if there is nothing wrong."

Dr. Sommers was gentle in spite of her large hands, and her bright, open face seemed to reflect her attitude. After examining Jenny thoroughly, Dr. Sommers wrote on her history that Jenny complained of low back pain with neck flexion or with extension of her knees when her hips were flexed, and the complaint of low back pain came without leading questions. That is one of the symptoms of encephalitis. Her impression of Jenny's history and physical was "subacute illness which includes low grade fever, headache and lethargy." She confirmed Jenny had a severe case of photophobia.

The neurologist was sincerely concerned and stuck close by Jenny. She did many tests, including a Lyme titer. When Jenny's pediatrician, Dr. Masser, returned, she didn't want the neurologist to pursue her concerns, since Jenny would soon be transferred to Overton.

Thanks for Listening

Sometime in the coming year, I found a letter tucked into Jenny's Bible. She had written it by hand to Dr. Masser in December 1988, but never mailed it:

> Dear Dr. I'm so tired, my body doesn't seem to be able to shake this.
>
> I'm scared not because I have diabetes [discussed as a possible diagnosis] because I have no energy, and I still have to force myself to eat or I wouldn't. I'm falling so far behind in my school work. Last week on Tuesday, we decided to go to one class, French, just to get out 45 minutes. I was so tired after that class I couldn't hardly stand. I went home at 1:00, and slept till 10:00 a.m. next morning. I did get up once to go to the bathroom, and I fainted. I suffered the next two days.
>
> When I do get some energy, I get up, sit up, watch TV and bang, I get real dizzy and so tired and I pay.
>
> It's like a cycle, get ahead a little bit, and then head in reverse again.
>
> I just want to get well...Thanks for Listening.

It would be the next summer, a few weeks before Jenny's 16th birthday, when I sent Jenny's December letter to Dr. Masser along with a letter of my own. By then, Jenny was in intensive care in New Jersey, bedridden with low grade fever, the mentality of an infant, unable to talk, left leg and foot turned inward, hands drawn up. She was fed through a G-tube 24-hours daily, had severe headaches, total memory loss, swollen joints and cried continually. Remembering all the abuses Dr. Masser had imposed upon my child, I vented my frustrations and disgust in my summer letter, concluding, "...the next time a teenager or child tells you she is sick—Listen! Get down off your pedestal and care!! I never want this to happen to another child."

New Year's Eve, 1988, Jenny was experiencing excruciating head pain. Confined to her bed, she seemed "out of it" when all of a sudden she jerked hard, opened her eyes and "didn't have a clue" who we were. I was overwhelmed. My daughter had no idea I was her mother. She didn't know her dad. She didn't know her brother, Tommy. She didn't know Pastor Dave. The horror of it all haunted me. "What is wrong with Jenny?"

Pastor Dave was concerned for all of us. He had been there not only as our minister, but as a friend. He knew I had been with Jenny night after night in the hospital, and insisted I go home and rest on New Year's Eve. His intuition that Jenny's problems were physical was confirmed for him that night. Later, Pastor Dave told me what he witnessed.

"As I sat with Jenny that night, all the curtains were pulled, no light was on, no TV played, no noise of any kind could be heard. All of a sudden Jenny covered up her ears and started screaming."

When he ran to her and asked her why she was screaming, she said, "Noise." Jenny was in the very end room in the pediatric department. Pastor Dave didn't hear anything, so he went to the door and looked out. "As far down the hall as I could see, a lady was running an electric sweeper," he said. "I didn't hear it until I opened the door, yet she heard that sound and responded in terrible pain." Drawn up in a fetal position, covering her ears, Jenny tried to hide from any sound that hurt her.

3. Another Town—Another Hospital

Dr. Masser had talked to a diabetes doctor at Overton Hospital who would be Jenny's primary doctor. Our hometown ambulance service agreed to transport. They were tremendously kind to Jenny, and in years to come, I would appreciate them more and more.

Jenny was loaded up and I rode in the back with her. The EMTs had been given Jenny's medical record from Miseracordia for Overton. As they read her papers, I wondered, "What are they thinking?" It broke my heart to know Jenny was ill and had been labeled by an indifferent physician. Later, I would learn patients have the right to read all their medical charts and to have copies of their records. When the patient is a minor, the parents have the rights.

My hope stayed focused—this new medical facility would surely give Jenny proper treatment. Obviously, my motherly intuition wasn't working on this one. Dr. Masser had written in her clinical summary that the doctors should investigate the hypoglycemia and also anorexia or psychosomatic illness. Jenny was traveling with a label.

When we arrived at Overton in central Ohio, confusion reigned. The complexities of this large teaching hospital overwhelmed me. The doctor came in, introduced herself, then went out into the hall to talk to other residents. As this new doctor looked over Jenny's records, I heard her say, "I can't understand why the pediatrician sent her to me. This isn't a case dealing with diabetes." Because glucose tolerance tests had been obtained under the conditions of decreased eating, she felt the results were somewhat invalid. She re-ordered tests which came out normal. This was not an endocrinepathic condition, in her opinion, so she transferred Jenny to a neurological service.

All I did was repeat and repeat and repeat myself. From day one, I recited Jenny's medical history to every person on her case. As a parent of a very ill child, I felt like the doctors and other staff members never talked to each other. It was maddening.

A neurologist, the most overbearing man I had ever met, came in and ordered me out of the room. While I had a bad feeling about him, I thought I had to leave. Too reserved to stand up to people, I simply evaporated. As a parent, I had the right to be with my child. But I didn't know any better then.

The day would come when I didn't leave her if I was uncomfortable with a situation. If a doctor can't examine a child in front of a parent, something is very wrong. I had worked in a doctor's office for years, trusting the doctor's ability to diagnose and treat. Ever since Jenny had gotten sick, my faith in medical professionals had been shaken and my distrust in their judgment continued to grow.

This doctor immediately ordered psychological care, along with an adolescent medicine doctor. The resident on Jenny's case seemed compassionate, as was the resident working with the neurologist. But they had little pull. On admission, Jenny was diagnosed with chronic weight loss, fatigue, headache, and photophobia with memory loss and confusion.

She was still feisty enough to describe one resident as "fish face" and she worried about doctors and nurses who had treated her badly. "Will they hurt others?" she asked. The neurologist's exam showed Jenny did not know her brother's age and was unable to answer other questions concerning the recent past. She walked poorly, displaying a staggering gait, and she suffered severe photophobia.

The adolescent specialist wrote—*the origin of her symptoms is organic.* The psychologist felt Jenny's symptoms were very real to her in that she was consistent in her memory loss and in her hypersensitivity to light and to sound. He stated that her symptoms were consistent with a neurological explanation.

A gastro-intestinal specialist was also called. He determined that the endoscopy showed erythema of the esophagus, marked erythema of the pylorus, and some focal erythema of the duodenum. Esophageal, gastric and duodenal biopsies all were suggestive of signs of inflammation. He prescribed medications. When the neurologist decided Jenny had symptoms consistent with encephalitis, he ordered medicine for her pain.

During this hospital stay, Jenny continued to be very sensitive to noise. The slightest high pitch set her off. Beepers on the IV machines were especially terrible for her. When she heard one, even from clear down at the end of the hall, she grabbed her head and cried. We tried to keep things quiet, but that was impossible. Certain sounds seemed harder on her than others.

She suffered extreme head pain, and her photophobia was still severe. Much of the time, we kept towels or washcloths over her eyes to protect them from the light. Each day seemed like a long, endless night. She had regressed to the level of a seven-year-old child.

Home, Again

Connie, Scott and their kids had moved back home to Ada. When it was time to take Jenny home, Aunt Connie brought her station wagon to the hospital. We padded the back end with sleeping bags to make Jenny as comfortable as possible. The trip felt like it took a month.

Just as we pulled into our driveway, a train approached on the tracks next to our house. Its whistle blew long and loud for the three village crossings. We tried to get Jenny into the house quickly, but we had a terrible time. As blunt Connie would say, Jenny was "no light weight." Barely walking, Jenny experienced excruciating pain from the noise of the train.

We were home again, but Jenny no longer had a memory of home. While at the hospital, we had observed her memory getting worse and worse. We repeatedly identified family members. She had no memory. If we said, "This is Tommy, your brother," she believed us. But, she usually forgot soon after. She had lost everything, and on top of her losses, the doctors didn't believe in her.

During her cousin Gail's first visit after Jenny's memory loss, Gail answered a question with the word "sure." Jenny didn't know what that meant. They colored together that day. "She colored real pretty, but it was just a little circle," Gail said. It was tough on Jenny's younger cousin to see Jenny so sick.

The medical expenses kept adding up, but I couldn't worry about that—our priorities had been quickly realigned. My one thought was to get my child's health back. How fragile we are when our child's health is at risk!

"Why isn't this happening to me instead of our child?" was the one question that obsessed me.

An outpouring of affection to both Jenny and our family continued. Jenny received volumes of cards, flowers and gifts. When she was aware, she appreciated every little thing. However, there was only one thing she wanted. To get well.

The people in our small town expressed concern and help in many ways. During the previous hospitalization I found money in my suitcase left by friends. So many had made the hour and a half trip to the hospital in Clark, and their concern never went unappreciated.

Fellow church members at the County Line Church of the Brethren were generous with prayers, food, money, cards, visits, flowers, phone calls and other expressions of love. I always knew our church helped people, but I never realized just how much until our family was on the receiving line.

Our pastor and assistant pastor were always with us. One time, during Jenny's memory loss, the assistant pastor gave her a hard time. He took one of his business cards and wrote "Bengals" on it and told Jenny she had always been a Bengals fan, when we were actually Cleveland Brown fans. Another day we laughed when he did an impression of one of Jenny's neurologists.

During the next 12 days at home, Jenny tried hard to get well. She was ever so sick, but I thought I could do nothing except what I had been instructed to do. Jenny was willing to try anything, but she didn't have any strength.

On January 26, 1989, Jenny hadn't gone to the bathroom for 19 hours. Wild with worry, I called Dr. Masser and was told to bring Jenny to her office. Jenny was so weak and lethargic it was difficult to get her there.

After the exam, the doctor told me to take her home and give her liquids. If she didn't void by eight o'clock that night, I was to let them know. By the time we returned home, Jenny was totally exhausted and didn't have the strength to eat.

I tried to get liquids down, but she was becoming unresponsive. It was hard for me to get past the fact that Dr. Masser was the doctor who had slapped Jenny, but we needed immediate medical help so I notified the doctor and Jenny was readmitted to Miseracordia.

Dehydration

Jenny's admitting diagnosis was dehydration, with an admission weight of 138 pounds. Along with her general condition, her weight was a worry. Doctors ordered 1000 cc of fluid by IV. When Jenny hadn't voided after 28 hours, a catheter was inserted. Only 400 cc of urine was obtained. Jenny was becoming more and more unresponsive. Nancy Miller, a night nurse, would become one of many exceptional people who would make a positive impact on Jenny's life.

Nancy was one in a million. A strong personality was hidden beneath her pleasant face and graying hair. She was deliberate in her nursing, tender of heart, and spoke in a down-to-earth manner. Her support was incredible. She told us she had spent a lot of nights with Jenny and knew something was *really physically wrong*. Nancy felt that if a doctor spent time with

Jenny and got to know her, they would realize Jenny wasn't a psychiatric case. Surprisingly, Nancy was from our hometown and we hadn't known her before. I thanked God for sending special, caring people to help Jenny.

Cathy and Pastor Dave were so worried about Jenny that they spent the night. About 2 a.m. Jenny took a turn for the worse and Nancy called the pediatrician. Jenny was not responsive to deep stimuli and no longer voided through the catheter. Dr. Masser arrived.

During an examination of the central nervous system, she said Jenny was totally unresponsive to verbal stimuli, superficial pain or even to deep pain. The doctor decided to have Jenny transferred back to Overton in Clark, in the morning. I hated the idea, but I didn't know what else to do.

A resident and a nurse from Overton were with the intensive care van when it came to pick up Jenny. They seemed caring, but I was leery. I didn't want to see Jenny go through the hassle and mistreatment she had gone through before. It was at this point that I changed and began to aggressively participate in the decisions made for Jenny's care. The passive momma no longer existed.

Racing to Overton

Friends took me in their van, following the ambulance. When we found Jenny, she was still in the hall on a gurney. A nurse who had taken care of Jenny before came up to us and said the neurologist felt the problems were all psychological. He hadn't even examined Jenny! A herd of stampeding buffalo could not have pounded my head more violently. How could a doctor be so unprofessional and insensitive?

The nurse felt badly about the situation and told me how worried she was about Jenny. The neurologist's opinion left me devastated and my friends were filled with rage. Again, a medical professional had the inside track and Jenny remained labeled.

Finally, Jenny was put in a room. Her principal diagnosis on admission was *unresponsive*. She was running a temperature of 100.3, which was definitely a fever for her. Normally, she carried a temperature of 96 to 97 degrees.

The neurologist took the attitude that it was a waste of time to have Jenny there unless we put her into the psychiatric unit. He wrote in her record...*this patient is in a deeply, unresponsive state which appears to be worsening or a reoccurrence of an illness which has been ongoing for sometime.* He noted she was discharged previously with amnesia.

The psychologist on Jenny's case told me the other doctors wanted to put Jenny in the psychiatric unit. He said he didn't agree, but they kept dumping it in his lap. His compassion and concern were a welcoming reprieve.

At one point, nurses put Jenny in the hall to eat, stating, sometimes—when a child is placed out in public—the patient is so embarrassed, they will then start to eat. This "technique" did not make a difference.

Ritalin was tried, and stopped after 24 hours because of Jenny's increased crying. As far as the psychiatric unit, I flatly refused. They could bring in any psychiatrist they wanted, but Jenny was not going to a psych unit. I knew her well enough to know this wasn't a mental health problem.

One day as I sat in the lounge, a black lady got out of the elevator. It was easy to see it would be unwise to try to mess with this woman.

Her daughter, Sammy, was a patient across the hall from Jenny. In no time, we became fast friends. Debbie taught me a lot about being the mother of a sick child. She was a nurse and didn't put up with anything.

"Never let anyone push you around," she said. Believe me, she operated on that principle. It didn't take her long to realize Jenny was a very sick girl. Others saw this too. Several nurses strongly advised us to get Jenny out of there in order to get her appropriate care.

They said there were other places to go, and as long as she stayed in Overton, she would never get better because the primary care doctor felt she was a psychiatric case. These nurses were convinced—Jenny was physically ill and very ill.

Our insurance case manager was also supportive. She felt Jenny wasn't being diagnosed correctly. Again, I was told not to be discouraged. There were other places to get help. Often insurance companies seem like the enemy and people have to fight for their coverage. In our case, the insurance case workers were courteous and helpful.

A System Afflicted with Dementia

One day I was told arrangements had been made for me to meet with doctors who wanted to discuss a psychological work-up on Jenny. I had no problem with this and thought nothing more of it. When nurses started asking me if I was prepared for this meeting, I had no idea why they were so concerned.

Two nurses on Jenny's case appeared in street clothes. When they explained it was their day off, but they had come to be with me for support, I started to get a little nervous. They told me I was a strong person, and it was time to show that strength. The psychologist arrived, smiled, and told me he would be there for me. We walked to a conference room where I waited in the hall while they held a long meeting.

When I was invited in, I was seated in the middle of the room surrounded by two dozen people involved in psychiatry. I couldn't believe their firing squad accusations. They grasped at everything and anything—Jenny must have been sexually abused by her father, or a teacher or a minister. Surely some horrible trauma had happened and was hidden.

God must have given me strength because I had a calm, sound response to each question and accusation. Jenny and I had always talked about everything. She was open and honest and our relationship was like that. She would have told me if sexual abuse or some other trauma had happened to her. Much to my disgust, I began to feel, when some doctors don't know what is wrong, it is easy to just classify the case as a psychiatric problem. Then they are off the hook.

The meeting lasted about an hour, but it felt like an eternity. When we left the room, the nurses gave me warm hugs, saying I had done a great job for Jenny. Even the psychologist said I couldn't have done any better. I had been blunt and up front. After all, I had nothing to hide and neither did Jenny.

Pastor Dave couldn't believe medical professionals were ignoring her symptoms and making these charges. "The doctors didn't listen to what Jenny or her mother said, or look at the facts of her medical history. They had made up their minds when they talked to me," he declared. "I must have sat there over an hour with three of them. I am sure I did not persuade, did not make a bit of difference in their thinking." Pastor Dave was deeply hurt.

It was during this second admission at Overton that I became frustrated with student doctors, especially one. He came into Jenny's room, identifying himself as a medical student. Then he told me he was an intern. He finally upgraded his status to resident and *in attitude*—to God. Disgusted, I had to acknowledge this was the attitude of those who constantly poked and probed Jenny, as he did. She had few good veins. When an IV was in, it was to be left alone.

One day, the nurse had just put in an IV after several tries when a medical student came in to draw blood. Our minister was with us. Since the room was small, I decided to take a break. When I came back 45 minutes later, the student was still poking away. What amazed me the most was that he had started on the arm with the IV.

Enough was enough. I went to the nurse and told her I wanted that man out of Jenny's room. She had no idea he had been there that long and immediately went to see Jenny. Furious, she told him to get out of Jenny's room and never enter it again. He had messed with the IV and tortured Jenny in the process.

Nothing came easily for Jenny. Many times procedures were messed up. It was nothing for her to be stuck 17 times in her arms, hands, feet, groin, neck, fingers or ankles in order to get an IV in. We were thankful for some great nurses and a fine, supportive psychologist. They were the only thing that made the situation bearable at Overton.

On February 2, Jenny was treated with an antibiotic because bacteria were found in her urine. She was given a strong IV to build her up.

Doctors also wanted to do some more things concerning psych. When a psychiatrist came in from a larger psychiatric unit, dexamethasone was tried. It was discontinued when it appeared to make Jenny more lethargic.

A group interview was set up with the psychiatrist, other doctors, and Jenny. They decided to videotape the consultation. They told me they would be giving Jenny a medicine commonly known as a truth serum, and then Jenny would reveal "some big, dark secret." It was their opinion that Jenny would "disclose what was causing her mental problems."

When a thiopental interview was attempted, it didn't give the results expected. The psychiatrist came out of Jenny's room and told us they had come up with zero, and he had no desire to go further. Desipramine was begun after the interview in case decreased responsiveness was secondary to severe depression. They tried several other things, but nothing gave them the results they had hoped for.

At this time, Jenny's left leg continued to painfully turn inward. Mentally, she had regressed to a very young age. Only one thing was happening. She was getting worse. According to the psychiatrist's report, "Psychiatric or function etiology is unlikely at this point in view of the patient's clinical picture, mode of presentation, and current symptoms. The possibility of the symptoms being secondary to a major depression or a conversation disorder may be entertained, but it is highly unlikely."

In Jenny's four visits to the physical therapy department, she required a two-man transfer lift from wheelchair to mat. Her head slumped to the right with her arms extended in front, her eyes were closed and she made no eye or sound contact. She only resisted these procedures once.

Another idea was considered. Our hometown water tower had been painted the previous summer. According to one of our neighbors, their son had become sick and they were trying to find out what was wrong with him. Jenny was tested for different toxins. Nothing tested positive.

Someone at home told me Dr. Eastman, who had been our family doctor years before, was concerned about Jenny. Tall, with a full white beard, he made a striking figure. Desperate, I called him, searching for anything we could do to help her. After Dr. Eastman and I talked, we agreed I should bring Jenny home and he would take over her care. He questioned me a lot, and I felt, perhaps, this was our answer.

One fortunate thing happened. The staff neurologist left due to a schedule change and we ended up with another neurologist. In his discharge paper he wrote:

> In view of the history and extensive work-up, no clear organic etiology can be determined for Jenny's current condition at this point.
>
> Likewise, no clear psychological cause can be determined. It is felt at this time that whatever has caused Jenny to have this deterioration in her mental status and level of function, it is of paramount importance to take steps to improve Jenny.

She was discharged from the teaching hospital on February 10, 1989, and transported back to Miseracordia by our hometown ambulance.

When Jenny was in second grade, she had experienced stomach pain. After going to doctors in the area, I had asked Dr. Eastman what to do. He stated that Jenny wasn't a complainer and notified a surgeon who set up surgery immediately. During surgery, they discovered mesenteric adenitis and removed some lumps. Jenny had recovered well and I had been thankful for all Dr. Eastman had done. I was hoping for similar results this time.

4. All Communication Lost

It was a Friday night when the ambulance transported Jenny from Overton in Clark, back to Miseracordia in Lamont, closer to home. She had lost all communication. Why talk if no one believes you? I couldn't blame her if she was refusing to talk, but this was more than refusing to communicate. She was now semicomatose.

Unbelievably, this was her fifth admission in ten weeks to Miseracordia in addition to the two admissions to Overton. Her symptoms included a low grade fever, deep pain and head-aches, her left leg was turned in, she was sensitive to light and noise, she had memory loss and was lethargic. This time her admitting diagnosis was encephalitis.

After a doctor examined Jenny on Saturday morning, he wanted to call in a pediatric specialist and another doctor dealing with handicaps. Later, the pediatric specialist asked me to come to the lounge where he could speak to me. He had never examined Jenny, but proceeded to tell me she needed to be in a psychiatric unit, and, if I agreed, he would treat her there. If I refused, he refused to see her.

How can a doctor who has never seen a patient know what is best for that patient? Dr. Eastman had called in these doctors. Could I still rely on him to help? When the pediatric specialist made this major decision without examining Jenny, I became firmer in my belief—too many doctors protect each other through an unwritten policy of "Do Not Rock the Boat." This was an attitude which certainly left the patient hanging.

On Sunday, Dr. Eastman said he wanted Jenny seen by a psychologist from out-of-town. My heart wasn't in it, but I agreed. This psychologist proved to be considerate. He said psychological treatment, given Jenny's condition, including not being able to talk, would be ineffective until she recovered some physical strength.

Another doctor examined Jenny's leg. The bone scan revealed increased activity and arthritis in the left knee and left ankle. This doctor was concerned about Jenny going home. With the posturing of her left leg, Jenny would develop internal rotation contractures and flexion contractures in the sole of her foot. Essentially, she would be unable to walk. Here again, this was a doctor who didn't know Jenny. All I could conclude was this diagnosis would put her in a rehabilitation unit.

One day, Jenny's father, Jon, was there when Dr. Eastman came to visit, and the doctor convinced Jon to admit Jenny into a psychiatric unit. When I found out, I was upset with Jon. How could he let some doctor push him into this when he knew it wasn't best for Jenny? In the past, Jon had always looked up to Dr. Eastman, and he couldn't believe this doctor of all people would follow the popular diagnosis. Jon felt badly he had allowed himself to be talked into something he knew was wrong for Jenny.

Jon was working three jobs at the time. He was a full-time advertising salesman for a newspaper in our county seat, and worked part-time as an announcer at a Christian radio station in addition to cleaning Dr. Porter's office.

After his bad experience at the hospital with Dr. Eastman, Jon buried himself even further into his work. The best way he could handle Jenny's illness was to live on the edge of it. I understood. Everyone handles critical situations differently. Working long hours was Jon's way of taking care of our family.

The day after our encounter with Dr. Eastman, the doctor was in a furor. He told me Jenny would never get better until I accepted the fact she was a psychiatric case. Refusing to put her in a psychiatric unit, I told him it would be a miracle if Jenny didn't turn into a psych case with doctors like him.

"I am taking Jenny home," I said flatly.

"You can't because she is on an IV machine."

"Then I will take that damn IV machine with me!"

As far as the feeding machine, I had no problems dealing with that. Then he told me to put Jenny in a nursing home because I would be unable to take care of her. Now I was furious. No way was my girl going to a nursing home. Our words riddled the air.

Finally, he consented, "She will be discharged tomorrow."

The next day, my friend, Teri, was there when Dr. Eastman came to do the release. Jenny had acted like she had an earache and I asked him if he would check her ears before we left. He roughly jerked her head around. His actions were so unbelievable Teri was disgusted. Believe me, I had no problem letting him know how I felt. Dr. Eastman, a doctor I had trusted, a man I had looked up to as a father, had also let us down.

Jenny was discharged on February 24, 1989. I didn't know what to do next, but I had no doubts about taking her out of Miseracordia. It was right to take her home. Jenny was sick and no one would listen to us or believe her except the psychologist at Overton. "He listens and believes me," Jenny had once told me. In my heart, I knew Jenny was a very special girl. God had to help us.

Difficult Months at Home

After taking Jenny home, my work was cut out for me. I felt I had to get Jenny better and then find a good, caring doctor. The next months were difficult—her condition continued to worsen and she needed diapers while semicomatose. We placed a hospital bed in our living room, facing the street. All waking hours, Jenny cried in incredible, constant pain.

I would get her out of the bed and put her in a wheelchair and prop pillows around her to help hold her up. Her left leg turned completely inward. The inside of her left foot lay flat on the floor. I couldn't begin to move it. If I tried, she cried out. She required 24-hour care and was on 24-hour tube feedings. She tried so hard to eat, but I don't think she even understood the act of eating.

There was a change in the management at our insurance company because Jenny's case was so involved. The new case manager worked hard getting Jenny the right kind of wheelchair, one that would hold Jenny up all around, including her head, since Jenny no longer had any self support. The wheelchair had to be ordered special. Then the case manager was changed yet again, and getting her specialized wheelchair became another ridiculous situation.

During this time, we tried to keep our household as quiet as possible to allow Jenny to sleep and rest. She was so uncomfortable, even the ringing of a phone would wake her and she would start crying. The phones were shut off, except for one upstairs.

Tommy was wonderful. Jenny was lucky to have such a great brother, and we were blessed to have such a caring son. He was always there, helping me help Jenny. He knew how to run the feeding machine and how to handle other duties of her care. Baths were given to her in bed because it had become too hard to move her. We did range of motion exercises to help her extremities so they wouldn't lock up. At times, she could say something, other times—nothing.

When her communication first began being difficult, Jenny said, "Mom, sometimes I want to talk so bad, but it just won't come out." One day, as she was losing the ability to speak, she said, "Don't give up on me, Mom." Her eyes pleaded with me.

It felt like everyone in the house was walking on egg shells. We couldn't stand to hear Jenny cry, but we didn't know what more we could do to help her.

"It broke my heart when I walked in and she didn't know me," Pastor Dave said. "She couldn't even identify a cake of soap." I put my arms around Pastor Dave and told him, "She doesn't know me either."

Grace, a nurse at our pharmacy, gave us unflagging support, even if it was only to let me unload my frustrations at times. Nancy and Cathy, who never deserted us, were terribly distressed by Jenny's prolonged illness. "Why can't an answer be found?" they questioned. Both capable, confident nurses, they were frustrated by the lack of answers.

Teachers came offering help, only to be shocked at Jenny's condition. Just a few months earlier, Jenny had been an honor student. They knew her as a happy, energetic, loving girl. It was hard for them to see the change.

It was Tommy's 12th birthday on March 30, and birthdays had always been special to Jenny. When the family came down for supper and cake, I went to get Jenny out of her hospital bed and bring her to the kitchen.

She whined, begging me not to move her. Exhausted and weak, she even cried. This wasn't Jenny. She had always been there for her brother.

I put her in the wheelchair and propped her head up with pillows. I had been praying for her ordeal to be over. I didn't want anything, any pictures, to remind me of how bad she looked and how sick she was, but it was Tommy's birthday and we took her picture for the first time since she had become sick.

Suddenly, Jenny fell over the right side of her wheelchair. We got her back into the chair and I took her and her feeding machine back to the living room and put her in bed. I had always tried to keep everything as normal as possible, but there wasn't any point in putting Jenny through anymore. Tommy begged me to let her rest.

In a photo album, there is a picture of Tommy's birthday cake with 12 candles blazing. In the background, Jenny is slumped over the arm of her wheelchair. Her symptoms on his birthday are recorded under the picture: *Semicomatose, joint pain, NG tube feeding, infant mentality, severe headaches, left side paralysis, no body control.*

Somehow, Jenny managed to try to smile at me at times. With her uncanny sensitivity to others, I felt it was an effort to make me feel better. That day she didn't smile.

Gradually, Jenny was drawing into a fetal position. Her left leg was still red behind the knee area. On a couple of occasions, she began having ear pain. I took her back to Dr. Porter, who had originally said she had a bad case of the flu. He now said she had ear infections and prescribed medication. He felt the nose tube could be causing irritation. Whenever Jenny had an ear infection and was put on an antibiotic, she seemed a little better in other areas.

For the most part, she didn't talk, but would blurt things out at improper times. It didn't make sense. It was as though her brain was malfunctioning. There were times she sat up in the recliner, but mostly she slept. Her ear pain decreased with the antibiotic and an anti-inflammatory drug also seemed to help.

Upon returning home from a doctor visit one day, we were caught in a downpour. Attempting to get Jenny into the house, I realized too late I couldn't do it alone. Usually, Tommy was there to carry Jenny, but he wasn't home this time. Jenny was hanging out of the car door when a neighbor man came and carried her inside. Somehow, someone always came through.

Endless Admissions

On May 4, 1989, Jenny seemed more uncomfortable than usual. As I worked with her, she cried out "Ooh" and "Ow" and tried to touch her left arm and knee with her right arm. When I pulled her sheet back, I was shocked to see her elbow swollen, red and looking like cottage cheese.

Surely our luck was running out. I had tried hard to prevent bedsores by doing range of motion and moving her every two hours. Now this!

She continued to reach for her knee. Pulling her sheet down further, I found her other joints were in the same painful condition. The doctor was unavailable so I was told to take her into emergency. The ambulance came. Another painful transport.

When we first entered emergency, the ER doctor was concerned and couldn't understand how Jenny had gotten into this condition. Jenny was still having headaches. After examining her, he wanted a CAT scan and other tests, realizing she was very sick. But first he called Dr. Porter, who suggested calling the pediatric specialist, the one who had refused to help Jenny unless I agreed to the psychiatric unit. The ER doctor had no idea of the atrocious treatment Jenny had received at Miseracordia.

Thank God, Jenny's Aunt Connie was with me. The ER doctor asked us to join him in a room where he proceeded to tell us Jenny needed a psychiatric unit. How could a doctor who had examined her thoroughly—one minute determine something was physically wrong—and suddenly reverse gears and agree with a doctor who had never even seen Jenny?

How could the chain be broken on this "Doctors Stick Together and Kiss Up Club?" Connie and I were livid. "Fine," I said. "Then I will take her home." The ER doctor quickly called the other doctor again and they decided to admit her. This time her admitting diagnosis was encephalopathy, left sided hermiparesis and otitis media. It was decided Jenny was having ear aches from the NG tube in her nose, so a gastrointestinal specialist was called. He was kind and caring. Something we weren't used to in this hospital.

Jenny's doctor requested that Jenny have a percutaneous endoscopic gastrostomy (a PEG tube placement) since it was not anticipated that she would be able to return to normal feeding in the foreseeable future. While Jenny was having the procedure, we were fortunate that a friend from our church was her nurse. It was comforting to have our daughter with someone we trusted.

Jenny was also seen by an ear specialist who advised continuing the antibiotic. If there were further problems, they would insert tubes in her ears. Jenny was given medicine for her joint pain. This time her discharge diagnosis was the same as the admitting diagnosis. On May 7, she was transported home by ambulance.

Just two days later, Jenny was re-admitted to the hospital. She was running a higher fever and had persistent, intolerable ear pain. Her admitting diagnosis was upper respiratory infection and severe ear pain and headache. She was given a different antibiotic, and physical, occupational and speech therapy were begun.

The doctor discussed having Jenny go to a rehab center to help her function physically. I told him I had no problem with that if it would help her move around easier.

At this time, I was still dealing with an unorganized insurance case manager who called and asked what color wheelchair I wanted. Jenny didn't care if it was purple, pink or red! I told her, "Just get that wheelchair ordered. It's about time you conclude the arrangements." Everything had to be approved by the insurance company before they would pay their percentage. That was fine. But I felt, let's do it!

Jenny was signed up with a sincere, young student nurse named Beth, who not only spent a lot of time with her when on duty, but also came in on her spare time. For some reason, she was drawn to Jenny. Beth had a sweet disposition and I knew she would become a good nurse. We had no idea that we would ever see Beth after this particular hospitalization, but she would later surprise us by coming into our lives again.

One day I came back from the snack shop to find a note on Jenny's bedside table from Metta, the speech therapist. When she talked with Jenny in her room, Jenny had cried and would have nothing to do with her. The therapist requested I be in Jenny's room the next day so she could talk with me. The nurse explained Jenny did better if I was in the room.

When the speech therapist came the next day, my first reaction was negative, and the situation felt very uncomfortable. Thankfully, my first impression was wrong. She ended up putting all her expertise into her work with Jenny and became a trusted friend. In the recent past, Jenny had met very few medical professionals she trusted.

For the most part the occupational therapists were kind and worked well with Jenny. But one time, as I walked into Jenny's room, a physical therapist and an assistant had Jenny in a wheelchair and they were upset. They said I needed to talk with my daughter because of her actions.

This was puzzling. Jenny never caused problems if she could possibly help it. She wasn't the girl we once had, but I knew there was more to the current situation. Bending near her, I told Jenny I was going to physical therapy with her and she should try very hard.

Every time one particular therapist touched her, Jenny resisted. I just knew that lady had done something to Jenny. Later, I was told she had gotten rough. Perhaps, in her mind, this was "just a psych case" and she didn't want to bother with Jenny.

Only God knew how I wanted to educate these people to be sensitive to their patients. "We always felt she was far more aware of what was going on than some people thought," Jon said. Jenny never did like that lady, even though she couldn't remember why. When that therapist tried to be sweet with Jenny later, it was hard to take. Jenny was never left alone with her again.

For some reason, there were never any openings at the rehab program, and on May 19, we transported Jenny home. There seemed to be a little improvement after ten days of antibiotics while in the hospital. When the antibiotics were stopped, she continued on another medication.

As for the wheelchair, enough was enough. Jon drove to Clark with Cathy's husband, Erwin, and picked it up. Jenny needed it, and I wasn't about to let the delay continue. When I had time to think about it, it amazed me how I had changed since the previous fall. I had learned to stand up for myself, and, even more so, for Jenny.

After taking Jenny home, she seemed to crumble. We were doing all the therapies at home with the therapists from the hospital, but I could tell she was getting weaker and weaker. Physically, she looked ravaged. She began running fevers again, her headaches had increased in intensity, and the pain in her joints—now considered arthritis—was so terrible she was desperate for relief. She had complete memory loss, was unable to walk, talk or eat, and her body was so stiff she was unable to bend. Her daily decline was obvious.

One day when I had worked especially hard with Jenny and she was in so much pain, I thought I couldn't stand it anymore. At that time she was talking little. I walked out of the room and cried and cried, overwhelmed and lost that I couldn't make my girl better.

When I calmed down and returned to Jenny, she said, "Mom, send me away. It's okay." That snapped me out of my negative thinking. She cared so much about us that she couldn't stand to see us hurt. She felt it would solve things for us if she was put away. Right then, I made Jenny a firm promise: "I will never give up on you."

Breaking Points

Still, there were times I got frustrated. On a couple of occasions I totally lost control, sadly, at Tommy's expense. One time he was in the bathroom, sitting on the floor putting on his socks. I went to the bathroom door and when I found it locked, it set me off and I knocked the door off its hinges. Startled, Tommy just sat there. Then I had to call a friend and ask him if he would come and repair the door and frame. Why did I react so terribly to a locked door?

The next time I "lost it" I had asked Tommy to do something unimportant and he kind of just horsed around. Something clicked and all of a sudden I picked up an antique chair in his room, carried it through the house, out the front door, and threw the chair clear out to the street, smashing it in what seemed a million pieces. Jenny was propped up in the recliner and saw me go through the room. It was so unlike me. I hate fighting and turmoil, but breaking that chair made me feel better. We seldom yelled in our home, but I found there were times I could take only so much. Apparently, that was my way of releasing some of the stress, and, thankfully, I didn't hurt anyone. One thing was sure. Material things no longer meant as much as they had before Jenny's confusing illness.

One Saturday afternoon when Jenny was in severe anguish, we decided to get rid of the hospital bed and bring down her own bed. Maybe she would get some of her memory back if she had her things around her. We brought down things she had on her bedroom walls and added cards sent to her and decorations. Jenny still noticed balloons and loved flowers. Two friends with flower shops kept her in good supply of both. Now the room looked like Jenny.

People continued sending things and visiting, letting us know they were concerned. Pastor Dave's love was genuine, and he was always there, even when he was having kidney stone pain. Jenny's grandparents had different ways of showing their love. Jenny's condition took a toll on Grandpa Epley's health. He cared so much for her.

Grandma Epley sent food and flowers. Jon's parents didn't want to see Jenny that way, so they didn't come often, except for holidays. We didn't see a lot of the family except for Aunt Connie. Perhaps, it made them feel uncomfortable. Very seldom did I ask for help. When I did, I asked Connie. If I needed anything badly, I knew I could pick up the phone and call any family member. Still, I had a hard time asking.

5. An Enemy Named Lyme

One day my friend Cathy made a call I would never forget. She told me she knew what was wrong with Jenny. Surely this was just another big balloon that was about to burst. Big hearted Cathy had felt frustrated as a nurse. She knew something was *really* wrong with Jenny and all she could do was watch helplessly with us as Jenny got worse and worse. This day, the tone of Cathy's voice was different. When she came down to the house, she brought the May 22, 1989, issue of *Newsweek* magazine.

She told me Jenny had Lyme disease, and I had no idea what she was talking about—I had never heard of Lyme disease. Cathy told me to read the cover story, "Tiny Tick, Big Worry." I had to admit the symptoms and medical information described Jenny's situation. She had the bites and all the symptoms, but I reminded Cathy that Jenny had a Lyme titer done in December 1988 by a neurologist. Cathy didn't have an answer for that, but she was certain it was Lyme. A therapist agreed. When another nursing friend concurred, Cathy volunteered to find out more about the disease. She learned...

Ticks infected with the Lyme disease bacteria, *Borrelia burgdorferi*, spread the bacteria when they bite humans. Mice, deer, other mammals and birds are part of the tick's life cycle. Lyme is likely transmitted during the immature nymph stage or by an adult tick. The nymphs are no larger than a period on this page. The adult tick carrying Lyme is only slightly larger.

Without our knowing it, Jenny had shown most of the early and late symptoms of Lyme. Because so many of the symptoms imitate symptoms of other diseases, doctors who do not know Lyme disease, or who do not take seriously detailed patient histories, including travel, often misdiagnose the disease. This is why Lyme disease is known as the "Great Pretender."

Three things are key: 1. To have a clinical diagnosis early. 2. To seek treatment from an informed physician immediately. 3. To understand how to prevent exposure to Lyme. (See Other Resources).

Jenny did not have the benefit of any of this. It was not until later that we would become knowledgeable about the characteristics of her enemy. We had been living with and ineffectively fighting Lyme disease without knowing its name.

Cathy called the Massachusetts's Health Department and talked to a doctor who suggested another Lyme titer be drawn and sent to her. Jenny's doctor did the test and sent the blood sample. Cathy also called a woman whose son had Lyme disease and understood our situation. They talked for quite a while. She was a great help and suggested a specialist in New Jersey whom Cathy contacted. When the doctor wasn't in, Cathy left a message and my phone number.

That night the doctor from New Jersey called and asked for me. Never dreaming she would call right away, I had made a run to the grocery store. The specialist told Jon I should call her the next day before 3 p.m. When I got back home from the grocery, I was shocked to learn she had called, considering that some doctors don't return calls even when they know the patient.

The next day, I called Dr. Paige. She came right to the phone and patiently listened to the unfolding of Jenny's story. She never rushed me. Her concern was real and she was appalled at all that had been done to Jenny. It was no time to mince words, and I told her exactly what the doctors had said and done. The minute I mentioned a psychiatric diagnosis, I figured that would be the end of her help. She would be just like the rest.

Dr. Paige was all business. As she listened, she picked up on something that turned out to be incredibly important. She told me Jenny may never, ever have a positive Lyme titer because of the tetracycline she was taking for acne when she was bitten. The doctor explained the medicine can interfere with the test.

Since Dr. Paige was from out of state, her hands were tied. With the information I gave her—and if I sent Jenny's records—and if all was as she expected—she said she likely would treat her for probable Lyme disease. If I could find a doctor who would talk to her from our area, she offered to help. I agreed to call her in two days.

There was just one thing that I withheld from Dr. Paige, which left me a little unsettled. Physically and emotionally exhausted from all that had happened in the previous months, I did something I knew wasn't right. Afraid I would get everything she said mixed up or forget what she said, I taped the conversation without asking her permission. I wanted our nurses and therapists to hear the information from the doctor's mouth. Underneath it all, I always wondered if the time would come when Jenny's nurses and therapists would begin to doubt Jenny too.

I went to Dr. Porter's office personally to request his help in treating Jenny for Lyme disease. Since diagnosing Jenny's symptoms as the flu the previous fall, he had tried to make her comfortable and always responded to her symptoms with concern rather than harshness like so many other doctors. I explained Dr. Paige's opinion—that Jenny needed treatment for Lyme. He listened, but refused to treat with IV antibiotics, so I dropped it and decided to do something else.

"Did Jenny get better when she was treated with antibiotics for ear infections?" the New Jersey doctor had inquired. Jenny did improve on antibiotics and then she would slide back again. I would learn later why this information about improving temporarily on antibiotics was vitally important in determining Jenny's diagnosis and treatment. Jenny was bravely fighting her symptoms, but her enemy was proving to be an overwhelming foe. Terrorized we were losing our daughter, we were willing to grasp at anything that could give us hope.

At Last, A Cooperative Doctor

In talking with another nursing friend, Carol, I asked if she had any suggestions. She knew Jenny well and couldn't understand what the doctors were doing. Carol worked for a Dr. Scott in our county seat. She said she would talk to him and get back with me soon. In no time, she called and told me Dr. Scott wanted to examine Jenny. After he checked her over carefully, he told us Jenny had a lot of neurological problems and considering the fever, joint pain, memory loss, fatigue, headaches, confusion and the overall deterioration, Jenny deserved to be treated for probable Lyme disease. He agreed to contact the New Jersey doctor to work out a plan of treatment.

It was decided to start Jenny on IV Rocephin, an antibiotic, and we needed nurses. We lucked out when Nancy Miller, a great Christian lady, could come. As a precaution, we took Jenny to Houser Memorial, fifteen minutes from home, for the first IV in case she had any reaction. Everything went well and she was given 1 gram of Rocephin IV daily, beginning June 7, 1989, upon the recommendation of Dr. Paige in New Jersey.

For six months I had been doing Jenny's total care, with the exception of about a month. It was decided I needed to have a nursing assistant occasionally, so I could get out a bit and make grocery runs and do other errands. We had some nice aides, but even this service became a frustration instead of a help.

When a certain aide came, Jenny fussed if I left. I couldn't figure this out. At times I had noticed marks on Jenny and never knew what caused them. I had an uncomfortable feeling about this aide, so I made up my mind—I would find out why I didn't trust her. One day I told the aide I would be gone longer than usual. I made it clear she should not plan on me returning for quite a while.

Before I left, I placed Jenny in the recliner with pillows propped around to hold her up. She looked comfortable. In no time I returned, slipping through the back door which I had left unlocked, to discover Jenny falling out of the recliner. Her upper body hung over the side of the wooden arm. The aide was in another part of the house playing computer games. As I walked quietly into Tommy's room, the aide yelled out at Jenny to stop whining. She looked crazed when she saw me.

"Get your stuff and get out of my house," I yelled. Then I notified the hospital home health unit—I did not need aides. If necessary, friends or family would help.

First Home IV

Nancy Miller came on June 8, 1989, for her first visit, and Grace brought all the pharmacy supplies. Tons of paper work had to be done. Since Jenny's IV had been started at the hospital, the nurses simply used an attachment on her arm and the IV was easily accomplished. It continued to be difficult to put in an IV, and we learned to treasure each IV that worked well.

Her diagnosis was post encephalitis and possible Lyme disease. Jenny looked terrible. She was in excruciating pain and she had deteriorated unbelievably. We put side rails on the bed to prevent falls. I always kept her in clothes, usually jogging suits. With the hot weather, and Jenny running a fever and in constant pain, I tried to make her more comfortable. Her dad's T-shirts served as her new wardrobe.

A bedside commode was used. It was now impossible to carry her to the bathroom, the bed pan was uncomfortable, and getting on and off the commode exercised her. We bought a shampoo board. She had always been a nut for grooming, having squeaky clean hair and taking frequent baths.

Grooming was the part of our daily routine that helped her feel better. Shortly after the IVs were started, Jenny required 24-hour-care. I would lay down in bed with her to get a little sleep or rest on a nearby couch. She couldn't communicate to let us know her needs. Her joints were so bad that she moaned when we moved her, and her fever continued to climb. Over the counter pain medications did not ease her suffering.

I questioned, "Why isn't she getting better when she is on IVs to help her improve?" I was told the doctors expected this. Patients often get worse before they get better.

We bought a blanket cradle to keep the bed covers from touching her since even the slight weight of blankets caused her discomfort. An over-the-bed table was rented to help the nurse. It was a shock to realize how much Jenny needed. An overwhelming amount of supplies were purchased.

Sometimes I felt sorry for Tommy. He was a great brother and helped so much with Jenny. When they were young, Tommy had sometimes resisted Jenny mothering him. But, they had always been close and nothing had changed that. If he had been jealous of the time she needed, he could have made life miserable for everyone. But he didn't. He just wanted to help Jenny get well.

Somehow, I needed to spend time with him. A baby monitor was purchased for Jenny's bed so I could go outside and play tennis and other games with Tommy. Football was never one of my interests, but that was another way of spending time with him. After watching many TV football games at Tommy's side, I became a fan.

During one of Jenny's hospitalizations, a couple from home who had lost a child wanted to help. Knowing how tough times could be, they gave me a money gift and told me to decide how to use it. Instead of paying medical bills, I had bought Tommy the computer system the home health aide had used. Tommy whiled away many solitary hours on that heaven-sent gift. I was thankful I had been able to do something for him.

Jon tried to spend time with Tom, but he continued to work heavy schedules. Sports saved Tommy. He loved football and track and his junior high coaches were the greatest. Given the stress at home, I was aware drugs or alcohol could have been an escape. Thankfully, this never became a problem.

Sunday morning, July 2, 1989, Jenny began to have seizure-like movements. Her temperature was 101 degrees and her joints were in terrible pain. She had developed a rash that month that looked like the rash she had when she first got sick. Something was as wrong as wrong could be.

When I called Dr. Paige on the east coast and described Jenny's symptoms, she understood what was happening. When Nancy came after church to give Jenny her treatment, she became concerned and notified Jenny's local doctor. He told us to keep an eye on her and get back to him. Later that night, she got much worse, jerking all over.

I called the ambulance and we took her to Houser Memorial in Keyes, a short drive from home. Only once had I questioned actions at this hospital. Usually they had treated her professionally, with concern, dignity and respect.

The doctor gave her Dilantin, Valium and phenobarbital, but the medications didn't help. She just worsened. The doctor realized her situation was out of hand and she needed a larger facility. An ambulance was called to transport her to Granite, in Clark. When an EMT told the driver to hurry, I knew it would be a faster trip than the normal hour and a half driving time. Jenny was jerking severely.

Upon arrival at Granite, the emergency room doctor said it was his impression and that of another doctor that *Jenny suffered from Lyme disease.* Blood work and a CAT scan showed a questionable temporal lesion. It was not until the next day that her seizures settled down. At this time Jenny was being given 1 gram of Rocephin every 12 hours.

6. A Pitiful Case

Jenny was placed in the neuro-intensive care unit where an infectious disease doctor spent a lot of time examining her. When he talked to Dr. Paige out East, she advised him to switch Jenny to Claforan IV.

"This is a very pitiful case," the new doctor said. "I have no idea where the psychiatric diagnosis came into the picture." He was blunt and said he didn't know if Jenny was going to make it. Then he said, *"I don't think this is Lyme disease because Lyme does not get this bad."* It was his opinion it was more likely a progressive virus that had affected the brain. He had no good news. He felt her prognosis was extremely poor.

Jenny's MRI showed no definite abnormality, but there was slightly more enhancement of the membranes enclosing her brain and spinal cord than he was accustomed to seeing.

After Jenny was moved into a regular room, she was seen by a neurologist new to her case. It was Wednesday, the day the New Jersey doctor was off, but I could feel God with us. When the neurologist suggested a psychiatric work-up, I knew right then I wasn't putting up with anymore idiocy.

My energy was up and I left Jenny's room and immediately found a pay phone to call Dr. Paige in New Jersey. When I reached her office, I couldn't believe it. I was told, "She is trying to locate you." We talked and I explained to her what was going on. In no time, arrangements were made to transfer Jenny to New Jersey.

When Jenny was placed on Rocephin, it was with the understanding we were to make arrangements to get her to New Jersey so the doctor there could see her. When Jenny started seizing, no one would transport her that far because of her unpredictable condition.

After I got off the phone, I started towards Jenny's room and ran right into the neurologist. He said he wouldn't see her until the next day. "Get Jenny's papers ready for discharge," I ordered. The doctor looked stunned, but he only responded, "Okay." I wasn't worried about his feelings and opinions, and he knew I was serious. Our insurance company made arrangements with an air ambulance company in Florida for the flight to New Jersey.

Air Ambulance

We left Ohio on July 6, 1989, and Nancy Miller, whom we had first met as a night nurse at Miseracordia, decided to go with us. She was unbelievably good to Jenny, and became a welcomed supporter in our fight with Lyme. Nancy cared intensely about her patients and always felt something more had to be done to find out what was so terribly wrong with Jenny.

After going home to pack, I rode back to Granite Hospital with Nancy and her husband. Jon and Tommy were also there. Shortly after the air ambulance arrived, the flight nurse efficiently checked Jenny. Even though the jet was compact, the pilot had no problem with Nancy going with us.

While Jenny, her supplies and our luggage were loaded, Jon and Tommy looked over the jet and asked a hundred and one questions. There was only one unresolved problem. I had never flown, and I was scared to death. Jenny couldn't go by herself, so I had to accept the fact *we were flying*. There was no other way.

In spite of my apprehensions, the flight didn't seem to take long, and we landed safely at a county airport where an ambulance crew was waiting. My feet were on the ground again! Nancy road in the back of the ambulance and I sat up front with the driver. Heavy road construction made for a bumpy ride, and I worried about how Jenny was handling it. I was grateful the EMTs were gentle and friendly.

I had been warned that people in the East could be rude. What an unnecessary warning! We were treated with kindness and love the whole time we were there. The only oddity was, occasionally, a waitress in a busy restaurant might pitch a menu at the customers. Personally, I found this more humorous than annoying. Other than that, people were wonderful.

As we pulled up to Healthside General in Jersey Meadows, New Jersey, I was discouraged. The entire place was under construction and in turmoil. We were instructed to take Jenny directly to the pediatric intensive care unit. Nancy and I looked at each other and decided looks weren't everything. If they could make Jenny better, I would have gone to a shack.

The intensive care staff asked if we were the people from Ohio. Jenny was admitted to a six bed unit and immediately settled into bed. They couldn't believe she was in such poor condition. Along with the nursing staff, there were several doctors in the unit. They worked under the leadership of Dr. Nkomo, a fine African doctor with dark curly hair.

During my first conversation with him, his accent was difficult. I couldn't understand a word he said. Other than that, he seemed like a giant, cuddly teddy bear. When I got to know him, I realized he was extremely intelligent and personable. And, eventually, his "northeastern" African accent became second nature to me.

It was one in the afternoon when Jenny was admitted. The staff was prepared for her and her orders were ready. Jenny's temperature on admission was 100 degrees. She was dull and responded mainly to painful stimuli and a little touch stimuli. She had spastic extremities and was uncommunicative, although she would pat her stomach with her hand if she had to go to the bathroom.

As they took her history, they questioned us about trips we had taken. For some reason—the trip Jenny, Tommy and I had made to Georgia the previous summer was forgotten. I did tell them she had been out in fields near home taking pictures for a photography class.

She had dearly loved that class and wanted to learn so much and do a good job. Since she couldn't drive, I drove her around the countryside to help her get her pictures. Sometimes, Jenny could be so naive it was refreshing. We were by a farmer's field one day where she found a herd of cows. She just had to capture them on film so she walked way down a lane to the fence and started taking pictures. When she returned to the car, she was delighted. She told me the cows were so excited that one jumped up on top of another just to see her, so she took their picture.

It was obvious Jenny had not been around farm animals much. When I explained to her what they were doing, that they weren't jumping up to see her, she was in a tizzy. She had to develop those pictures with her classmates and she was the only girl in the class. Then, figuring it would result in a lot of laugher, she said, "Oh, well. It will make for a happy day in photography."

As the New Jersey staff did their work up, it was felt that, perhaps, Jenny had been bitten while out in the fields on her photography jaunts. It wasn't until much later that we found out differently.

Based on symptoms and history, Jenny was started on another antibiotic, Claforan IV, for treatment of what was thought to be Lyme encephalitis. A rheumatologist was called in to examine Jenny and give his advice along with others. He talked to both Nancy and me. Nancy told him Jenny had swelling of both knees, particularly the left, both elbows and both ankles.

We never hesitated telling everything, which included how the doctors back home had labeled Jenny. But, part of me thought that if I never mentioned it, possibly they wouldn't have the same hang ups.

Unchained, Unshackled, Unfettered

For some reason, when I met Jenny's primary doctor, Dr. Paige, I felt a hundred pounds lift from my shoulders. What a relief. To feel such incredible trust and faith in someone in the medical field. I never questioned her actions. Going into this thing, Jenny didn't have a positive Lyme test, but she had the bites and all the symptoms. The staff had never seen such a deteriorated stage of Lyme. I was told, "Her treatment will be experimental. We will try to do what is best to get Jenny well."

What else did I have? We were losing her. The last infectious specialist who had seen her in Ohio had told me there was no hope, to prepare for her death. Yes. I understood everything. Her treatment wouldn't be according to protocol or medical books. But she deserved help and we had finally found a place that would make an effort to give it to her.

Jenny needed the best and deserved the best. I knew this was the right place and these were the right people. These doctors made a connection between Jenny being on tetracycline from March 1988 to December of 1988, and her negative Lyme titer.

Jenny was pale and in a lot of pain. Dr. Nkomo described her condition as *"progressive, diffuse cortical dysfunction with vegetative state."* He ruled out chronic encephalitis, chronic Lyme encephalopathy, chronic viral encephalopthy, subacute sclerosing panencephalitis, Creutzfeldt-Jakob syndrome along with isolated granulomatous angitis of the central nervous system, systemic lupus erythematosis with central nervous system involvement as initial manifestation, as well as other vascular disorders of the brain such as moya-moya syndrome or some other bizarre condition.

He wrote on her chart, "This child has been labeled as possible psychological impairment and a psychiatric admission was suggested, but, ultimately, I believe the truth came out when an infectious disease consultant during her recent hospitalization stated there was something seriously organically wrong with this patient."

He wrote further: "This is certainly a sad case and I am not sure how much we can do at this point regardless of the primary diagnosis. I would like to think that this is Lyme disease and this is a treatable disorder, and it may well be Lyme since she was out in the woods and developed a rash reminiscent of an ECM rash with an area of some sort of insect bite. Her initial flu-like illness was certainly suggestive of Lyme, but the progressive downhill course would suggest that if this is Lyme, we have progressive encephalopathy."

Dr. Nkomo agreed to treatment with Claforan, but at a stronger dosage. Along with his partner, this doctor visited often and followed Jenny's case closely.

Since admission, Jenny had experienced seizures off and on, but on Sunday, July 9, she began having serious seizures. Her doctor came from home to check her, and an anesthesiologist was called to prepare to intubate her and put her on a respirator. Before they had to put her on a respirator, they were able to get her settled down. She was given phenobarbital, Dilantin, Klonopin, Haldol, Valium and Ativan for her seizures.

At times, we could tell she was beginning to seize. Her right thumb would start jerking, then the jerking would climb up her arm until her face would jerk in places. Usually a convulsion followed. On July 10, her Claforan was increased to 3 grams every eight hours. On July 11, more purposeful movement was noticed, such as scratching her head. A bone marrow test was done on July 12. Jenny whimpered and cried some during the test. Did she know they were only trying to find ways to help her? Her mentality had regressed until she was infantile-like and helpless, as immature as a baby.

Jenny's 16th Birthday and a Visit from Tommy

July 16 arrived. This definitely was not what I had in mind for my daughter's 16th birthday. It broke my heart to see her. Volunteers at the hospital, people who didn't even know Jenny, brought her a darling black stuffed dog and a card. They had heard about Jenny and wanted to do something. That little stuffed dog is still in her room. Balloons and flowers and cards were sent to her the whole time we were in New Jersey.

Back home in Ohio, Tommy and Jon were lonesome for us. Jon felt he had to stay on the job, so we made arrangements for Tommy to come to New Jersey alone. I was terribly glad to see him and he was happy to be with Jenny, especially for her birthday. Tommy's life had changed in a flash and he felt lost at home.

During his visit, Jenny needed a transfusion and Tommy was a match. We made some adventurous trips to the Red Cross. Much later, Tommy would tease, "Jenny, you are really lucky to have my good blood in you." The transfusion was done with no problems. The week that Tommy stayed was a week he never forgot, including a trip to see the roaring ocean.

On July 16, Jenny moved herself off the bed pan for the first time. On the 17th, the doctors put a triple lumen catheter in because there was so much difficulty getting in an IV. With her seizures, the staff had to have an access available.

During the week Nancy stayed, we had a Bed and Breakfast close to the ocean. After she left, the staff made it possible for me to stay in the intensive care unit and I took showers down the hall. One night a nurse told me there was a Ronald McDonald house in a nearby town. She wasn't sure if I was able to use the facilities because it was for another hospital and for the families of cancer patients.

My clothes needed washing and I needed to rest, so I asked if she could find out if I would be welcomed. There was a major difference about this hospital and staff. I had no fears of leaving Jenny for a while. All the people who were taking care of her could be trusted.

Arrangements were made so I could stay at the Ronald McDonald house anytime I wanted, even if it was just for a few hours. This wonderful home was equipped with everything anyone could need. The private rooms had private baths. Residents shared the kitchen, laundry and an entertainment area and I met many wonderful, helpful people there. Some of us still correspond or call.

There was a taxi driver named Sam who was wonderful to me. His daughter had once been very ill and he knew what it was like. The staff at the hospital teased me about "spending time" with Sam. He became a valued fatherly friend. With some of the other taxi drivers I learned it was necessary to pray for a safe arrival. If I went to the Ronald McDonald house, I went late at night. By early morning, I was back on my way to the hospital. It was wonderful to get a little fresh air and rest and clean up with leisure.

On July 21, Jenny turned her head toward the doctor for the first time when he talked to her, but a cough developed and her temperature went over 101 degrees. The next day a chest X-ray revealed something on the left lower lobe of the lung, so she was treated with 400 milligrams Erythromycin every eight hours and 30 milligrams Codeine every six hours for cough as needed.

On the 24th, Jenny was still running a fever and began having vaginitis, which can be a result of antibiotic use. She also got oral thrush. Both problems were treated and cured with no further problems.

On July 28, the Claforan was discontinued and tetracycline was begun because Jenny was allergic to penicillin, the doctor's first choice. She was given 500 milligrams tetracycline every six hours. By this time, we could see slow improvements and she was more awake. Still, she cried now and then. In spite of all the same symptoms, I knew she was improving.

New Problems

New problems developed on August 1. Jenny's arms were turning inwards badly, she was less active, sleeping more and becoming rigid. The doctor said she had signs of pseudobulbar syndrome. He explained that if he took my arm and twisted it like Jenny's arms were twisted, it would break my arm. Something had caused her brain to malfunction and they began treating her as a head injury patient.

"Even her crying could be caused from this," he said. Some patients yell, cuss, scream and cry when coming out of a coma. Jenny's primary doctor requested an orthopedic doctor just to be safe. They immediately stopped the tetracycline and started her back on the Claforan. For some reason, the Claforan seemed to break through the blood/brain barrier—a selective filter which limits flow of certain substances to the brain.

The intensive care doctor explained that the IV medication doesn't just go in and hit the disease and the disease is gone. Rather, it seems to pound on the brain continually until a little gets in and then it just beats down the bacteria, knocking it out of commission.

"It takes a long time," he said.

Jenny's primary doctor also put her on an IV steroid called Solu-Medrol to try to relax her arms. On August 4, surgery was done to put in another central line. Since she was in an intensive care unit, they could only leave the lines in for a few days. They couldn't take the chance of an infection.

On August 5, the doctors determined Jenny was suffering from pseudobulbar syndrome. Her arms were twisted 24 hours a day. On August 6, her right hand began swelling and her left foot was internally rotated to 90 degrees. The staff took her out of bed and placed her in a special chair for an hour.

The orthopedic specialist wanted to put Jenny's arms and left leg back into correct position and splint her because he was afraid, if it wasn't done, she would be that way forever. Attempts to splint her arms and left leg were eventually stopped.

Jenny responded to a command for the first time in a long time on August 7. On the 8th, both hands were severely swollen, but she was more awake, smiling, less cranky and following more commands.

Her arms were still tender and turned inwards. By the 12th, she opened her eyes more, moved around more, and her joint tenderness was decreasing. That day they decided her cough could be from the central nervous system.

That was also the day she got her first positive urine *Borrelia burgdorferi* antigen, her first positive test for Lyme They decided to keep her on Claforan until her antigen came down and also until her symptoms improved. People from speech therapy brought in a teaching board. Since she couldn't communicate, they thought pointing to things on this board might be one way for her to get her messages across.

On August 17, Jenny was taken to surgery to place a Hickman catheter, a more permanent IV line. The risks of the surgery—bleeding, a collapsed lung or death—were explained to me. Again, I knew it had to be done. Jenny needed the IV.

Everything went well during surgery, but at 11 that night, Jenny began running a temperature of 102 degrees. She was watched closely because we had been told we could take her home the following day. Arrangements had already been made with the Florida air ambulance.

The following day, when her temperature dropped to 98 degrees, Jenny was discharged. Everyone had been wonderful, but I missed being home with my family. As much as I hated to get on that air ambulance, I was thankful to be heading back home with Jenny. It was August 18, 1989. Three months shy of another Thanksgiving Day. Nine months since I first became aware that Jenny was sick.

7. A Flight into Madness

It was such a good thing. A natural thing. We were going home. But it was not to be. We made the flight back to Ohio, where an ambulance from our hometown awaited our arrival. However, it would be seven weeks and another flight to New Jersey and back before Jenny would enter our home.

When we landed at an airstrip only 15 miles from home, I told the EMTs we needed to contact Jenny's Ohio doctor, who would be following orders on how to continue her IV treatment. Jenny seemed to be running a fever, and I felt she needed to be checked before going home. When we contacted Dr. Scott, he told us to bring her straight to the emergency room at Houser Memorial to make sure everything was okay. On our way to the hospital, the ambulance passed within a few miles of our home.

Jenny's temperature was 103 and the doctor wanted her admitted. As badly as we missed home, I knew not to take chances and Jenny was taken to intensive care. I was allowed to stay with her and the entire staff responded wonderfully to her needs. When I did go home one night, I was called because her temperature had gone over 105.

The doctor felt Jenny had a fever of an unknown origin with Lyme encephalitis and a seize disorder with clear central nervous system dysfunction. He placed her on an antibiotic called Cipro and her temperature went down. In a short time, Jenny's temperature flew up again and blood cultures were taken through a Hickman catheter.

Later, she experienced six grand mal seizures in three hours. Nurses eventually got them under control with medication. Jenny also developed a severe rash all over her body. The results of her blood cultures were positive, so the Hickman catheter was immediately removed. She was placed on 100 milligrams of Benedryl every six hours. Dr. Scott talked with

Dr. Paige in New Jersey who felt the rash could be from the antibiotics. Both the IV antibiotics and the Cipro were stopped, since Jenny's fever had gone down other times when antibiotics had been stopped. The rash gradually decreased, but it took quite sometime.

On September 2, the doctor noticed two swollen lymph nodes under Jenny's scalp, which he planned to biopsy. Dr. Scott thought the increased pain was arthralgia, nerve pain in her joints. When her pain medicine was increased, she experienced more seizures. It was overwhelming to realize Jenny was gradually declining again.

"Jenny appears to be more sedated, very lethargic, weaker and her cry seems to be more neurological," Dr. Scott wrote on her chart. He noted less rotation of the arm and felt this was a neurological change. Jenny had been off Claforan for a few days. I didn't know if that was the problem, but everyone could see Jenny was getting worse. Soon she became unresponsive.

After talking with Dr. Paige out east, Dr. Scott agreed that a transfer back to New Jersey would be advisable. Lyme was conquering her again. The nurses at the hospital told me I knew my daughter and to do what I thought was best. Returning to New Jersey was best.

For the first time, there was a battle with the insurance company because they needed to have a meeting to discuss their part of the air ambulance cost before the trip. I didn't intend to wait a few days for them to have their meeting so, on my own, I made arrangements to fly back to New Jersey. In my worst dreams I never thought I would have to get back into an airplane again.

We landed in New Jersey on September 8, to find an ambulance crew waiting for us. It felt like we were the sorry cast in a poorly rated TV show. Jenny was extremely uncomfortable and responded little. The intensive care unit staff couldn't believe we had returned so quickly. When Jenny's primary doctor had called in new orders, the unit staff wondered what had happened. It was late when we arrived and they quickly settled her into bed in the six bed unit.

The doctors questioned me about Jenny's condition and I filled out all her papers. The diagnosis for this admission was *progressive neurological deterioration and Lyme encephalopathy*.

They were aware that Jenny had been hospitalized all the while we were home because of persistent high fever, accompanied by seizure activity.

Initially, Jenny's temperature rose to 105. It remained in the 102 - 103 degree range for the first six days of this admission at the New Jersey hospital.

Her doctors were concerned that Jenny didn't have a central line. I explained it was removed due to a positive blood culture. The staff began their work with determination to get her well.

It was beyond my understanding, but I always felt relief in the Jersey hospital. "God surely led us here," I thought.

Back to Ground Zero

The doctors immediately started Jenny back on Claforan IV treatments. They had seen her deterioration before and hoped this would again make a difference. Other tests were also done. By the next day, Jenny was flushed, but no rash appeared. She had carried a fever since admission.

The doctors discussed their options. The idea of desensitizing Jenny and then giving her penicillin was a thought, but since Claforan had done so well before they decided to give her Benadryl 1/2 hour before each treatment to see if that would work.

It did, and Jenny had no problems as long as this method was followed. Another problem was her muscle tone. It was down in all her extremities. An infectious disease doctor examined her head lesions, tender lymph nodes, approximately 4 - 5 centimeters in size.

A Special Phone Call

September 12, 1989, would turn out to be the best day I had had in quite sometime. I had gone back to the Ronald McDonald house when I got a call from the hospital. First, it scared me. They never called unless something was really wrong.

"Don't be upset," Jenny's nurse, said. "Just listen carefully." I waited and then I heard someone say, "Mom." It was said quickly, but I understood.

"Jenny, is that you?" I cried out. I couldn't believe it. It was Jenny! She hadn't talked for so long! Her voice was soft and she sounded young, but that one word was a miracle. It would keep me going for a long time.

Deep inside, I always felt Jenny would get better, but when everything seemed to go wrong, I would get down. My faith was not without its hours of faltering, torment and questioning. What a terrific nurse to take the time to enable Jenny to talk to me.

When Dr. Paige came in the next day, the nurses couldn't wait to have Jenny greet her. They told Dr. Paige, "We have a surprise for you." She stood by Jenny's bed, waiting patiently. It took Jenny a long time to concentrate and then to speak. Finally, she erupted with a "Hi!" Dr. Paige was delighted. Smiling, she patted Jenny's hand and praised her for speaking so well. Normally all business, Dr. Paige seldom showed her soft side.

Slowly, Jenny began saying more words and speech therapy was begun. Jenny was becoming more alert. It was a lift to see her look around her room, noticing her environment, checking it out. At times, she even seemed to be humming to music. Still, she was lethargic and would cry intermittently.

The infectious specialist met Jenny and asked endless questions. There was something about him that didn't impress me. He didn't feel Jenny was doing well and made some suggestions even though he had never seen her before. What was he comparing her condition to? I could see she was doing better.

She *was* responding to her medical care. He wasn't satisfied and wanted to send her to New York for brain biopsies, worried possibly something else could be going on in addition to the Lyme. I couldn't agree to biopsies. Jenny had been through so much and finally she was improving.

"Why add a questionable procedure to the equation?" If she wasn't improving, that would be another story. Her brain lesions were getting smaller. I told him I just wanted to leave things the way they were for now.

A News Article Worth Reading

Another triple lumen catheter was placed in Jenny on September 14. The following day, she seemed more orientated, understanding, following what was being said around her. She even smiled more. We had received a newspaper from home that carried a large article about Jenny. It also had her picture. The unit doctor was on one side of her bed and I was on the other as we held the newspaper over Jenny, sharing the article.

Then we noticed Jenny was moving her eyes back and forth. Jenny was reading! She had always been sharp and loved books. What a triumph! Jenny hadn't lost her ability to read. Once, Dr. Paige had told me she had no idea what would happen. No promises had been made that Jenny would improve.

She said the disease seemed to have hit Jenny's entire brain and she could possibly end up a vegetable. That earlier conversation remained suspended in the shadows, but I never stopped believing Jenny would get well.

The joints in her upper extremities were less stiff and she tried to say more words, but was unable to do so. When she couldn't speak like she wanted to, she got a little frustrated. Mostly she said, "Hi!" It seemed like we had to say a word over and over and finally she would blurt it out. Her ability to communicate would come and go as if her circuit board was scrambled. The times she could respond were precious. Sometimes I would get to the hospital before 7 a.m. if I slept at the

Ronald McDonald House. I would walk over to her bed at that early hour to find her resting, looking around. Then, she would see me and a big smile would light up her face. On the occasions when she welcomed me with "Hi!" it was like sugar water running through my veins. Jenny had always been sensitive, and tried to make people feel better. Perhaps, somewhere deep inside her, she knew I needed encouragement from her. If she did, she was right!

By the middle of September, Jenny had not experienced any more seizures, not even the pseudo-seizures. Things seemed to be improving slowly, even though she wasn't talking as much. The doctor explained that in conditions like this Jenny could take one step forward and then suddenly take steps backwards. Then she might take two steps forward and even three steps backwards. It was important to appreciate each improvement, and not to expect a lot—now—or maybe ever.

By September 23, she began to wave with one hand. Another triple lumen catheter was put in with no problems. Her left side still did not work, even though the nurses worked hard with her. When Jenny did anything, it took her a long time to think it through, and then it was done in a very quick manner.

Upon request, she would try to move her extremities. The doctors felt she was determined to move her fingers, but she usually couldn't without assistance. They also observed she was attempting to follow commands. In her medical records the doctor wrote, "She is making every effort to recover from this illness."

As the end of September drew near, Jenny was taken to surgery to insert a Groshong catheter. Her doctors felt it would be better, since it would not need heparin put in after flushing the tube. If Jenny continued to improve and had no fever from the surgery, she could go home in a week. The doctors were uncomfortable about letting her go home before that, given that the previous time she had run a high fever and had other problems after a surgery. They were not about to take any chances.

The doctors said Jenny's progress was tremendous. I clung dearly to the hope her progress would continue.

A New Family

During her long stay, the intensive care staff became a family to us. I did most of Jenny's personal care, since I wasn't doing anything else and the staff was busy enough with the other five patients.

All the nurses had worked diligently on Jenny those long days she was critical. To show my appreciation, I tried to help make things easier for them when I could. While Jenny slept, I would rock the other kids and do little things to pass the time.

One day everyone working the unit was hungry for pizza. Dr. Nkomo said he would buy if I went to get it. Well, people in New Jersey drive a little differently than people near our small town in Ohio.

"Watch for the circles," I was warned. It didn't take me long to figure out what they were talking about. At the rotary intersections it seemed like six lanes got squeezed into two lanes all at once.

I soon found out I should just *gas it and go*. Checking out the traffic didn't seem to help. While on my pizza run, I got stuck at a shoot-out at a gas station. By the time I got back to the hospital, I had the pizza but very little appetite. Dr. Nkomo assured me shootings didn't happen often and I could safely go on the next pizza run. I didn't think so.

Our time in New Jersey was one of meeting caring, giving people like Bev Maloney, who paid for a rental car for me. That helped with expenses and made it easier to travel back and forth to the Ronald McDonald House. Then there was my taxi driving friend Sam and his family, and Teri and Eileen from Florida and Patty at the Ronald McDonald House, and Loretta and Walter. Their son, Christopher, was in the bed next to Jenny. Walter entertained us with the "Winnie the Pooh" song, a musical interpretation not to be missed.

There were times I would go back to my room and find envelopes containing money on the door. I had no idea who they were from. One had a note instructing me to buy Jenny something special. I bought her a heart shaped opal ring, which she wore from then on. During our two long stays in New Jersey in 1989, Jenny and I couldn't have been more thankful for the support we received from friends and strangers alike.

It was unbelievable how far Jenny's recovery had come, but Dr. Paige was right. We never counted on all the steps going forward. There was a long journey ahead but her improvement was wonderful.

To help Jenny learn about her family again, I made a family album. Through photos she had a condensed presentation of her life—family, friends and activities. She loved looking at it.

People soon learned that if they mentioned her album, they were caught and ended up looking at it with her. Putting a headset on her, I let her listen to solos she had sung. She was enjoying music again.

I did everything I could think of to help her remember her past. Her friends would write her letters. She would read them, but she didn't know who they were from or what they were talking about.

Nurses took extra time fussing over her, painting her nails in lightening strikes and stars and cutting and curling her hair. They even put make-up on her once. Her recovery thrived on their tender, loving care.

Once in a while the staff and I broke into hearty laughter, like the day a young patient on the loose fed Jenny's hospital account charge card into the bookkeeping machine. *"Ka-cha-boom, ka-cha-boom, ka-cha-boom"* it rang up false billing after false billing.

Another day, Jenny was staring at her window as I approached. What was Jenny to think? Her nursing supervisor was making funny faces at her through the window pane. This clowning around nurse was not only pregnant, she was balanced out on a ledge high in the air. This was definitely "going out on a limb" to cheer up a patient.

For the second time, arrangements were made for Jenny to leave New Jersey by air ambulance. It was October 6, 1989. Jenny's discharge diagnosis was *Lyme encephalopathy*, and she would leave with a variety of medicines.

A remarkable thing happened before we left the hospital. Jenny's primary care doctor came in to discharge her, and before she left she bent down and gave Jenny a kiss. The nurses were astounded. They had never seen Dr. Paige show her emotions like that.

Then I handed Dr. Paige an insurance form to facilitate payment for her services.

"Forget it," she said softly, handing the form back. "You'll need your money—other expenses will be so much." I couldn't believe it. Dr. Paige astutely diagnosed Jenny's problem, took the time to help and care for her, and then didn't want any payment. Truly, God had sent us to her. Humbled by her generosity and kindness, I thanked her from the bottom of my heart.

As we loaded Jenny into the air ambulance, one of her nurses turned around, kissing Jenny and then me. She was crying as she left. How did we ever end up in New Jersey? What a wonderful medical family had encircled us, lighting the torturous, dark tunnel that had encased Jenny.

As we were flying home, I remembered a physical therapist from an Ohio rehab center where Jenny had been scheduled to go. The therapist knew I wasn't thrilled about Jenny traveling for rehab at that time. When she visited, she looked Jenny over and said, that with Jenny being so sick, she needed continued medical care instead of physical therapy.

"We have to treat what is causing the disability before anything else," she said. Clearly, she understood my concerns. Medical people in our area couldn't. There was no doubt in my mind—we had been divinely guided to New Jersey.

This flight home was so rough that my bottom was off the seat more than it was on it! I thought we were never going to land in Ohio. When the pilot decided to take a short nap, it really helped my fear of flying and I didn't hesitate to wake him up.

"Everything is okay. The plane is on auto pilot and it takes care of everything," he said.

"Would you make me feel better and just stay awake?" I asked. Normally, it only took 1 1/2 hours to get home. As we began our descent, I looked out the window. It sure didn't look like our home airport. And it wasn't. We had landed in Pennsylvania until the wind settled down. I couldn't believe we had to endure another take off and landing.

Waiting in the Pennsylvania airport, Jenny said she had to go to the bathroom. Later, I gave her a hard time about her male nurse having to carry her bed pan through the air terminal to dispose of its contents. I thought of the antics she had pulled as a youngster. "Did she do that on purpose?" I wondered. It would be just like her.

Eventually, we landed in Ohio, where our hometown ambulance was waiting for us. What a wonderful sight. It had been an eternity since we had been home. Our family looked great, but they were a bit shocked with me. I had left 25 pounds in New Jersey.

It was October 6, 1989. In less than eight weeks it would be Thanksgiving again. It was hard to take in all the suffering and struggles Jenny had endured since the previous November. Even though Jenny was a lot better, my work was cut out for me. Only three investments concerned me. Putting time into helping Jenny get well, becoming Tommy's full-time mom again, and having our whole family together. When Jenny smiled, the EMTs could see she felt better, and we all headed home with lighter hearts.

8. More Hospital Ward than Home

Before we left New Jersey, I made arrangements for nursing help at home. I explained what we needed and the nursing service agreed nurses would be at our house when we arrived. As we pulled into the driveway at home, a crowd was gathered. Even more people were inside. Evidently, all the nurses were to be there, so things could be explained at one time. The nurses bombarded me with dozens of questions as they tried to set up the IV system. It was overwhelming to realize these professionals were depending on me. I was drained and exhausted.

Grace from the pharmacy sat out in her car smoking a cigarette. There were entirely too many people inside for her taste, so she waited and came in when really needed. I was weary with medical papers to tend to, hauling things into the house, and trying to answer all their questions accurately. My energy must have come from knowing how happy Jon and Tommy were that we were home. Tommy, especially, couldn't wait to spend time with Jenny when no one else was around.

Before we left New Jersey, Jenny's nurse had made me prove I could change Jenny's dressings in a sterile procedure. We would not be allowed to leave the state until I could do this. Surrounded by medical people, I knew I had to do it correctly or become a permanent New Jersey resident. Now, at home, I was grateful I could explain everything to the new nurses. All these people were leaning on me, since I was the only one who knew what Jenny needed.

Schedules for the nurses were set. Each treatment lasted four hours and Jenny had three treatments a day, so nurses came and went for a total of 12 hours each day. I helped with Jenny's care while they were there. During the other 12 hours, I did all her care. The nurses were wonderful, but the nursing supervisor who came to the house once a week liked to keep things stirred up. Nurses that connected especially well with

Jenny wanted to work more hours, which I requested. But the family did not have any say in nursing assignments. The supervisor didn't like requests for specific nurses.

It was critical for me to be able to do all the IVs. There were times when the nursing schedule got messed up and either two nurses would show up or none. One time it was midnight and no one came, so I just went ahead and did the necessary procedure since I knew how. Bad mistake on my part with that supervisor! She was used to a hospital atmosphere, not home care. In home care, nurses deal with the entire family, not just the patient. I felt sorry for the nurses working with Jenny and wished one of them could take over as supervisor.

When we left New Jersey, Dr. Paige had asked me to send videotapes of Jenny so they could monitor her progress. She was still considered an experimental case, given they had never seen Lyme disease deteriorate a patient to the degree it had in Jenny. With money donated by people in our county, we were able to purchase a video camera. It was a help both in Jenny relearning and in documenting her progress.

Another thing the New Jersey staff strongly requested was getting lab work done every week. Watching the results of her blood work would prevent any surprises. The doctor came from our county seat to examine Jenny when it was too difficult for her to travel even 15 - 20 minutes to see him.

The next few months were rough. Jenny went through a stage similar to a stroke victim, and I was thankful we could record her condition with the video camera for her New Jersey doctors. Her situation was so sad I could never have described it in words.

Beth, the student nurse who had befriended Jenny, came to visit. It was a great surprise for Jenny. Again, someone we hardly knew took the time to be with a former patient. I remembered my prediction. Beth was going to make a very, very good nurse. Friends and strangers alike continued to express care and concern. Our church family especially helped with prayers, food, money, flowers, visits and other expressions of love, and Pastor Dave never deserted our family. Sometimes he stopped in alone, sometimes with family members.

Jenny and Tommy also gained an honorary grandparent in Lee Jackson, a lady from our church. She was another willing helper. Just listening to her delightful southern accent gave us a smile. Churches from all over the area found ways to put love into action. And the entire time of our absence, while we were in New Jersey, ladies from a club I belonged to provided a meal every night for Jon and Tommy. When we came home, my cooking was kept to the essentials and Jon and Tommy missed all that great food. Exhausted from working with Jenny, I didn't worry much about the kitchen.

A hospital atmosphere took over Jenny's room in spite of our efforts to bring many of her personal things down from her bedroom. Now, her room included her regular bed, a commode, an IV pole and machine, a feeding machine and pole, an over-the-bed table, a wheelchair, shampoo board and medical supplies from wall to wall. Physical, occupational and speech therapies were all done at home through home health care. The therapists were wonderful and we were appreciative things were being done to help Jenny. Previously, many of these same therapists had watched in horror as she regressed.

One day I was taken aback when a friend brought me some materials on Lyme from Dr. Eastman, whom I earlier thought would help Jenny. He had heard Jenny was being treated for Lyme, found some information on it, and asked my friend to give it to us. I appreciated the papers, but wished he could have shown concern earlier when we needed it so badly.

He even told an acquaintance that he knew I hated him. Seemingly, he didn't know me very well. There are some people I would rather not spend a lot of time with, but hate only festers. If people could walk in each other's shoes, they would be more sensitive. Some troubles are like walking on hard lava rocks in thin soles under the heat of a noonday sun.

Arrangements were made to take Jenny to a rehabilitation unit in another town, but Jenny did not want to go and became upset. One of the nurses was there when the doctor told us of his plans. He didn't care how Jenny felt and said it was going to be done. I talked with Dr. Paige in New Jersey and she told me not to push Jenny.

"Jenny has given her all and will push herself to the limit," she said.

"Sometimes, when a person is pushed too far, it can cause even more problems." Dr. Paige told us to back off and I agreed.

When I told our local doctor, he was not pleased and notified the insurance company I wasn't doing what was best for Jenny. The nurse could see how upset Jenny was and she knew there must be a good reason for her behavior. We had been burned by many short-sighted doctors, and I was still cautious about putting too much hope in the average doctor. My gut feeling was that rehab wasn't the thing just then.

When the time was right, Jenny progressed in therapy on her own drive. Once again it was brought home to me how important it is for doctors to take into consideration a parent's knowledge and insight about their child. Parents should not hesitate to be a vital part of their child's treatment plan. While I was ever present on the medical scene, Jon provided support by staying on the job.

Each Day—A New Adventure

Jenny now had a strong desire to learn more and more. It was like her memory bank was empty and she needed to put things back into it. She had to be re-taught everything. We had given her sponge baths for so long she was a little apprehensive the first time I gave her a tub bath again. She had no idea what was going on. Once she relaxed and realized how good it made her feel, she wanted to take baths all the time. At age 16, she was learning again how to brush her teeth, comb her hair, and do other simple tasks. She was awkward and clumsy, but that never stopped her.

In quiet times she played board games, card games and watched movies. Her nurse, Anita, said, "She loves movies with emotional endings. We laugh as we watch each other cry." Jenny continued to care about the needs of those around her. Petite, kind and easy-going Anita was always touched when Jenny would ask about her and her family before Anita could find out how Jenny was doing.

"She thrilled to see friends and hear how everything was in their lives," Anita said. She watched Jenny greet each day as a new adventure. "She had the ability to make others feel good about themselves. Many evenings when my shift was over, I did not want to leave her," Anita said. Jenny and Anita were so close it was comforting when Anita prayed with Jenny during an IV replacement on an emergency room run.

"Beaches" meant Best of Friends

Jenny and Cindy Nelson had known each other since they were babies. Cindy's mom, Cathy, and I had become best friends in high school, and after we married and had children we still remained close. It only seemed natural that Jenny and Cindy became best of friends too and Tommy hung out with the Nelson boys.

"We were always over at each other's house, staying over night, having family cook-outs and stuff," Cindy said. "I would take all my Barbies down. When we played Ken and Barbie getting married, she was my bridesmaid and I was hers.

"She would string words like 'DAAADDDD' out," Cindy said. "When Tommy would want to know what we were doing in Jenny's room (just girls doing the hair thing and playing school), Jenny would say 'TOOOMMMMY! Get out!'

"One day we started digging around in this big closet in Jenny's bedroom. I was like the little devil and she was like the little angel." Snooping through the closet, they came across my wedding dress and tried it on. "You would have thought we had found a pot of gold, taking turns playing the bride," Cindy said. "Our moms had been best of friends forever and Jenny and I pledged that nothing would ever destroy our friendship either."

When the movie "Beaches" came out, Jenny was very sick, having recently returned from New Jersey. I rented the movie and the girls watched it together. They loved it so much, I kept renting it until we finally bought a copy. "We sang and cried together," Cindy said, "but we always knew one of us losing the other—like the story in the movie—wasn't going to happen to us. We promised each other. We'd find out how to get Jenny cured."

The Nelsons invited us for dinner. When the night arrived, Jenny was feeling really poor. We hauled Jenny from her wheelchair to Cindy's bed where she rested while we ate. Energetic Cindy, with her dark hair designed in the latest style and make-up just so, decided Jenny needed some entertainment and sang and danced to every song on the "Beaches" tape, including a spunky presentation of the bra scene.

Propped up in bed, Jenny attempted to video tape the show, but she was laughing so hard a lot of the carpet and ceiling got recorded. "We had made a pledge to each other—to be there for each other—always," Cindy said.

In spite of that sincere promise, there came a time when Cindy pulled back from Jenny.

"I couldn't figure out how it was killing me so much that she was so sick and she was so strong," Cindy said.

"I was angry. She was this person who loved God, respected his wishes, sang Gospel, everything. And she had this disease.

"I was down. I couldn't take it. There was a period when I couldn't go and see her. I blocked myself away. I didn't want to talk about it. I didn't want to believe it." Many times Cindy would pass the house and see an ambulance there. "I couldn't change it. I wanted her to be happy, but I didn't know how to deal with it."

When Cindy came by again, she learned sign language so they could communicate. Eventually, the day would come when Jenny was back in school, and the girls visited more and passed notes in the hall to each other. "You are a very good friend." "You are a best friend." "You are a very caring person," Jenny wrote.

Years later, the evening of Jenny's graduation from high school, Cindy came down to the house. Cindy still styled her thick brunette hair meticulously, and she loved having a chance to fuss with Jenny's fine hair. "We were kids in adult bodies," Cindy said. "If you would have given us time, we could have broken out the Barbie van."

Get Ready, Get Set, Go

One day Jenny decided she wanted to go somewhere quicker than I could get her there. She slid out of her wheelchair onto the floor. In no time, she was all over the house, crawling with her right side since her left side was still paralyzed. "Scooting across the floor on her own steam instead of getting help is chancy with the IV tube and central line," her nurse, Wanda, said.

We put carpeting down to protect her from breaking a bone or hurting herself on the hardwood floors. Long term steroid use could result in easily broken bones. While Jenny was willing to take some risks, she confided to Wanda her concern about "what my death would do to my family." Wanda was generous with her time and sincerely interested in Jenny, so it wasn't surprising Jenny confided in her.

When she was in public, Jenny had to wear a mask. We assured people she couldn't give them anything, but Jenny couldn't take the chance of being exposed to something they could give to her. If others were a threat to her, Jenny felt "they should wear that dumb mask for awhile." I told her, "Tough,

Jenny. It doesn't work that way." She hated that mask. It made her sweat, causing terrible damage to her make-up job, and bumps popped out on her face. Thinking the fresh air would help her, I made Jenny comfortable in her wheelchair and took her on long walks. Sometimes she didn't feel good and fussed when I got her ready. I was convinced it was good for her, and unless it rained hard, we took walks between treatments.

Each treatment began with IV Benadryl 1/2 hour before the Claforan to prevent reaction. Then came the Claforan, which ran over two hours, then IV Solu-Medrol and finally flushes. From start to finish it took at least 3 1/2 hours.

One time we went to a local snack shop to visit with friends and Aunt Connie, who worked there. Several people were smoking. The smoke bothered Jenny, and she had no problem letting people know how she felt. She sat in her wheelchair, coughing and waving her hand around trying to move the smoke away.

Embarrassed, I took her out of there when she wasn't about to stop. Was she being spunky or immature? Before she was sick, she would never have made such a scene. Rather, she would have tactfully and quietly left the room.

The school sent a tutor to the house. When Jenny began re-learning things, it was like a chain reaction. A good student when younger and learning material for the first time, she now moved a lot quicker when relearning the same things. I don't know if she got bored and craved more stimulation, but we needed to change tutors. The first tutor was a teacher in the lower grades. Did Jenny feel too old for that?

When her nurse, Jane, arrived one day, Jenny was so very ill. Jane lay down with her on the bed, stroking her hair, speaking softly to her. When she asked Jenny how she was, Jenny answered, "I'm fine, Jane. How are you?" (Jenny couldn't even hold her head up.)

"With Jenny it is never a rhetorical question," Jane said with great admiration.

When the school band came and played for her outside her window, she loved it. Other times another friend, Bert, came down and did Jenny's nails with stripes, dots and other designs. She spent a lot of time with Jenny. Bert was going to nursing school and knew she could learn a lot from Jenny.

One of Connie's favorite stories is about a day she came when I was running behind. She asked if she could finish getting Jenny ready. I said Jenny needed her contacts put in. "Well, to me, there is nothing stupider than sticking something in your eyeball. I don't understand that," blunt and to the point Connie would recall years later.

"I thought, 'Oh! God! Jenny please forgive me, I'm going to try this.' She couldn't talk but she made me know she felt I could do it.

"The first one went right in and Jenny was pleased. I thought, hmmmmm, another one to go." Connie genuinely loved Jenny. Not because she was family. Just because she was Jenny.

Throughout the years, Jenny endured countless painful procedures without complaint.

"I believe she is the only patient to ever thank me for giving them an enema," Nancy laughingly observed.

Another day Nancy was alone with Jenny when she received word that her granddaughter was very ill. The speech therapist came and went. Jenny told Nancy to leave too. She promised to stay on the couch and not move until I got home. Nancy explained she couldn't leave her, but she appreciated Jenny's thoughtfulness.

There was one time Jenny reversed her attitude toward Nancy so much that she refused to let Nancy into her room. I felt badly, but Nancy, the nurse, understood abnormal behavior is often normal in a head injury, a classification Jenny fit into given her earlier comas. Nancy decided Jenny had overheard her say something to the supervisor and Jenny thought what she said wasn't right. I couldn't believe Jenny's actions, although she was having her period and her symptoms always got worse then.

With Jenny's illness we never counted on anything. Her recovery was like a step ladder. Steps up—steps backward. When her Lyme symptoms took over and brought her down, we needed to be patient until she got better.

9. A Struggle to Tell a Strange Story

While we were in New Jersey, I had received a call from a friend who told me Heather Lyle, an eight-year-old girl from our hometown, had died. Heather and Jenny had become sick at the same time. I didn't know the Lyle family well, other than introducing myself to them once at a hospital where both the girls were being treated.

Even so, I called them from New Jersey to express my sympathy. They seemed like fine people. I prayed during that whole conversation that Heather's mother, Chris, wouldn't ask about Jenny. I was incredibly glad Jenny was doing better, but I almost felt guilty since the Lyle child had died. It wasn't fair. How could this nice young girl who had so much life ahead of her be gone? I struggled endlessly with this question.

After we had been back home for some time, Jenny gave me an evening I would never forget. Communicating with her was difficult. Because of her apraxia, she couldn't open her mouth or move her tongue. I was resting on the couch around 2 a.m. and she was in her bed. Jenny made a noise to wake me up.

Exhausted, I went in to her. Pointing with her right hand, she tried to tell me something. "We will talk about it in the morning," I assured her. She would have none of that. Never had I seen her so determined. Whatever it was it was important to her, now.

She kept pointing to a picture on the wall that Heather Lyle had colored for her."Yes, Heather made that," I told her. Shaking her head—no, she pointed to her wheelchair. When I told her I would put her in it in the morning, she tried to get out of her bed. I had no idea what had gotten into her, but I got her wheelchair and put her into it. With gestures she implied she wanted to go into the other room. As we moved into the family room, she pointed to a wooden cross art piece my father had made for our family. I still couldn't figure out what she wanted. Finally, after many guesses, I said, "Yes, you and Heather both got sick at the same time." She shook her head, no, and headed over to the family albums that we had looked at so often.

She flipped through the album until she found a picture of family members at Lookout Mountain in Tennessee. Then she tried to bite her wrist. Her message evaded me, but determination was written deeply on her face.

For a long time, I tried to figure out what she was trying to tell me. Had she been bitten at Lookout Mountain? When I asked her that, she was emphatic. Yes, that is what she meant. Then she found a picture of her with her date at homecoming the fall before she got sick.

She cried, "Ooh" and "Ow" as she pointed to her knees and elbows.

Was she telling me she had joint pain way back then? We had always figured she had been bitten while taking pictures in the country near home for her photography class. As soon as I had the complete message, she wanted nothing more than to get back to bed where she immediately fell sound asleep. The next morning, she had no memory of the incident.

At first, I was unsettled. The whole thing was bizarre. Then I thought, maybe God wanted us to know what really happened and this was His way to tell us. People might think I was out of my mind by this time, but I knew Jenny's message could only be interpreted this one way.

If Jenny didn't think about talking, her mouth would open. If she thought about it at all and wanted to do it, she absolutely had no control. Her brain wasn't working in that area. Relearning the simplest of motor skills was difficult, but she worked hard. Independent and stubborn, she often refused help.

While it sometimes seemed to take her forever to do a task, I knew, eventually, she would get each thing done. People who got to know Jenny admired her for never giving up. Kids respected her and showed it in different ways. Jenny had never been a quitter and she didn't want things handed to her now. Daily, she pushed herself to get well.

Our high school holds an annual Music Feast each fall and that year they dedicated their program to Jenny. We took her to the school for the evening in her wheelchair, wearing her mask. To me, she looked much better.

Others were shocked at her appearance and had no idea what to say. When her old friends came up and recalled something they had done with Jenny, she would just look at me. She had no idea who they were since she had no memory.

During the program, she tried to move her wheelchair out of the gym. I wasn't sure what she was doing, but I pushed her out and we went way down the hall to an empty room. Suddenly, she slid herself out of the wheelchair onto the floor. A friend came along and helped me.

Did she feel different because no one else was in a wheelchair? Did she want to show them she could walk when she couldn't? We finally got her back into the wheelchair and back to the music program.

My heart was sad for her. In spite of all the goodwill and friendship, I think she felt like a failure that night. There was no happiness in her.

Mountains to Climb

Most people had no idea of the mountains Jenny had to climb. Walking, talking, eating and just being normal, how we take these things for granted. Never once did Jenny express that she couldn't or wouldn't do something. She tried until she did each task.

One time, Metta, her speech therapist, arrived when the front door happened to be locked. I was in the bathroom and couldn't answer the door. Using just her right hand, Jenny managed to get her wheelchair with two IV poles and machines to the front door. But when she reached the door, she had no idea how to unlock it.

"Damn it, Jennifer! Open the door!" Metta yelled, shivering in the cold. Jenny tried and tried, but that was one thing we had not retaught her, how to unlock the door. When I finally let frozen Metta in, she said, "Would you *please* show her how to unlock the damn door?" I never could imagine what it was like for Jenny—to have no memory.

Even though her mind was essentially a blank slate, there was one thing she didn't forget. Someone was talking about Jesus, and she knew about Him. Jenny had always had a close relationship with God and for some reason, she never lost a sense of that. Jon was usually on duty at the radio station on Sunday mornings, so it was up to Tommy and me to take her to church as often as possible, even though getting her there was never an easy task.

On occasion a friend would loan us a van. It would have been easier to stay home, but church had been important to her so it was worth the effort. Two friends would help unload her when we arrived.

There were times she had no idea she was in church. She would be so exhausted in making the trip, she slept during most of the service. When Jenny was still in the hospital, Pastor Dave told her, "When you come to church, I will wear the sweatshirt that Sammy gave you." It read, "Don't worry. Be happy." Pastor Dave never forgot that promise. One Sunday, he did just that. He wore that sweatshirt while giving his sermon.

A New Way of Talking and Living

Jenny was determined to talk and often made attempts to tell me things by pointing to items. Both of us were frustrated. One day, I remembered how she had seemed to read that newspaper while in New Jersey. I picked up the big family dictionary and gave it to her. She opened it, and proceeded to flip the pages, pointing to specific words until she made a complete sentence. That method didn't last long because she became upset with me. I would forget the first few words and then we had to start over. Metta, her speech therapist, and another friend taught her sign language. There, again, Jenny was far smarter and faster than her mother. She learned signing in a flash. I was unable to learn it at all. Now she knew it, but couldn't use it. No one in the house understood what she was signing.

There was no doubt she was still a smart girl even though she was trapped in a long process of learning to relearn. What a thrill it was to watch her pick up on things quickly, no matter the challenge.

I didn't leave Jenny too often, especially with Jon since he was uncomfortable taking care of her medical needs. One night I ran to the grocery store and when I came home I had to laugh, even though there was a horrible mess.

Before I left, Jenny was hooked up to the feeding machine with no problems. While I was gone, something came loose and formula was flying everywhere. It was like the blind leading the blind.

Jon and I agreed. I would never leave Jenny alone with him again. Tommy never had problems with her medical care, but he was around the house more. Many times, I had to decide. Laugh? or Cry? Thankfully we were able to stay positive most of the time. Our family had always taken delight in humor.

One time as I was taking Jenny down the porch ramp, I turned around to do something and forgot the wheelchair. Jenny's chair zipped down the ramp, flipped over and she landed face first in a mud puddle. When I turned her over and saw her mud splattered face, I broke out laughing in spite of myself. I guess that could be classified as "earthy" humor.

Another time, I was taking her up the ramp when I hit a piece of ice and fell. The wheelchair, with Jenny in it, rolled on top of me. I thought I would never get untangled from that huge, heavy thing, and no one was near to help. Jenny sat there, bubbling with laughter. It was her turn to pay back her mom and she sure was enjoying it.

We also had a lot of laughs with the clerks at a local bank, who invested valuable personal time in Jenny's recovery. Because Jenny had become frustrated when people couldn't understand her, she taught herself to talk by using the back of her throat, like a ventriloquist.

Since we were together so much, I could understand her garbled efforts. When we went to the bank, the clerks would try hard to understand what she was saying. Usually, Kelly Connor was the only one that could figure out Jenny's message.

All in all, they gave her a lot of good times, and Jenny would respond with a wide smile. People felt good when Jenny's warmth radiated. She had always picked her friends wisely, and the girls at that bank were definitely good pickings.

One night, Jenny was resting on the family room floor watching television. Tommy, quiet, reserved, even-tempered Tommy, came in the room and grumbled, "Why can't she get off her butt and help wash dishes?" as he knocked her for a loop onto her butt. That made Jenny mad. A challenge had been sounded.

Able to use her right hand only, with concentrated effort she pulled herself up into her wheelchair, refusing to let anyone help her. Unable to control her steering, she crashed into the doorway as she headed for the kitchen. Jon and I stayed in the family room while the two kids did the dishes. I had never heard so much slamming and banging in my life. Would we have any dishes left, I wondered. When they finished, they went off to Tommy's room, *together*.

That was the only time there had been such fussing between Jenny and her Tommy Tiddle Mouse (her childhood name for him), with the slamming of dishes taking the place of heated words. For the most part, Tommy treated Jenny just like he did before she was sick. She laughed easily when he teased her with his subtle sense of humor. He was simply the best thing for Jenny.

We tried to live as normal a life as possible, but sometimes that was hard. Having almost lost Jenny many times, we were on edge. But no matter what her condition or symptoms, we never, never pitied her. She would have hated that.

One time I asked her if it bothered her not to remember her past. "Mom, you can't do anything about your past," she said. "But you can do something about your future. I want a future." Through it all she usually had a good outlook. We agreed. There was a reason for everything that happens, and, perhaps one day, we would know that reason.

Jenny loved kids, especially babies. I decided to start baby-sitting again to help with some of our expenses. When I started taking care of a little girl named Emily, it was wonderful therapy for Jenny. She worked hard to help with Emily, even when she could only work with one side of her body. Jenny would hold Emily while I pushed the two of them in her wheelchair. As Jenny got better and I took in more children, she would take the little kids into her room, paint their nails, tell them stories and let the little girls play in her make-up and jewelry.

"This little life is so special," she would say. She loved being near any little baby. "Jenny enjoyed watching them grow and change," Anita observed.

Television and old movies helped Jenny pass away many hours. She enjoyed "Hello Dolly," "The Sound of Music" and "Grease." She always laughed at the "Rainman" K-mart underwear scene. Sentimental stories like "Ice Castles" grabbed her. The theme of reaching for a goal in spite of insurmountable obstacles reflected her own struggles. She understood the words, "I felt a power in me." She also came away with this message: "Not trying is pointless and cruel. Not trying is wondering your whole life if you gave up too soon."

Later, much further in her therapies, she would outline the book "Joni" by Joni Eareckson. Her meticulous note cards detailed struggles in Joni's life, which Jenny related to. "...it's a miracle she lived...depression and disappointment...life isn't fair...focusing on the Lord for it takes a strong person to endure all she went through and still find a reason to go on!"

Tapes and videos of groups in the high school music department were watched over and over again. Jenny found happiness in the simplest of things. While baking cookies with Tommy and their cousin, Eric, Jenny started a flour fight. When it was over, her sky blue eyes peeked out from a white powdery face. It was a mess to be thankful for.

10. A Visit with Heather

Just before Christmas in 1989, Jenny wanted to go shopping at the mall, and she asked her friend, Cindy Nelson, to go along with us. Once there, I loaded Jenny into her wheelchair and she asked me not to go near the slipper department. Jenny was still so naive. She didn't think I had a clue she was shopping for slippers for me. The girls went on their way and I headed in the opposite direction. When I met them later, I knew something was wrong the minute I saw Jenny. Cindy was pushing the wheelchair and couldn't see Jenny's face. She was unaware there was a problem.

We rushed for the car to get Jenny to the hospital emergency room with Cindy in the back seat next to Jenny. All of a sudden, Cindy sounded terrified. "I don't think Jenny is breathing," she cried. I drove like a crazy person.

The emergency staff swiftly worked on her the minute we got to the hospital. When she came around, she was surrounded by medical personnel. Later, Jenny kept trying to tell us something. When Cindy and I couldn't understand her, Jenny tried even harder to get her message across.

Finally, I understood. Jenny was saying she had talked with Heather Lyle and she needed to see Heather's parents. Heather was the little girl from our hometown who had died while we were in New Jersey. I put Jenny off by telling her to wait until we got home, hoping she would forget. But, no. When we arrived home, that was the first thing she said. Still, I tried to put her off.

How could I call parents who had lost a child, and tell them my daughter had talked with their daughter? They would have thought I was nuts. In my heart of hearts I knew there was only one other time Jenny had been so determined to get a message across. That was the night she told me she had been bitten on vacation at Lookout Mountain. Jenny was angry with me, but I just couldn't bring myself to call Heather's family.

"Mom, I promised Heather I would do this, please call," Jenny begged. Talking from the back of her throat in a guttural slur, she repeated and repeated her plea.

My friend Cathy, Cindy's mother, knew the story—that Jenny said she had talked to Heather. The next day Cathy happened to see Heather's mom, Chris, in town. Cathy, observing that Chris looked worn out, felt the need to encourage Heather's mother to contact our family. Cathy leaned over and told Chris to call our house if she wanted to feel better.

When Chris called and asked me what was going on, I was dumbfounded and didn't know what to say. Finally, I explained Jenny had collapsed, and after being treated in emergency, Jenny wanted to talk to them.

Chris wanted to come over right away, but I had too much work to do on Jenny right then. Also, I thought maybe I could have Jenny tell me everything and I could write it down for the Lyles. It would be difficult for them to understand Jenny talking from the back of her throat.

The next day when the Lyles came over with their other daughter, Chris looked exhausted. As Jenny talked to them, the power of God could be felt in her room.

Jenny told about going to the mall, even though she now confessed she had felt ill before we left home. At the mall, Jenny and Cindy saw a large porcelain angel with moving hands holding a light. Jenny wanted to buy this angel in the worst way for me, but it cost $60 and Cindy had told Jenny, "You can't afford it." Jenny felt she just had to have it, and asked Cindy to get more money from me. Then she felt dizzy. The next thing she remembered was me shaking her, yelling her name. Again she felt dizzy and weak.

The night before the Lyles came to visit, Jenny had again described her visit with Heather, and I wrote down every detail. It took three pages. Part of her experience follows:

Then, all of a sudden, there was a light. White, gold and yellow. Very bright! All I could see was this blinding light... A little girl walking around. Her hair was long and brown and so beautiful.

She had this white dress. It was like satin or silk and so beautiful... then she started walking toward me. Instantly, I knew who she was.

She was beautiful...she had a pretty smile on her face. I looked down at her and she said "Hi Jenny!" She knew who I was.

The girls had never met, but Jenny explained to Heather's family that she knew they had both been sick at the same time. Jenny continued her story.

Heather looked up at Jenny and said, "I want you to tell my family how happy and healthy I feel and how free I am. I feel so much love." Heather told Jenny to tell her mom, Chris, to get some rest and not to worry about her.

Jenny repeated Heather's words. "My mom will know this message is really from me if you tell her I finally learned to skip." Chris began to cry.

Heather's mother hadn't been able to sleep since her daughter had died. She had been praying God would let her know somehow that Heather was okay.

"Why did I live? Why did Heather die?" Jenny questioned. I had no answers.

Perhaps God gave her the answer. She felt God was talking to her through Heather when she heard these words, "I want you to go back to the world, because you have a goal to meet. There is so much you haven't accomplished yet."

While I couldn't answer many of Jenny's questions, I came to realize that after that experience, Jenny never had any fear of death. "I'm not afraid of dying," she said. "I'm afraid of living like this the rest of my life." I could not see into the future. I did not know that someday this experience would give me comfort. Jenny had already felt the peace of Heaven.

Doctor Problems Continue

Our problems with doctors near home never stopped. Since I refused the out-of-town rehab suggested earlier, I knew it would be necessary to find another doctor for Jenny. The nurses suggested a few doctors, but we knew Jenny had been labeled. Who could I trust to be good to her? I made some calls. Asked a lot of questions. Then one office called back.

The doctor wanted to take over her case, but he proved to be like so many others. It started out great, but in no time he became arrogant and wouldn't even listen to Jenny's nurses. How could he not believe them? The nurses took care of Jenny and knew what was going on. They had no reason to lie.

Jenny kept complaining that her Groshong line was hurting. It had been repaired once because of a little split. That time the nurse came and repaired it on our family room floor with sterile supplies and procedures. Later, we went to the emergency room for an X-ray to check placement. The nurses worked with Jenny constantly and knew she was not one to complain. They felt strongly there was a problem with the line.

Finally, the insurance nurse told us to take Jenny to Dr. Lang, a surgeon. Wearing reading glasses and rumpled clothes, he looked more like a student than a surgeon, but he was wonderful to Jenny. When he put dye down the tube, he discovered the tube was leaking fluid throughout her chest. All her medication had been leaking out into her tissues. He immediately removed the tube, replacing it with a new one.

This doctor had no experience placing a tube like that, but he did a fantastic job. Not only was he top notch in his work, but he had a wonderful warm manner. Jenny was always awake for this procedure. It was comforting to have him pray with her before surgery and tell her how good and brave she was as he worked.

Later, the tube cracked at the top and was repaired by putting an extension on it. That made the tube longer, so we tried to wrap it around in a circle and tape it to prevent it from being bumped or pulled. The way Jenny crawled on her right side worried me. This Groshong catheter lasted quite awhile, but one day, just as I had feared, the tube pulled out a little while she was crawling. I notified the nursing supervisor, who couldn't believe it was pulled like that, so she called one of Jenny's nurses to come and check it.

Out of all the nurses on Jenny's case, the supervisor continued to stir up conflict. She caused stress for nurses and even fought with the doctor once about us going to Clark, where Jenny had been hospitalized before our trips to New Jersey.

We had wanted to go to Clark to see the psychologist who believed in Jenny. Jenny needed someone to help her deal with this unpredictable disease called Lyme. The nursing supervisor had refused to permit us to go and butted heads with the doctor. I wasn't about to stand for that. We went.

When the Groshong tube pulled out, we had to go back to Miseracordia where a surgeon had been absolutely horrible to Jenny. Our minister stayed with us in the waiting room. When the doctor came back from surgery after putting another tube in, he was just plain mean. He said Jenny was pulling her tubes out. I explained it came out accidentally when she was scooting to get around. He told me that was stupid. Later, the nurses said he had yelled at Jenny the entire hour of surgery. Naturally, the nurses were upset.

Jenny asked me why doctors had to act like that. "Mom, I stayed real still and never moved to try to help him, but he just kept yelling at me." I explained it wasn't her fault. It was certain doctors, and she shouldn't expect any changes. I knew in my heart, Jenny would always be labeled a bad person at Miseracordia. I also knew that doctor would never work on my daughter again. Who would willingly expose their child to abuse?

1990—Challenges and Hard Work

After a while, I was doing all the treatments and care. The only nurse that came was the supervisor, who continued to cause us grief. I saw no reason for her to be there, but the insurance company insisted a nurse come. Finally, the insurance case worker and I agreed, the supervisor wasn't the right person.

Arrangements were made with hospital home health to send a nurse two to three times a week to make sure everything was going well and to help if I needed anything. Nurses from that group had helped us earlier, and they had been wonderful.

Jenny and I preferred to keep everything low key at home, and, as in any chronic illness, money remained a concern. "Mom, just do it yourself," Jenny would say. "We don't need anyone else." So many people had hurt her she no longer trusted easily and didn't want to adjust to someone new.

At that time, a typical day for me consisted of getting up at 5:30 a.m. after a night of little sleep. First I would bathe, dress and make myself some coffee. Then I began preparing IVs, injections, machines, feeding tubes and canned nutrition. Jenny and I would get her to the bathroom, which included washing her face to start her day.

Once she was back down in bed, I would hook up her machines and start her treatments. All tubes were flushed after each treatment. Treatments were done at least three to four times a day and lasted two and a half hours each.

Range of motion and other exercises were done in between treatments, and dressings were changed and she was given a bath and her bed was made. Some days Jenny needed to be taken to a doctor or to a hospital for treatments. In addition to nurses visiting, the pharmacy made deliveries and there were continuous phone calls and visits. By now I baby-sat two to four kids daily, along with my housekeeping tasks. Even though Jenny's treatments finished around midnight, I needed to be available several times a night. Her care was the main structure of our day.

Throughout each restless night, there was time for worry. What unexpected thing would happen next? Would there be a medical crisis? Seizures? Tubes malfunctioning, requiring emergency surgery? A machine breaking down? We made the most of each day as best we could.

On a cold winter day, Jan arrived. She wore deep purple eye-liner and a big, dark heavy coat. Jan looked about as happy to be at our house as we were to have her there. It wasn't that I didn't want her, I didn't even know her. But the air was tense. Jenny didn't trust anyone connected with Miseracordia. She never refused to let Jan work on her. She just tuned her out.

Our first home health nurse had been sweet and really stood up for Jenny. I knew deep down, even though Jenny felt I could handle things by myself, the insurance company had to play it according to the rules. They had to have nurse coverage, and truthfully, I really needed someone to lean on.

Jan and I talked. After we got to know each other, Jan turned out to be a special caretaker. She stood up for her patient's best interests no matter if toes were stepped on. Warm and sincere, many times she took care of difficult problems.

The first part of 1990 brought many changes. Jenny was hospitalized twice to regulate her seizure medication. We changed doctors again and gained a new nurse. Jenny improved but still took steps back occasionally. We continued with the same treatment. One positive development was Jenny's relationship with Metta, her speech therapist.

The kids in school didn't know how to deal with Jenny's situation, so one day Jan and Metta went to school with Jenny to speak to her classmates. They showed videos of some of the things Jenny had gone through, and explained Jenny needed to wear a mask on her face in public to protect her. Jan described Lyme disease and its treatment. They talked about Jenny's neurological problems and helped the kids relate to Jenny.

Jenny giggled when she noticed the guys checking out Metta in her short leather skirt. Metta treated Jenny really fine, but if someone walked in on them and didn't know how they dealt with each other, they would have thought otherwise. They did a lot of sharp-as-a-tack teasing. How they loved to give each other a hard time.

Metta is a loving, generous, and challenging taskmaster. I was thankful for her unique relationship with Jenny. In time, Metta took Jenny out to eat, shopping, and on wheelchair walks. After Metta got Jenny interested in East Indian bracelets, Jenny wore them with bright dangling earrings. "She needs them to spruce her up," Metta said.

Jenny especially loved riding in Metta's new car, and dreamt someday she would drive it. They even talked about taking a road trip to Chicago.

Because of her experience and expertise, Metta was able to push Jenny far out on the edge of the learning curve. Metta told me Jenny taught her a lot about life—that you shouldn't hesitate in doing special things with special people. Tomorrows are not guaranteed.

A Happier Birthday for Tom

A home video shows Tommy having a truly "Happy 14th Birthday" in 1990. Jenny was alert and involved in the celebration. She set the kitchen table and later cleared it off, even putting things into the trash bag by maneuvering her wheelchair with her right side only. "I hope you drive a car better than you do a wheelchair," I teased.

Later, when she had improved a lot, she wrote notes critiquing her progress in that video: "Miss Independent, helping mom do dishes. Right hand—thumb loop to keep my hand from clutching up. Hard job—putting on table cloth." But she did it! She described frames 3743 through 3894 with this note: "Tom's B-day. Me—telling a joke."

A month earlier she had analyzed the video of a therapy session: "Mouth opens automatically when you [I] bring food to mouth or for brushing teeth, but won't open when talking." She also commented people would be surprised at how much she could do using only one hand and her teeth. Every day we watched a series of hard won "Super Bowl" victories.

A year later, on Tom's 15th birthday, the camera records Jenny singing. I had asked Tom what special thing happened to him, and he had shyly answered, "I'm the first freshman in our school to letter in track."

Later, outside, the video camera recorded Tom walking over to Jenny, taking her face in his hands and kissing her on top of the head. Reacting to the camera in her face, Jenny stuck her tongue out at the lens, then smiled and sweetly said, "Good night, everyone. Have a nice evening. Drive carefully on the way home."

11. Therapies and Laughter

Most of the therapists in outpatient were wonderful. In occupational therapy Jenny learned to do personal care and feed herself. Working with only her right hand and her mouth, she learned to open things as difficult as a make-up powder case and lipstick and toothpaste tubes. Then, peering intently into a mirror, she applied her lipstick and powder.

Her first snack using a specially designed spoon and bowl was flavored yogurt. Its soft texture was easy to pick up, and she managed to keep it on the spoon all the way to her mouth. By the time she got to this stage in occupational therapy, her neck was stronger.

Originally, she had lost all muscle control in her neck and body, requiring the use of a head brace on her wheelchair. The occupational therapist worked diligently, stretching and exercising Jenny's arms and hands and fingers and neck. Only through retraining and strengthening of her muscles would she regain control of her muscles, and more importantly, we hoped she would regain her independence.

In speech therapy Jenny was making great strides for a person whose ability to communicate had been trapped behind a paralyzed tongue. Metta reported to the doctor, "Jenny's progress for continued improvement in speech therapy is good based on both the patient's extreme motivation, her family support and good attendance in therapy." Jenny's modified barium swallowing study showed dysphagia, difficulty with swallowing.

When Metta came for speech therapy, girl talk often bantered back and forth before work began. Jenny managed to communicate her love of humor even with her humming voice from the back of her throat. Between the two of them they cooked up the idea that Jenny should have her feeding tube removed in surgery and not tell the visiting nurse. Then, when the nurse came to check her, Jenny would say, "I don't know where the tube is. Can't you find it?" For a sharp-tongued taskmaster, Metta was also swift with praise, when earned.

Metta's commentary during their sessions varied. "What a brat. That sounded like a chicken with a sore throat. What kind of noise was that, Jennifer? Excellent! One more time. Good! One more time. One more time. Say 'Hi' to your doctors in New Jersey. The last one was your best! Hurry up about it please, Jennifer."

A notebook carries Jenny's commentary as she later reflected where she had been and where she was going.

Since I broke foot [my] physical therapies have slowed down. But in time the foot will heal. Mentally I have taken off. Writing with speed.

I have even started lower case cursive letters. And can write my signature. Metta was here this afternoon. We worked with bite block, moving my tongue up roof my mouth, trying to flick making sound.

Metta and I are determined for me to learn how to talk with my mouth open. Responses are quicker.

Five days later Jenny wrote...

Well I tried to type my journal on the computer, miserable machine only saved half of what I wrote. When I write I know what's ending up on the paper. Metta came...worked with similar and differences questions, bite block. Sounds want to come out of my nose. Using back of my tongue easier [to] make sounds come out my mouth where it should. She's impressed with progress I'm making.

After Jenny and Metta had been working together for a long time, we told Metta Jenny had a surprise for her. For the most part Jenny was still talking from the back of her throat.

Looking at Jenny with no great expectation, Metta said, "Okay. What's the surprise Jennifer?" Jenny looked at Metta, concentrated, and clearly said, "Metta."

"Oh, dear God," Metta said as a big smile spread across her face. Both overwhelmed and pleased, she bowed her head, covering her eyes with her hand. She needed a moment to take in the grandeur of Jenny's one word love message. Metta knew better than anyone the effort Jenny had put into training her tongue and mouth to form that one word. As soon as Metta recovered, the taskmaster returned, "Say it again!"

"Metta." Jenny said. "Do you have to think about it? Or does it just come?" the teacher, tutor, therapist, friend asked. "Say something else," she demanded and Jenny clearly said, "Mom."

Jenny greeted Jon with "Hi, Dad! How are you?" one day when he came in the back door during a speech session in our kitchen. Jenny had worked long and hard on that too. Another day, with great concentration, she told Metta, "I—have—money."

A twinkle appeared in her eyes as she broke out into laughter saying, "Take—me—shopping." What a blessing—to hear Jenny's spontaneous laughter flow throughout the house again.

Another day Pastor Dave sat in the corner of the kitchen with delight in his eyes as Jenny, dressed in a bright purple blouse and gosh-awful big earrings, thoughtfully pushed each letter of the alphabet across the tip of her tongue in a soft deliberate voice for Metta. When Jenny finished, she shared a hug with Pastor Dave. "I'm so proud of you," he said.

The time came when Jenny bounced back and forth, speaking from her throat for a word or a sentence and then speaking correctly with her tongue and mouth for a word or a sentence. It depended upon her level of concentration and her stage of relearning. If she rushed to talk, it came from her throat.

As more and more comprehension exercises were introduced, Metta told Jenny to make up 10 sentences. For each sentence, Jenny was given a one word start. Metta gave Jenny a hard time when her sentence using "kiss" was "I want a Hershey kiss." Surely, she could have desired a kiss from some handsome movie actor, Metta teased.

And just that fast, if Metta didn't get the results she wanted, she would bark, "Life's a bitch, Jennifer. This is work. Do it over." Metta knew just how to balance the sugar and spice and keep Jenny challenged. For one of her sentences Jenny said, "I love you, Metta." Her therapist responded sincerely with, "I love you too, Jennifer."

"'Gum, gum, gum,' she begged from everybody when she finally learned how to move her mouth again," Connie laughed. "The first thing, when anyone would come in, she'd say, 'Gum!'"

Her work with her tutor, Bonnie, was coming along well. Jenny wrote in a notebook:

> Bonnie came worked 2 hours. Reviewing continents, locating them on map. States and capitols. Learned few more. Helped me on computer, I think I'm going to need more help.

In physical therapy, Jenny and the therapists laughed so hard I thought they would all fall down. Until Jenny could support her head, it slumped to one side. When she was out of her chair, three people worked with her at a time. One braced her right arm and held up her chin. Another provided support by grasping a large belt placed around Jenny's waist while scooting her stubborn left leg forward. The third person worked from the front. All of them were encouraging.

When better, Jenny looking at the videos of her earlier therapy work and analyzed her efforts and progress.

Me on couch watch t.v. at one time in my bath in bed, all I'd have to look foreward to what is going to Be on t.v. me talking underneath my breath, tongue paralyzed, didn't move lips. talked quickly.

Metta and I discuss men. I was tryin to fix Metta with someone. Lips move slightly, notice some movement. Concentrating to move my lips. left foot turned in. fingers in mouth after while did lick my lips. telling a story when Metta took me shopping, talking to nurse, Wanda underneath my breath.

More personality, acting more and more like a regular teenager. face broke out and very heavy due to heavy i.v. steriods and lack of movement and exercise always in bed or lying on couch. wasen't up a conceterable amount. Very long story!

With OT. therapist, in wheelchair, working on neck control. at the time didn't have any strapped in. combing my own hair, putting on makeup - trying to become as independent as possible. lst time stand up in PT. fully supported, slouches, can't hold my head up...a lot of work. Joined by Metta.

1st time I took step. they had to hold my left foot ground, because it wouldn't stay down. Popped Gt. out [Groshung catheter slipped out from the waistband of her clothing where she kept it tucked.] P.T. taking more steps. Learning how to walk trying a brace on [left leg] to help keep my left foot down.

Seeing how straight I can stand. Tutoring succession, outside...Responses still very slow, reading sightently, [silently] on my own! Reviewing a story.

Equestrian therapy gave Jenny a tremendous boost in overcoming some of her handicaps. While riding, the patient uses the same muscles as if they were walking—with the motion of the horse helping the inactive muscles to relax. At first, she looked like a floppy rag doll on top of the huge animal, and it took three to four people to support and work with her. During her first sessions, she wore a helmet, mask and neck brace.

In six weeks she was able to hold her head up unaided and no longer needed the neck brace. "We have never had a patient improve so quickly," the director of the program said. "We just fell in love with her and her determination." Jenny was thrilled when she no longer needed to wear a mask.

No one had to push Jenny. Once exposed to their knowledge and instructions, Jenny challenged herself. She was her own best cheerleader, and put everything she had into her therapies. When Tommy went along to a session, he would walk along side another patient's horse as a support person.

Eventually, Jenny learned to hold the reins and direct the horse as she sat tall in the saddle holding onto the saddle horn. Equestrian therapy included exercises for arms and neck and adjusting to body balancing. Patients squeeze their legs to instruct the horse to trot. A great part of this therapy is retraining the muscles in the pelvic and nerves in the walking motion. Each thing she accomplished gave her greater control of her mind and body. She worked in this therapy for 22 weeks.

It was a thrill to see Jenny respond—through agonizingly hard work—to the challenges in her various therapies. And what a joy to watch her warm inner spirit connect with these loving, patient helpers. Several of her therapists wrote notes in her 1990 yearbook:

Jenny, To a very special person who is turning into a beautiful woman by the week. I'm glad just to meet you and I'm very lucky to be working with you. I wish you continued good luck in all you do and hope all of your dreams come true. God Bless. Love. Stacy, O.T.

Jenny, To a wonderful young lady who I think is great! Keep up that neat personality. God Bless you in all you endeavor.　　　　　　Love Ya Lots. Linda, P.T.

Jenny, It's been a tough few years but you've come through with flying colors! I know and you know that God does answer prayers. We have to be patient and wait and work. There is a blessing for me getting to work with you and to get to know your Mom and Dad and Tom. I will be watching to see you grow to reach all your goals—I expect invitations to all your graduations! Continued good success and God's richest blessings always! You will always have a special corner in my heart.　　　　　　　　　　　　Love, Marguerite

Dearest Jennifer, What can I say? You've heard it all a million times—you're an incredibly hardworking, determined and smart person.

But best of all is your cheery personality and sense of humor that makes working or just spending time with you always a treat. I've never been as proud of someone as I am of you. I know you've got all the guts and determination to accomplish whatever you want so JUST DO IT!! I wish for all your dreams and aspirations to come true. I wish you a life full of love, happiness and many challenges to motivate you and keep you working. Just remember—take care of yourself and listen to your instincts. God Bless Jenny dear.

　　　　　　　　　　　　　　　With love, Metta

12. One Last Trip to Jersey

In May of 1990, we received a call from the New Jersey hospital. A night was being planned to honor Jenny's doctor for her work and dedication in treating Lyme disease. The evening was to be a surprise, a time to show Dr. Paige how much people appreciated her commitment and accomplishments. We had desperately flown Jenny to New Jersey as a last resort. In Dr. Paige, her associates and the hospital staff we had found a safe harbor. It would be a privilege to join others in honoring her.

When the nurse called and asked if we could possibly be a part of this special evening, I knew it wouldn't be easy. Jenny was still in her wheelchair with its head support so it would take a lot of arrangements, and the thought of flying was still frightening to me. Our church friends and others supported the effort and travel plans were made, including arrangements in New Jersey. Someone even picked us up and took us to the Ronald McDonald House.

It was wonderful to see everyone, especially with Jenny doing better. Jenny still couldn't walk, talk correctly or eat, but she was aware. Our generous friend, Bev, who had rented a car for me earlier, had a car waiting for us.

We were asked to be on the Sally Jessy Raphael show while out East, but declined. It was more important to make a visit to the doctor's office for an examination after the event. We also wanted time to visit the pediatric intensive care unit where Jenny had spent so many months. The staff was delighted to see Jenny and to observe her progress.

The night honoring Jenny's doctor was remarkable. First of all, Dr. Paige was, indeed, surprised. And, while she was pleased to see Jenny, she expressed concern that the trip and all the running around might be too much for her. Even during the festivities, Dr. Paige asked questions and checked Jenny over.

I wondered if she ever stopped worrying about her patients. Jenny and I enjoyed meeting her husband and their daughter.

It was incredible to gather together with hundreds of people of diverse occupations and from many parts of the United States to show appreciation to this fine doctor. We were honored to be a part of the evening. It was the one way we could thank Dr. Paige for the care she had given Jenny and for the way she practices medicine.

The mayor of the community commended Dr. Paige as one who "cares deeply and sincerely about her patients" and demonstrates "great compassion and humanity." Several Lyme patients personally expressed their appreciation to Dr. Paige. Speaking from the back of her throat, Jenny tearfully thanked Dr. Paige for recognizing and treating her Lyme. Where would Jenny have been without the intravenous antibiotics and all the other treatments prescribed by this fearless fighter of Lyme disease?

Notes of Affection

Throughout her lifetime, before Lyme and during Lyme, Jenny impulsively sent off loving notes and cards. Friends, family and acquaintances responded in kind. In 1990, a friend sent this handwritten note, typical of the response Jenny's magnetism had on others:

> Dearest Jenny, I love your courage, your spunk, your determination, your smile, your gorgeous eyes, your pretty hair, your graceful hands, your joyous laughter. In short. I love you.

Some of the treasures I hold most dear today are notes and letters written to me by Jenny.

> Mom, (two tiny dots and a bold curved line represent a smiley face)

I Love You! (words underscored twice)
Thanks for all you do. You're the Best. (smiley face)
Love, Jenny (heart)
P.S. Get Some Z's! (underscored twice)

A homemade card (before Lyme) decorated with string art and a rainbow and tulip:

Mothers aren't a piece of junk you can pitch or throw away. Mothers are the most valuable things on the earth today. We all think you are special in many different ways. Because you are everything I ever want and so much more! I Love You!

Love, Jennifer Sue Umphress

A note to Jenny from one of the singers with The Cathedral Quartet:

Jennifer, Thank you so much for the card you sent me! It was very thoughtful of you and I do appreciate it! Take care and have a Merry Christmas.

In Christ, Ernie H.

On a Christmas card her speech therapist, Metta, wrote:

Jennifer, you are truly a very special and extraordinary person.

A young veteran in our hometown framed his Bronze Star Medal of Valor and gave it to Jenny with this note:

We have many ways of recognizing great acts for brave men and women in struggles. But what have we for brave little girls? It may be inadequate but you have earned at least this in recognition of your courage.

"Jenny didn't have to do anything to attract people," Tom said. "She was just very special being herself. She wasn't false. Jenny was very honest in whatever she said." She encouraged people to look at their choices. "People just grew towards her. It wasn't anything she did. I think they looked up to her for what she had come through and what she had accomplished." Her brother knew her well.

Summer 1990

Jenny and I decided to visit Debbie and her daughter, Sammy, in June. We had grown close during a hospital stay for the girls. It took some time to load up supplies, the huge wheelchair, all the IV equipment, and clothes for even just a couple of days. But it was worth it. We had a wonderful time.

Debbie's apartment *with stairs* was not exactly handicapped accessible. Getting Jenny up and down was a chore. Once settled, Jenny quickly decided she wanted a hair-do "just like Sammy" in spite of the big difference in their hair texture. Sammy's hair was tight and curly. Jenny's was Jenny's.

In spite of Jenny's thin, sandy blonde hair, Debbie could not have been more accommodating. With Jenny spread out on the floor, Debbie lathered Jenny's head with a thick hair dressing and then proceeded to create gobs of braids all over Jenny's head. My junior miss was proud as proud could be of those startling braids. Debbie had created just the look Jenny wanted.

When the girls announced they wanted to go shopping at the mall, off we went with one looking like salt and the other pepper. They had a ball that day, especially when they hid the car keys and acted like Debbie had lost them. We were so furious we thought about leaving them, but they would have just turned that into another adventure.

Back home, Jenny continued to crave learning. Metta had her work on the computer, using a program dealing with her cognitive disorders. The process of cognition, mentally acquiring knowledge, can seem like an insurmountable challenge.

Recovery and the speed of recovery depends upon the injury, damage or situation of the patient. First, the patient must be able to understand each new command. Then they need to dig deep within themselves in an effort to call up the ability to respond. After the command is understood and they are willing themselves to speak or write and their thought process has been stimulated, it still takes great effort to communicate.

In one particular exercise, a question would be asked and there would be three possible answers. It was impossible for Jenny to handle the whole computer keyboard, so I put tape on the a, b and c keys to make it a little easier. We had to time her responses. At first, it could take up to five minutes for a response. By July, she was getting her responses down to less than two minutes. Tommy sat for hours timing her.

"What do you want to learn more than anything?" a new tutor asked. Jenny said she wanted to learn to write so she could communicate. In July, when she began to write, her first papers were indecipherable. I had no idea what she had written, but she worked hard until, gradually, her writing improved. Jenny felt her steps forward were slow. To everyone else, she was coming along fine.

First she learned to print and then she learned cursive again. By the time her handwriting was fine tuned, it looked exactly like it did before she was sick. How could that be?

Earlier, she had a tutor who was impatient with Jenny's slow response time. "Jenny is a visual person," she explained knowingly. "If she had read this, she would have retained it. But since I read it to her, she is not remembering it." Then the instructor dramatically smacked out a rhythm with her open hand on the picnic table in our back yard. It sounded like "Boom, Boom, Boom" to our fragile Jenny as the tutor demanded a quicker response with her thick black eyebrows raised in a "I dare you to figure it out, kid" expression.

"Mom, is that lady with the program or what?" Jenny would later question. "Where did she learn this beat system?

It's okay for music, but you don't have to read to the beat. If she would just quit that stupid pounding...why doesn't she let me think about it for a minute?" As is often the case, the student had more common sense than the teacher.

Three Birthday Parties

That July, we celebrated Jenny's 17th birthday. First, family, friends and her youth group at church gave her a surprise birthday party. The smile on Jenny's face was full reward for everyone.

Balloons and cake and other treats and trimmings made the event festive. Her best buddy, Jenny Y., helped her say "Thank You" when she opened her gifts.

The therapists gave her a party at the hospital which included a risqué cake. When Metta asked her if she understood the Twinkie and frosting-made anatomy decorating the cake, Jenny looked like, "Well, of course. Do you think I'm a dummy?" Her third party was held at home. Tommy didn't say anything at the time, but he was a little jealous of all the attention and parties Jenny got that year. He was too young to understand it was an effort to make up for all she had missed.

"Someday you are going to drive me here," I said one day as I was driving Jenny to a therapy session at the hospital.

"Let's do it today," Jenny impishly responded.

She continued to appreciate everything people did, including the smallest of acts. One time Jenny wanted her hair fixed and a friend came and gave her a permanent. It made her feel so much better. She always had a lot of pride and cared about her looks. When she began to show an interest in grooming and her appearance again, she seemed more like our old Jenny. There was only one change in her likes and dislikes from before she was sick—she no longer loved wrestling. I was pleased. Her dad was disappointed. He still enjoyed the sport.

As she improved, Jenny renewed her passion for shopping. Sometimes when we shopped, she would drift away on her own. Off she would go with money in her purse, moving her wheelchair with just her right side, managing pretty well. When we would meet up, she often had made a purchase. I never understood how she was able to know how much money to pay.

After I found out what she had been doing to pay the clerks, Jenny and her tutor worked on counting money. It seems when Jenny went into a store and found something she wanted, she would take it up to the clerk, open her purse and tell them to take what money they needed—and they did.

Usually, when people came in contact with Jenny for the first time and saw how she looked—her left leg all turned in, splints on her arms, her left hand wrapped up, her head immobile in a head lock, tubes, and a mask on her face—it was obvious they felt uneasy. Sometimes Jenny got tired of people staring at her, or going behind her wheelchair and talking about her like she didn't exist. I tried to explain, often people do not know how to handle situations they don't understand.

Once, when a child looked at Jenny's mask and asked, "What's wrong with you?" I said, "She's going to rob a bank!" Jenny cried, "Mom!"

There was a store Jenny loved because the aisles were far apart and she could get through them easily. When I took her to a different store, Jenny decided to go on one of her independent shopping jaunts. Back at the car, as I was breaking that big wheelchair down into its eight pieces, I noticed something wrapped around a wheel.

Apparently, she had gotten caught up in the clothing displays. The items were snarled tight and it took some effort for me to get them out. I couldn't believe we had taken clothes out of the store without paying. I looked in my purse only to discover—no more money. Embarrassed to the core, I went back and told the clerks what had happened. They just laughed.

God forbid if I ever parked in one of those handicapped parking spots. "Please Jenny, please," I begged. "I don't want to push your wheelchair clear from the far end of the parking lot. Please let me use the handicap sticker."

"Mom, I'm not handicapped!" she'd say in exasperation.

As she improved more and more, she was a delight to be around and she let me know she appreciated the things I did for her. "You never, ever gave up on me, Mom," she would say, giving me a kiss and a hug. "I love you!" She didn't have any remembrance of me being her mother, but she told me she felt a closeness inside.

In one month's time, she went from not being able to hold a pen and not knowing the alphabet, to writing in cursive again. She was also working on geography and taking piano lessons with her right hand. At times, in between treatments, she was able to go out with friends. How she loved going out!

Sharing her Triumph

On an October Sunday in 1990, we pushed Jenny's wheelchair into church and placed her in the aisle at my side. "I looked out at the congregation," Pastor Dave said, "and there Jenny was walking up the aisle the first time since she was sick. I had no idea she could do that or was going to do that."

Holding Jenny's left arm securely, I guided her up the aisle by pushing her left foot forward each time she took a step with her right. She had to wear a mask, but she was dressed up and made up for her triumphant walk down that aisle.

"I doubt if there was a dry eye in the church," Pastor Dave said. She had practiced and practiced, just like she had practiced saying "Dave" until she could say it right. I slipped her mask down and Pastor and Jenny shared a long, loving father and daughter hug as people in the congregation stood up clapping, expressing praise and thanksgiving.

Pastor Dave had seen her, our teenage daughter, moaning and curled up like an infant. He had worried and waited through painful surgeries. He had held her hand through a hell-filled trial. It was only fitting that she share her moment of tri-

umph with him and our church family who had loved and supported her.

Reading from a handwritten note, Jenny shared Romans
8:28. "And we know all things work for the good for those who
are called for His purpose." The translation from her personal
Bible was: "And we know that all that happens to us is working for our good if we love God and are fitting into his plans."

Pastor Dave then asked her to tell the congregation of her
dream. Almost in amazement at herself, Jenny said, "I am going to be a doctor." Pastor's pride and joy could not be con-
tained and I stood back, looking at Jenny with wonder. Jon was
working the sound room at church for that service so he was
present for her grand debut.

Out of Tune but in Concert

On December 2, 1990, Kelly Connor, a local vocalist and
one of our bank clerk friends, was scheduled to give a concert
at our church with Jim Boedicker, who arranged Kelly's concert bookings in addition to his own musical ministry. Bubbly,
vibrant and classy-looking, Kelly easily wrapped others in her
warmth as she dynamically expressed her love of God through
song. Jim's personality was an interesting contrast to Kelly's.
Lanky and easygoing, his quick wit masked the far-sightedness
of his thinking.

Early the previous summer, Jenny could not hold up her
head by herself. "Every time I saw her, she showed me something she had accomplished," Kelly said, "so I would challenge
her. The next time I see you, you will be doing such and such."

Six weeks before the December concert, Jenny was mostly
only talking from the back of her throat. Then, one day just before Kelly sang in her own church, Jenny went up to her and
said, "Hi Kelly!" using her mouth and tongue. It wiped Kelly
out. Soon Jenny was talking more, and on top of that walking.

When Kelly saw Jenny stand up for the first time since she
was sick, Kelly said, "You're so tall!" Jenny towered over

Kelly. "Did I think she wasn't going to grow while sitting in that wheelchair?" Kelly reflected. Realizing how fast Jenny was improving, Kelly had brought a tape to the house in November and asked Jenny if she would sing a song with her and Jim for their December concert. Alone in her room, Jenny practiced and practiced. When the night of the concert arrived, Jenny had not practiced even once with Jim and Kelly.

"Jenny has graciously offered to help us sing tonight," Kelly said at the concert, and Jenny walked up the steps at the front of the church independently. Jim walked behind her in case she had a problem, but she was able to do the steps alone and he did not have to give her a helping hand.

Bending towards Kelly, Jenny whispered in her ear. "Jenny wants to say something before we sing," Kelly announced. Jenny held the mike up to her mouth and with a twinkle in her eyes, teased Kelly by speaking from the back of her throat.

"I've decided I'm not going to sing with you tonight, Kelly," she said. After much laughter, Jenny smiled and said softly in her new found voice, "I'm just kidding." She spoke for a moment, telling of the two years "my family tried to keep me alive, tried to tell others I was really sick." Then, with a positive attitude, she said, "I have a great life ahead of me."

Together Kelly, Jim and Jenny sang "There Is A Mountain I'll Cross Over." It spoke of mountains, oceans, valleys and roads to travel and how it is possible to do so with a friend. Jenny's huge hoop earrings bounced in rhythm as she held her microphone like a pro. A combination of bashful and confidence, she was quick to giggle and shared easy smiles with both Jim and Kelly.

After the song, she had hugs for Kelly and Jim and a huge hug for Pastor Dave who guided her down the stairs. As she walked, her left leg dragged a little and her left arm hung lazily, but she was capable of being independent and loved it!

13. Back to School

From the dawn of 1991, I looked back to summer 1990, when Jenny had told me she was going to school the following year. She knew there was no way she could make up enough work to join her junior classmates, so she was determined to graduate with Tommy in 1994.

Her logic was simple. Tommy was special to her and she would graduate with him. There was no way I could question her desire, so how could I question her decision? Once she set a goal, she felt she could rearrange the whole solar system.

When a friend gave Jenny a gift of money, she decided to use it for a class ring. The trip to buy class rings was an excursion and a half with three teenagers in tow. Tommy, Jenny and I took off with their cousin, Eric. Three teenagers—three class rings to select.

There was no doubt in Jenny's mind about what she wanted. She had her ring figured out to the finest of details, plus she wasn't shy about telling Tommy her opinion on what he should get.

Funny, carefree and flying high, Jenny felt great that day and the clerks could not have been more cooperative, so our mission was quickly accomplished. After we left the store, Tommy and Eric decided to take Jenny on a race across the parking lot in her wheelchair. As I drove the car to the next store, I made sure I didn't watch how they got Jenny around all the vehicles and obstacles in the parking area.

Jenny loved to be around other teenagers, to be included, to be treated normal. In some ways, her illness had taken a toll on her maturity. She fit in well socially with this class two years below her age.

That fall, Jenny decided she wanted a studio picture taken with Tommy, so one of my girlfriends came down to fix her hair. "Make me look different. Make me look older," she requested. "Make me look like the glamour shots." After her hair was fixed, I thought it looked a little uncontrolled. "Are you going to comb it now?" I asked.

"Mom, this is the style. I've looked in the magazines, you know." She was very satisfied with her new look.

With coupons for special photo offers in hand, we headed off for town. At the first studio, she begged them to hide her wheelchair some way. She still needed the wheelchair with the head brace. They did an okay job, but her wheelchair was not hidden. "Good grief, Mom," Jenny had said. "They are more expensive and do less work."

Then we went to a second studio where the photographers loved the challenge of doing a special shot for her. They unhooked and removed her head lock and used her right arm and hand to prop up her chin. Then they covered the back of her wheelchair with a fuzzy piece of material. Jenny looked absolutely beautiful with her bouncy new hair style. It was a Cinderella wearing the glass slipper magical moment.

We were "The Stuff"

Jenny continued improving, and she and Tommy started to do more and more things together. Sometimes, I would get a little nervous, but I had decided I shouldn't stop her. She had handicaps, but not letting her experience things would be taking life away from her. However, both the kids got into big, big trouble with me one day. We had gone out to Aunt Connie's mother's house and the kids were riding the motorbike.

"We thought we were *the stuff*," Tommy said years later. "Eric and I were only 15 and didn't have a license. We'd had a few wrecks, and had learned to not do that again."

That day, I was in the house when kids came running in to tell me Jenny and Tommy were out on the bike. There was only one helmet, and I knew Jenny couldn't stay on the bike by herself with her paralyzed side. I stewed and worried. When they finally returned, I found out how Jenny had managed to stay on. The kids had lifted her up onto the bike, and Tommy had taken Velcro straps and wrapped her paralyzed left leg to the motorbike. The other kids held her up while Tommy hopped on in front. Then he took Jenny's left arm, brought it around him and used her right arm to hold her left arm.

Tommy figured the bike *only went* 60 m.p.h. and they did four country miles. "Go faster! Go faster!" Jenny had shouted to him as they raced down the country roads. I was furious. When they got back, I challenged her about not wearing a helmet.

"Tommy needed the helmet more," she said. "I'm already a head injury patient, so what harm could it have done?" Later, both her physical therapist and I informed her of what harm it could have done. Tommy remembers, "That was the best time ever. It was her first time on a bike and she loved it."

Before the summer was over, Scott, Connie and their family took her boating one day. Once she decided to do something, she tried with all her power. "We tried to push her wheelchair through the sand while holding an umbrella over her," Connie sighed. "She was not allowed to be in the sun because of her medicines and she didn't like that supportive strap on her head."

I had crocheted bands in all kinds of colors to match her outfits so her head support strap would look like a headband and it would not be so obvious that her head was being held up.

Jenny loved practical jokes. After she learned sign language, she had asked her speech therapist to teach her to sign a particularly naughty message. Later, she signed that message for our minister.

Pastor Dave never asked her what the message meant, but he was so proud of Jenny's accomplishment one Sunday in church he demonstrated the signing Jenny had shown him. I thought I was going to die on the spot and prayed no one there could read signing. To this day, I don't know if Pastor was ever told what "he said."

While visiting at Jenny Y.'s house, our Jenny snapped a bone and ended up with a cast on her leg. Jenny Y. felt awful, but she had nothing to feel bad about. With the steroids Jenny was taking, her bones could easily break. Her bright yellow cast stuck out like a big yellow banana.

Seizures, Meds and Steroids

That year as she made more and more progress, Jenny continued to see a Dr. Sommers who worked well with Dr. Paige in New Jersey. Both doctors were neurologists and both were women. Their approach to medicine and their respect for patients clicked. It made a great difference.

Jenny's seizure medications had been gradually decreased and she had been doing well. Then, the doctors had decided to decrease the steroids again. It seemed like every time they messed with the steroids, Jenny started having seizures.

They had also put her on a pill to try to draw off fluid, especially around the time of her period. We were grateful for anything that helped, but if Jenny was going to have a crisis, it always came with her period. After she had improved considerably, her antibiotic was decreased successfully.

That August, Jenny had some problems with her Groshong catheter and the surgeon replaced it. It was getting more difficult to put the lines in because of scar tissue on and in her chest.

Again, these surgeons were gentle and kind, two qualities I treasured dearly in medical professionals. The surgeons could see how much she had progressed and really wanted to help her. We had learned through trial and painful error that a doctor who cares about the patient can conquer a lot.

By the middle of September, the doctors had decreased Jenny's steroids quite a bit and she began having seizures again. I didn't want Jenny to go back to Miseracordia since Dr. Sommers wasn't available. The poor treatment Jenny had previously endured there had been more than enough.

We finally didn't have any other choice, and Jenny had to go back. What a mistake. Jenny ended up in intensive care where things got even worse. Dr. Eakly, an infectious disease doctor, was called. Paunchy with thick gray out-of-style side-burns, Dr. Eakly, who thought he knew everything about eve-rything, outraged our dear Pastor Dave.

Dr. Eakly told us Jenny was no better than she had been on day one. Jenny had worked hard to improve and no one was going to tell her she hadn't made progress.

Pastor Dave told me later, "When I heard him saying to you, 'You just have to get a hold of yourself. You just aren't handling this well,' it was really more than I could take. I knew all your family had been through, all the endless hours. I'm not a physical person. Normally, I can get along with most anyone. I had to turn my back and walk away. I called my wife and said, 'You better put me on the prayer chain because I may hit a man.' My wife was shocked. She knew that was not how I handled problems.

"Jenny has experienced more adversity and heartache than any human being I have known," Pastor Dave said. He saw that in Jenny it was not the size of the challenge that was important, rather it was the character of the person.

An older lady who shared the room with Jenny was furious with Dr. Eakly for his rude and inappropriate remarks. "If I could have gotten a foot loose, I know where I would have put it!" she fumed.

In shaky handwriting Jenny wrote a note about this hospital admission.

...If I haven't told you already I'm in the hospital. My adrenal glands shut down, I went into seizures. Was in Intensive Care for a week, I don't remember. I'm glad I don't. I still have headaches and you can tell I'm shaky. I get to go home tomorrow! I did have an encounter with Dr. Eakly. I just politely told him to go to hell and take all the other Bozos on this case with him. [He was] questing [questioning] Lyme, putting New Jersey Doctors down. Psychiacalogical lable [psychological label]. I just can't handle it any more. Woman in PT finally encourage me, instead of always putting me down. Practiced with words, talking opening my mouth. Surprise say mom, Metta tommorow!

When Jenny's neurologist returned, things got much better. Dr. Eakly had refused to even discuss Jenny's case with Dr. Paige in New Jersey. I told him to never set foot in Jenny's room or have anything to do with her case again. Jenny was put on 100 milligrams of steroids a day and her seizure medications were increased. We were very glad to be out of there and to be able to take her home.

Earlier in the year, Jenny had been tested at a special education center in order to provide local school personnel with information about her programming needs. The school felt it best to send Jenny out of town "to a school of her kind."

That gave me a bitter taste—this idea of a school "of her kind." Jenny didn't suffer from a learning disability. Her memory bank was empty and she needed reprogramming. She had a keen ability to retain information newly introduced. Test results included this statement, "School instruction may aid in recovery and Jenny states a desire for school involvement."

Jenny wanted to go to school more than anything. Her goal was to graduate. Ada High School had never been involved with a situation like this, but I knew Jenny had a right to be there and she was going to have that chance if our family had anything to do with it. Anyone who spent time with Jenny saw the teacher in her. She was a vivid lesson in learning how to live.

Because Jenny was so capable and worked so hard and because I loved her, I continued to fight for her rights. She had come far from the days when she couldn't walk, talk or eat. In spite of her total memory loss, she was relearning. She had a right to be educated in the place she desired. When we met head-on, ignorant resistance from a school official, Jon wrote a letter to the school superintendent stating, in part, "We have been promised several things that remain unfulfilled."

Jon explained, "Jennifer has worked very hard, and has made tremendous progress. She is very anxious to continue her education..." After a formal meeting with the superintendent, details for her return to school were worked out.

News Clippings

Jenny's persistence eventually resulted in her G-tube and central line being removed. She was finally able to eat enough daily to function, and felt incredibly free without those extra tubes. Jenny's friends were able to take her places and she loved going to her brother's football games. When our freshman Tommy lettered in football that year, Jenny was button-popping proud of him.

That fall, the hometown newspaper did an article on her. Other newspapers had also reported on Jenny's case. A newspaper photographer captured her at a football game sitting in her wheelchair with a friend's two little boys on her lap. Proudly wearing a school jersey, Jenny peeked sweetly from between their pixie faces.

Shy and private, Jenny was reluctant about publicity. She hated to be the center of attention. But members of the community had been unbelievably helpful and supportive. They deserved to know when good news was happening, so we took the opportunity to cooperate with some newspaper stories.

Jenny's life with Lyme was also carried in the WTGN newsletter, the radio station where Jon worked and where Jenny served as a volunteer, and in a brochure distributed by our insurance carrier. The Ronald McDonald House newsletter carried her picture after our successful trip to New Jersey for Dr. Paige's surprise celebration.

A Mother's Life

During one of Tommy's out-of-town games, Jenny was near the viewing stand in her wheelchair when Tommy was injured. The coach came to the bleachers to tell me Tommy had a concussion. I was terrified. I had Jenny in a wheelchair recovering from total memory loss and my son was injured out on the football field. Connie took Jenny home while I went to the hospital. It was a relief to learn Tom had a slight concussion and would be okay.

One day Jenny was so determined to be at school that I finally drove her there. She still couldn't talk well. When she saw the school principal, she called out "Hey" to get his attention. He stopped in the hallway and watched as she worked furiously, independently, to get out of her wheelchair and stand by herself. The principal looked shocked. Then Jenny took a couple of steps. She had something to prove to him. When his face softened, I could tell he was touched by her hard work and enthusiasm.

Later Jenny said, "Did you see that look on his face? I thought he was going to pee in his pants." Jenny could still be a mischievous imp.

When we had been in New Jersey, Dr. Paige was frustrated with some patients because they didn't help themselves. "I can give them all the medicine in the world, but if they don't work with that medicine and help themselves, they will not get better." She had spent enough time with Jenny to know she was a fighter.

Christmas 1990, was much better than the previous Christmas. We were home and together as a family. The videos we took that Christmas record how far Jenny had come in her recovery. After the first of the year, Jenny became even more aggressive about going back to school. We knew she needed extra tutoring, but she also needed a social life with her schoolmates.

School Jackets—School Pride

It felt like the fireworks of the fourth of July in January, 1991. Jenny was learning to walk and to talk. Going back to school on a part time basis, she was a picture of sweet, smart and sassy dressed in a school jacket with her name on it. We had given it to her for Christmas.

That cold January day, both our kids were dressed in purple and gold school jackets when they left. Jenny had purchased a school jacket for Tommy for Christmas all by herself. Tommy was still the apple of her eye and she had insisted upon going alone to purchase his jacket.

"Where are *we* going?" I had asked her as she was getting ready to leave the house months earlier on a fine October day. "*You* aren't going anywhere," she had replied. "I just need help with my coat and get me out the door."

It frightened me to watch her leave the house in her wheelchair, ease it down the ramp alone, and then cross the street. She had her purse and she knew her mission. Shopping for a gift for Tommy *on her own.*

With her right leg and right arm, she pushed herself a couple blocks to the local clothing store where she ordered Tommy's wool and leather school jacket, explaining exactly the way she wanted the details.

It was the first item of 12 written on her 1990 Christmas list.

1.   *TOMMY*—letterman jacket ordered 10/29, purple, gold, 2 stripes, name, year, script in front, Back "Ada" script, White Bulldog $159.60.

I glowed with pride when she told me about her successful shopping trip. There had been only one bump in the road. "Mom, there's a dumb little step at the door of that store," she fussed.

That first school day in 1991 was a dream come true as both our kids went off to school. The day hadn't come easily for her, and it was a relief to know Tommy was near. Teachers, staff, and the kids were glad to see her back. She was a member of the graduating class of 1994, but the members of her '92 class felt she was still a part of them too.

First, Jenny took a music class which met early in the morning. Music was still an important part of her life and she greeted each person as she greeted each day—with a genuine smile. The director, Mrs. Knoble, welcomed Jenny back and worked patiently with her.

"Jenny tried to get the right notes," she said. "She knew she wasn't on key anymore and we would pound them out. When she missed a note, she was able to laugh. Jenny walked in grace."

In each succeeding year, Jenny loved being part of the music program more and more. Years later, her friend, Meagan, said, "In choir, Jenny would get her hips and knees going and start snapping her fingers. She would visit with the friend next to her. She had fun in the things she did, enjoying it all."

Slowly, Jenny added classes. It helped that the teachers were understanding. If Jenny had a seizure, it never failed to be with one of two teachers. The first time Jenny had a seizure in Mrs. Michele Elliott's class, her teacher came to our home after school to check on Jenny and make sure she wasn't discouraged and embarrassed. Her teacher knew how uncomfortable it was with all the kids staring, and she wanted Jenny to come back.

As a sophomore, Jenny's first class with Mrs. Elliott was Biology College Prep. Mrs. Elliott had explained to the student who sat behind Jenny that Jenny sometimes had seizures. She requested help getting Jenny safely to the floor if this should happen. She had also explained to a student observer that a padded tongue depressor should be ready to keep Jenny from biting her tongue.

The first time Jenny began to seize in that class, the kids were having a test. Mrs. Elliott was thinking—a 40-question test is a lot for Jenny. Jenny had never gotten her reading speed back. "What would I do if she had a seizure right in the middle of a test?" Just that fast, Jenny slumped out of her chair as Mrs. Elliott was looking at her.

Everyone reacted perfectly. A student got her down. They pushed the desk out of the way. The student observer got the tongue depressor. "Wow!" Mrs. Elliott thought. "This is great cooperation." Then Mrs. Elliott looked at Tom for instructions. "I felt such guilt. I thought, for God sake. I am an intelligent adult. I have worked in a doctor's office. I have been around sick people all my life and I am going to look to a 15-year-old boy and expect him to know what I am supposed to do."

Tommy knew exactly what to do when Jenny arms and legs were thrashing. They held them. "The temperature in that room must have gone up 10 degrees," Mrs. Elliott said, "just from the heat radiating from her body."

Mrs. Elliott asked Tom if he wanted to go home with Jenny and me when I came to pick her up. "No. I will be all right," he said.

"What a tough kid to be able to go on with his day," Mrs. Elliott thought, realizing he had probably seen seizures before, which he had.

Jenny earned a 96 in that test. "Her mind was there and then she had a seizure. I don't think she was embarrassed about it when she came back to school. If she was, she hid it very, very well," Mrs. Elliott observed. The school had mirrored Jenny's schedule to match Tommy's day.

"That is not fair to this boy," Mrs. Elliott thought. "He is a sophomore in high school and he is going to have the stress of looking after his sister all day long."

The next year, Jenny was in Advanced Biology, a lab oriented class (cat dissection, etc.) that required interaction between students. Before a quiz she would go over and over the

names of the muscles, telling Mrs. Elliott, "Okay. Let me practice before we do this. Okay. You say a muscle and I'll point to
it." She would insist the teacher go through every muscle with
her. "She just liked to achieve," Mrs. Elliott said. "A lot of students do a review, it just took her a little longer."

While Jenny's lab mates were considerate and made sure
she had a lab stool if she was weak, they enjoyed verbal joust-
ing about lab clean up. "Chris, I got out the cat. It's your turn to
clean the counter. I cleaned it yesterday," Jenny said. "Hey, I
don't do counters," would be the response. Clean up wasn't
clean up without splashing their share of water.

By the time her junior year came, she fussed when Mrs.
Elliott said they were not going to worry about lab make-ups if
Jenny was hospitalized. "No, Mrs. Elliott, that is not fair, that
is not right. I want my grade the same as everyone else."

Mrs. Elliott settled that. "Jenny, you can't make up lab
work. What am I supposed to do? Drag a dead cat into the hospital with you?" Laughing, Jenny finally agreed.

"Sometimes Jenny got confused in class. We would be dis-
cussing a subject and Jenny might be off in another chapter,"
Meagan said. Jenny would raise her hand, reading away from
the wrong chapter. Then she would just laugh at her mistake
and go to the right page."

Jenny took school very seriously. "Jenny would work on
things for three or four days before it was due and I would just
throw it together before class," Meagan confessed.

A half dozen girls considered Jenny to be their *very best
friend*. Mrs. Elliott said Jenny was "wise beyond her years as
far as what really matters. Girls would be all worked up about
petty fights, spats, gossiping, who said 'Hi' to their boyfriend,
who was supposed to save a seat in the lunch room. Jenny did
not mess around with pettiness. She was supportive, understanding and accepting, unconditionally."

Jenny kept pushing even when it took a toll on her body.
The doctors told her to slow down and take it easy, but Jenny

couldn't slow down when she felt well. She had her eyes set on graduating from high school. Every time she had a seizure, it caused her to take steps backward. Then she would try even harder to catch up with the class.

Her firm resolve inspired others, especially kids who tended to whine and complain. I don't know if they felt guilty when they were around her, but their attitudes improved. They saw how much she accomplished through her positive outlook.

Another thing happened each time she began to seize. Her contacts popped out like clockwork. She never had a minute's trouble except when she had a seizure. How Jenny hated having to tell the eye doctor she had lost another contact, but he would only tease her.

14. Learning by Heart

On March 14, 1991, the Christian television station in our area, WTLW-TV, contacted us, asking if we would do an interview with them. I was reluctant. Speaking in public does not fit into my comfort zone, but I saw how far Jenny had come. We were finally over the hump, and she had been cured of Lyme disease. So many people had lent support and encouraged us we decided this would be a way we could thank them. Jenny also wanted to show people that miracles do happen.

The TV show aired on May 2. It followed Jenny's progress in therapies, using clips from home videos. She also expressed her feelings and thoughts during the interview.

"People ask me if it makes me sad and makes me cry to watch the [home video] tapes. I guess I could look at it that way, but I look at it—that is how far I have come."

She seemed so mature when she reflected, "Life sometimes deals you a raw hand, but God is always there and you just have to keep hoping and praying and fight to get better."

When the program host asked her about her memory loss, Jenny said, "The past is the past. You can't do anything about it. But I have a future and I'm going to make the most of it. Sometimes I would think, 'God, it's about time. We've waited too long.' Mom always tells me good things happen to those who wait. Sometimes I just had to wait a little bit longer than a normal teenager. But it came."

Jenny giggled, rolling her eyes to Heaven when asked how birthdays are celebrated. I told a family story, a trick I tried to pull on her. "Having no memory, she asked, 'What happens on my birthday?'" I had told her, "You go out and buy your mother a really nice gift."

"Naive me," Jenny sighed. "I fell for it until told differently. Wise up. Don't believe *everything* your mother says."

Jenny "ragged" on me and took advantage of being on stage that entire interview. "At one time I couldn't talk at all and the only way I could talk was through a dictionary," she said, explaining how she found and pointed to each word. "I used a dictionary all the time."

Then, in a delightfully sarcastic tone she added, *"It worked okay if you wanted to say one word sentences. But by the time I said [pointed out] my whole phrase my forgetful mother would forget the first word I said—so I had to start all over again and say the whole thing. We went through a little bit of sign language, but that went right over Mom's head. So we stopped that."*

The interview included our whole family. Jon reflected, "We had to turn Jenny over to the Lord. Her illness was too big for us to handle." Even shy Tommy spoke on television. He was happy to have his sister back in his life, and he wasn't afraid to tell the world.

There was one big difference in their relationship since Jenny got sick. Before, Jenny was the big sister and Tommy the little brother. Now, Tom took the responsibilities of the big brother and Jenny was the younger sister. As they reversed roles, he became a super big brother.

We received many positive responses to the TV interview. People who were looking for hope in their life, for solutions to their problems, found encouragement. When Jenny set goals for herself, it seemed to make others fight harder to accomplish their own goals. Jenny never stopped setting goals. A strong believer in *God helps those who help themselves*, she had no compassion for quitters.

A Wish List for Wellness

The better Jenny felt, the more she wanted to do. In March 1991, she thought through her immediate "Wants to Do." Bake pie x 2, bake loaf of bread from scratch, get driver's license, get heater in car fixed, call friend (a guy) and ask him to go to movie, get a permanent (take along a friend), go out with mom and friends at bank, ask Vicki about a job, put rat poison in Dr. x@*%*#'s coffee, get a gift and card for another doctor, and last, but not least—do something special with Tommy!

For a few months, our life was fairly quiet. Jenny had seizures, but we dealt with them as they happened and continued with the same neurologist. Jenny liked her so well, it was nice having her as Jenny's primary doctor in Ohio.

A lot of blood work was required to keep Jenny's levels in therapeutic ranges in hopes of preventing seizures. Her treatment kept her on high doses of steroids, which Jenny didn't like because they caused stretch marks and built up her arms. I didn't like them because of all the side effects.

There were many dangers in using them, but her medical history showed, as long as they didn't mess with the dosage, she had fewer seizures.

Problems ahead of us included concern that Jenny's neurologist would be retiring and moving away. The past had tested us and we had to think of the future. We wanted to make sure she had a competent doctor.

In May, I received a call from a lady in a neighboring town. She had been treated for Lyme disease for 10 days by Dr. Eakly. After the treatment, she became terribly sick again. When she returned to him, he brushed her off and told her she was *cured* of Lyme and she should quit feeling sorry for herself. This came as no surprise to me, considering Dr. Eakly's atrocious treatment of Jenny and his disbelief in her Lyme diagnosis.

Eventually, this woman found a doctor in Indiana and suggested I consider him for Jenny. He had helped her and she felt confident in referring us to him. I discussed this with Jenny and asked her what she wanted to do. After careful consideration, she decided to make an appointment to see what the doctor was like before making any sudden changes. I totally agreed. She was doing so well, I felt in my heart Jenny was totally cured, and that was going to be the end of it.

A Crippling Frustration

For ninth grade science in May 1991, Jenny wrote a paper entitled: LYME DISEASE - A CRIPPLING FRUSTRATION. Were capital letters requested by the teacher for the title page as the writing style for science papers? Or did Jenny want those words to *blast off* the lead sheet just as they had exploded into her life?

She devoted ten and a quarter pages to text, an objective presentation of the facts along with an introduction, followed by subtitles: "About the Ticks," "A Little History," "Symptoms," "Detecting Lyme Disease," "Treatment," and "Helpful Hints to Avoid Lyme Disease."

Not until the last page does she give a personal slant to the subject.

"Something to Leave You With" takes the reader to Lookout Mountain, briefly reflects on how much she lost during her difficult struggles, "two important years of my life!", and praises those who gave her brilliant medical care.

She also believed and stated, *"I have made a complete recovery..."*

People who had watched her slowly progress from an infantile state to a student who could research and write a paper of this quality would have assumed she was cured. However, we still did not understand the insidious nature of Lyme.

Her clarion message was delivered in the three final sentences of her paper:

It's been proven that the best weapon against Lyme disease is public education. Please use precautions when walking in the woods, and take some extra time to spot check yourself for ticks. Lyme disease *is preventable!*

She provided the phone number for a Lyme foundation (see Other Resources), used pictures and graphs to illustrate her subject, and listed six references in her bibliography. Jenny knew Lyme disease, inside and out.

"Very informative—interesting reading," her teacher wrote as she commented on Jenny's "A" paper.

A Mother's Day Letter

Before Lyme, Jenny had been an extremely sensitive and thoughtful child. She was even more so now. Did Jenny somehow retain the intangibles—love, thankfulness, compassion, inner peace, pride, stubbornness, childlike humor, trust, honesty and a tiger-like fight for life? Or did they grow anew? For Mother's Day 1991, she wrote me a letter. Like the facets on a gemstone it reflected her spirit.

> Mom, Thank you for your continued support and love...You have a warm heart filled with love. Your encouragement and understanding have helped me through the toughest and most exciting years of my life...You are filled with so much love, it shines through your smile. I believe my smile is inherited from you. Your not only a wonderful parent, but also my best friend! If I searched the whole world over, I couldn't find a funner, daringer, sweeter, more compassionate person. I love you with all of my heart. How fortunate I am to be blessed with such a wonderful life...
>
> P.S. Thanks—for keeping me laughing.

In school she earned top grades in spelling. In her personal writings, she concentrated on expressing her feelings and did not worry about correcting her spelling.

Jenny and I spoke at several mother and daughter banquets. We showed a condensed video of the steps of Jenny's progress, and we both spoke about her recovery, including humorous and serious things. Jenny would end the program singing "Through It All." It was impossible to meet all the requests, so we tried to get to the churches that had supported us in some way.

Great Love from a Grandpa

Before Jenny got sick, my father bought a riding lawn mower. He brought it over to our house one day and let Jenny drive it. Lordy! Lordy! Looking out our window, I watched Jenny deviously ripping across the yard as fast as she could go with Dad looking like Charlie Chaplin, frantically trying to catch up with her.

"Here! Here!" he had yelled, just like he called his dog. Tommy had laughed, enjoying every minute of the riding mower escapade. Jenny had given her Grandpa Epley a lot of loving exercise that day.

Dad loved Jenny the first moment he saw her, but I know his love for her was engraved even deeper the day she came so very close to dying right in his back yard. Just before Tommy was born, Jenny packed her bag just so, including new clothes she felt she needed because the baby was getting new clothes. Then we took her to my folks, and I went into the hospital to have Tommy.

It was a chilly April 1, and Tommy was two-days-old when I went to pick up Jenny. Just shy of three-years-old, Jenny was in the house one minute and then disappeared. Searching the yard, I could faintly hear her voice answer as I repeatedly called out her name.

I walked around the yard, but I couldn't find her. After some frantic moments, I found her down a deep, narrow hole my father had dug in the back yard for a pole.

Dad had placed a board over the hole, but when Jenny walked on the board, it flipped up, she slipped in, and the board fell back over the hole. When I found her, she was purple and shaking, smashed tightly into the mud with water washed up to her chin. I yanked her out quickly in spite of my stitches from delivery. Was that the day Jenny learned how to be brave?

As a youngster, Jenny always gave Grandpa Epley a hug and a kiss. She was probably the only one who got away with it. And she loved his snow white flattop haircut. "Mom, feel his hair!" Jenny would say as she ran her fingers through his bristles. Well, I just wasn't comfortable caressing my father's hair.

Jenny had no memory of petting his hair before she was sick, and still she had the same habit after she was well. Could all your memory be taken away and impressions remain imprinted upon the heart?

Once Upon a Prom

Suddenly, it was prom time. Jenny had never gone to prom and her friend, Jamie Sizemore, a junior, asked her if she would go with him. Jamie was a special friend who had always been there for her, so she was happy to say yes. And, she just happened to have a dress.

The previous January, when Jenny was learning to walk again, she had begged me to stop in at a prom and bridal shop on our way home from the mall. A sparkle came to her eyes when she touched pretty dresses. She asked me if there was any way she could get a dress in hopes the day would come when she could go to the prom. I knew we didn't have the money, but I couldn't say no to her. It had been my dream too. The day Jenny could walk again and dance at a prom.

It was a cold January day when she tried on a certain beautiful black dress. It was perfect on her. She tried on many other dresses too, and the clerks were wonderful to her as she stretched and strained, getting out of her wheelchair again and again. But, the black dress was it. I would have had to be blind to not see she had fallen in love with that dress. Thankfully, the store clerks were agreeable to timed payments. It would take a long time to pay it off.

Because the steroids had a tendency to change her shape, the dress was altered several times before prom. Once she got the dress home, she must have tried it on 10 times—she always felt so good all dressed up It was the first time she had a glamorous dress.

By prom day, Jenny had saved some money and went to a beauty shop and had bright red artificial nails put on. She was high-fashion proud of them. It had been a long time since she had pretty nails, and she felt her hands looked ugly without them.

Jenny never could do her hair. She couldn't control the curling iron. After I fixed it, we finished it off with a special hair decoration.

When Jamie walked in, Jenny was impressed. He had bought a tuxedo and really outdid himself. "If you want to go with me, you had better pull yourself together," Jenny had challenged him. Jamie had never looked so good. They made a sharp looking couple, Jamie in his new tux and Jenny in her black dress with a beautiful red corsage from Jamie.

As the prom started, each couple was announced and they came out in a grand march. It was a whirlwind of proud parents and friends, clicking keepsake snapshots. The principal told me how proud he was of Jenny. Jamie beamed with her on his arm. It was Jamie's first prom too, and he wasn't afraid to show how thrilled he was to be there with Jenny.

"She loved to dance and she made me love it too. She wouldn't let me sit down on my key-ster," Jamie laughed. "Jen said, 'I am going to dance and so are you.'" Jenny had originally been a member of Jamie's class, the class of 1992. "When Jen came to prom with me, people were really happy to see her even though she was two grades behind," Jamie said.

People who hadn't seen her improvement were startled at how well she looked. It was a wish-upon-a-star night for two young people. They had agreed they were going as friends and seemed to have a better time than many of the couples that were dating seriously. They went to dinner before and to after-prom to finish off the event.

A Birthday Letter

For my December birthday that year, Jenny wrote a loving letter and enclosed it with the birthday card from both the kids. She made sure that my age was prominently written on both the card and the letter.

> Dear Mom, Well, we've both traveled a long rocky road and it seems like it's everlasting...So many things in my life keep changing, but my love for you will always remain strong! You've been my strength, as mine weakends, my inspiration, and hope. You've taught me so much about the real world, and about myself...I know my bond for you grows closer everyday. As if we are twins. I feel your pain as you hurt with me. If I looked the whole world over, I couldn't find a better mom, and a truer friend....Momma, I really believed you helped save my life in a very special way. You believed in me and stood beside me. You fought for me, and you keep fighting every day...When others tell me I'm so much like my mom, I hold my head up high, and tell myself I must be doing something right. Have a Special Birthday—for a very Special person.
>
>   "Love" Your Daughter, Jenny

A Gold Medal Winner for Life

The 1991 high school yearbook, *We*, carried a full page story with photo about Jenny and her fight to survive Lyme disease.

The author of the article described, in Jenny's words, how her behavior had regressed to an immature level, how her knowledge had been wiped out, and the joyful sensation she felt being able to learn again.

It tells of Metta, her speech therapist, who worked her hard and played hard with her. Jenny recalled a Metta challenge, typical of Metta's blunt approach: "Life is a struggle. You can't get everything in life unless you work your butt off to get it!"

I was humbled when Jenny described me as her inspiration. "Jenny gives the glory to her Mom, who was awake with worry when Jenny was sound asleep in a coma."

The rest of the article emphasizes her happiness at being back in school and her appreciation for the support and acceptance she found there. As to the future, " I am here, not to take up space, but for a reason...to help people."

15. A New Doctor

The first of June, 1991, came and Jenny had finished her freshman year. It had been much harder for her than the average student. She had so much to relearn, plus the regular lessons, but Jenny had stayed firm and determined. The teachers were not to give her an easy way out. She wanted to be treated just like everyone else.

Early in June, we went to visit the new doctor in Indiana, Dr. Adams, to see what he was like. Because of our many problems with previous doctors, we naturally didn't expect too much. Our attitude had leveled out to, "If we don't have our hopes up, then we can't be disappointed again." It took almost two hours to drive to his office. Then we had to fill out Jenny's medical history, since he knew nothing about her case.

Jenny didn't know Dr. Adams from the man in the moon and she was leery. I drew comfort from the Lyme patient who had referred us to him. She had told me he really cared about his patients and listened to them, realizing not every situation was a textbook case.

By now I knew Lyme symptoms did not necessarily follow researched descriptions. Each person presented symptoms in a unique way. While there were often similarities or patterns, no two Lyme histories progressed in exactly the same way, and unexpected symptoms and presentation did not automatically mean a psychiatric case.

After hearing of Dr. Adams, I had written him a letter telling him it was a relief to know there was a doctor fairly close to home who helped Lyme patients. For some reason, I never mailed that letter, and, when I wrote it, I never dreamed he would someday treat Jenny for Lyme disease.

Before we made the appointment, I informed our insurance carrier. The insurance company didn't care who we went to.

They considered it the patient's choice. I considered it the patient's right.

The first visit with Dr. Adams was expensive, but he did a complete physical and took a complete history. I made it quite plain to him that doctors in our area felt Jenny didn't have Lyme disease, and that she had been labeled as a psychiatric case. Since Jenny didn't have a memory of her life before she had been sick, and she had been too ill to follow the development of her case, I explained her entire history.

Dr. Adams was unbelievable. He listened. He cared. He appreciated how far Jenny had come. He was proud she was working hard on her education. And he was in total agreement with the diagnosis of Lyme. It was his opinion that the Lyme tests done earlier didn't carry a good rate of accuracy. Given Jenny's history of bites and symptoms, he agreed with the doctors in New Jersey.

However, Dr. Adams was furious about the high doses of steroids prescribed, and that Jenny had been kept on them. Bluntly, he told us how it was going to be. He had previously treated Lyme disease patients and said the disease was difficult to treat, but he pledged to do his best.

Along with his diagnosis he gave us an interesting piece of advice. "If you ever go to a doctor that says he knows everything about Lyme disease, run in the opposite direction." Jenny had already been betrayed by obstinate doctors who felt they knew *everything*, while viewing her symptoms through tunnel vision. I couldn't have agreed with him more. He made sense. What a relief to have complete trust in a doctor again. I hadn't felt this way since we had left New Jersey.

The first step of his program was to get Jenny off the steroids. Dr. Adams made it clear to us that this wouldn't be easy. It was going to be a really rough road, but he promised us he would ride it all the way with us and he did. The steroids would be slowly decreased. Dr. Adams also talked to Jenny's doctor in New Jersey, who offered her services if needed. It was nice to find a doctor closer to home that Jenny liked so well. She took to Dr. Adams right away and it didn't hurt that he had a southern accent and reminded her of a handsome actor from "Mad About You"—one of her favorite TV shows. When I learned Dr. Adams had a daughter Jenny's age, I knew we had come to the right place.

A Driver's License!

By summer 1991, Jenny had been free of tubes for quite a while and was trying to do many of the things average teenagers do. One of the most important things she wanted to accomplish was to learn to drive a car. For her, this was a goal. For me, it was a major sacrifice.

Because she had experienced so many neurological problems, learning to drive was difficult. Or, more accurately, absolutely horrible.

We owned both a standard shift car and an automatic, but Jenny never did anything the easy way. She decided it would be *more sporty* to drive a car that shifts.

Getting her brain, feet and hands to coordinate was almost mission impossible. If her dad had found out what his car went through while she learned to drive, he would have delivered a cow with curdled milk.

My attitude finally adjusted from panic to, if we didn't break it, if the car survived, Jon wouldn't have to know about the trauma. Sometimes Tommy would ride in the back seat. We all got mangled up from the jerk, jerk, jerking each time Jenny stopped and accelerated again.

Before she got her temporary license I had her drive through cemetery roadways. I always told her, "If someone who resides here ever objects to you cruising their area, we will have to leave." Not one soul kicked up dirt, so she hopped Jon's car all over those narrow, winding cemetery roads. Jenny passed her temporary license the first time. Then she practiced driving both in and out of town.

Next, we borrowed the bright orange parking cones from the high school. Talk about stressful. Jamie claimed she kept running *over* them as she practiced maneuvering *around* them.

"Jen, get it *between* the cones," Jamie sighed, when she really demolished one.

"Hush up. I'll get this!" was her typical response. And she did.

When Jenny received her driving license on her third try, she drove out to Kelly's house, grinning from head to toe. "I got it! I got it!" she yelled as she held up the keys. But she didn't like the fact that her license was restricted. It was only good for a few months at a time because of her seizures.

"That's life," I told her.

The following handwritten note is stored with Jenny's papers. It hung on our fridge door for a long time.

I, Jennifer Sue Umphress, Do solemly sware, to wear a seatbelt; while driving my car, or any other car; at all times.

I will not start moving the car until all my passengers are sucrerely in a seatbelt, for their safety.

If I break, this rule, I agree to give up driving for 1 month.

Signed, Jennifer Sue Umphress

Witnessed By: Susan J. Umphress

When Tommy got his license, I had him sign a written pledge too. It was an effort to make Tom and Jenny take the responsibilities of driving seriously.

Jamie knew that Jenny's driving license and cars represented independence, freedom and being normal like other kids. Her cars were her pride and joy. First she had a little Chevie, then a VW Jetta. Both used cars spent a lot of time in repair garages. Then she got a little white Hyundai Excel. It was the first brand new car in our family, and Tommy was as excited as Jenny.

Jamie was impressed Jenny always had gas in her car and kept up her car payments and the insurance. And she was heavy into spit and polish. Her cars were never dirty and she hounded Jamie about the condition of his car.

"Put your seat belt on. Your car is filthy. Clean out your car," she nagged.

"She would help me wash my car unless it was *really* dirty, then she made me do it myself," Jamie said. "If we washed it together, it always ended up in a water and soap war and the bucket getting thrown. We always had a good time."

Hospital Volunteers

The summer brought an incredible switch in medical roles. Jenny appreciated all the special care she received from people, and now she wanted to help others.

To do this, she decided to become a volunteer at Miseracordia. How could she subject herself to such pressure? This was the hospital where people had belittled and humiliated her, treating her unfairly more than not. Why would she want to be part of that institution?

"Two wrongs don't make a right," she stated firmly.

Just because some people had acted poorly did not mean they would dictate how Jenny would run her life. "I feel led to help people at that hospital," she said. And that is what she did. Tom decided to volunteer too.

The personnel in the volunteer office treated her like gold, and had nothing but good things to say about both kids. Mother's pride aside, I admired Jenny for this. One summer of volunteer work led into two and then into three. The kids met many special people during that time.

Angels and Emery Boards

Jenny's bedroom was both typical teenager and atypical teen. She had the luxury of having two fine, richly grained antique dressers, family heirlooms. A clean nut, she kept her room neat as a pin, rearranging it when the mood hit her and it hit her often. Rearranging furniture was a hobby—or obsession—we shared.

Shelves and dresser tops overflowed with "necessities" like angels and emery boards, rings and things, a little wooden sleigh with a white Teddy bear and a Raggedy Ann doll struggling to hold up a heavy head of red curly hair.

When Jenny was young, she received a homemade Amish dress and cap from Grandma Epley for a special festival, and a friend's artist son did a marvelous sketch of Jenny wearing the outfit. From the sketch on her wall, the little Amish girl and Jenny blended into one. She always loved her trips to the Amish with her grandparents.

Tape equipment, speakers and tapes of all kinds were stacked and organized. My mother often took Jenny to buy tapes at an area Christian book store.

The first time Jenny sang "Using Things and Loving People" in church, her solo had been requested by a person going through family problems. She sang it in a sweet innocent voice.

Her back-up tape for "Praise God" blurted from the speakers with a hot and peppy snap. She simply loved all kinds of music. And Tom and Jamie had reason to complain—she played everything loud.

When Jenny was better, Tom would drive us to town shopping and Jenny would sing non-stop to whatever was on the radio. Irritated, Tom would say, "Jenny, shut up. Quit singing that song. Do you have to sing that loud?"

As ornery as a pumpkin growing in a field of potatoes, Jenny would turn around to the back seat and give me a look to see if I noticed what was going on. Tom would change stations again and again to get her to stop, and she would know every song on every station.

A bedroom shelf was the perfect place for a pink hat with white polka dots and a white cap with two red strawberries. Since she no longer twirled a baton, she declared, "It's good to hold open my bedroom window."

A cross-stitch softly shared the message, "We are His people and the sheep of His pasture." A wall hanging from Grandma and Grandpa Epley read, "I said a prayer for you." Jenny's bookshelves spoke volumes about her need to learn, understand more about life, be more compassionate.

Titles on her shelves included: "The Directory of Religious Broadcasting," "The Student Bible," and two books by Joni Eareckson Tada: "Choices Changes" and "Secret Strength."

Others were "Life Can Be Hard Sometimes, But It's Going to Be Okay" and "I Almost Missed the Sunset," Bill Gaither's perspective on life. She had "A Dictionary of Biblical Words" and "The Daily Walk Bible."

It was an interesting mixture. From her childhood she kept "Bible Stories for Little People" and "The Bible in Pictures for Little Eyes." Pat from Dr. Adam's office had given her "Oh, the Places You'll Go" by Dr. Seuss,

"Dating, Picking and Being a Winner" and "What Your Dreams Mean" were resources for sorting out her personal life. Interest in school years included these selections: a "Thesaurus," "Researching Term Papers" and "Above and Beyond—Wisdom and Advice for the Graduate—Making Your Life Count."

A cedar chest, her hope chest, had been started before she had Lyme. As Jenny's friend Cindy knew, having a family of her own was a dream since childhood.

Dates with Pastor Dave

Jenny was so well that Pastor Dave started to take her out to breakfast. They had fun "making a date."

Everyone else just took it for granted they could eat out, Jenny would think as she looked around the busy restaurant. It was a big event for her.

When Pastor Dave realized how much it meant to her to do something normal like that, he tried to take her out once every three or four weeks. She loved it when people thought she was his daughter. Jenny would start their breakfast with a prayer. "Thank you David and I can be out together today." And she was thankful his daughters were not jealous of the time he spent with her.

They talked about school. When she earned a 4.0 average, Jenny decided, "I want to be a pediatrician." Later, realizing she likely wouldn't have the strength for such a tough course of study, she decided she would be a nurse and "help people so they won't be treated poorly like I have been sometimes."

"That was really, really upon her heart," Pastor Dave said. "She would name specific instances where one nurse would do a procedure and it wouldn't hurt and another nurse would be rough and uncaring. She could see the difference."

At some point in the next year or two she told him, "I don't think I can go into medicine. I don't have the strength or stamina." Pastor Dave was pleased Jenny gave serious thought to her future.

They talked about Tommy. "On her best day you could not have persuaded her that she had not robbed Tommy of so much," Pastor Dave said.

"He has to live on the edge because of me," Jenny said. "He has no security. Tommy can't count on anything."

"Tommy was as special to her as she was to him," Pastor Dave would later say.

She lifted Pastor's spirits. "Whether she felt good or bad, she didn't let her feelings dictate how she treated others. Her smile could make you forget anything you had on your mind," he said. "She was always mature spiritually. Jenny and I would lean on each other, her with Lyme and me with my kidney stones. What she would say to me were a lot of the things I said to her when I wasn't having problems. Often times we swapped scriptures. *And that He has begun a good work in us and will finish that work...* She said that to me as many times as I said that to her," he would later recall.

"How are you feeling today?" she would ask before he could even say hello. Pastor Dave realized he couldn't fool her. "I couldn't say I was feeling fine if I wasn't. She would know. She had a heart of compassion. She really cared about people."

There were times when Pastor was hurting badly that he saw tears in Jenny's eyes for him that he never saw for herself. If she thought he was too ill to be out visiting, she would ask him to go home.

Pastor Dave saw no pretense in Jenny. "Jenny was consistent. She didn't demand more of others than she did of herself," he observed. "She let others know where she stood. She was unbelievably honest. What you saw was what you got. *And we just happened to get an angel.*"

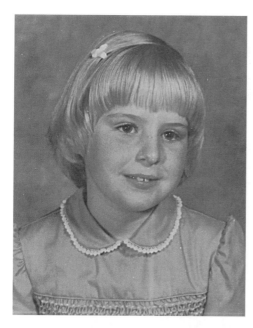

First Grade—1980
A picture of innocence.

Motherhood—My greatest joy.

"Big Sister" means
"Little Mother."

Summer 1985—Dancing with Grandpa Epley.

Lookout Mt., TN 1988—Standing next to Jenny (far right)
and Tommy. Our lives change forever from this day.

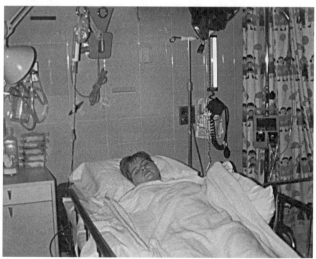

Summer 1989—Jenny remains in a coma after
being rushed to New Jersey by air ambulance.

Jenny wears her "I Made It Happen" shirt.
Roles reverse as Tom becomes the "Big Brother."

Jenny and I make a third trip east—to help honor her
New Jersey doctor. This time she gets to visit the ocean.

Even with her left arm helpless, she loves cuddling babies.

When Metta comes for speech therapy, girl talk banters back and forth.

154

Jenny pulls down her facemask for a special moment
with childhood friend Jenny Y.

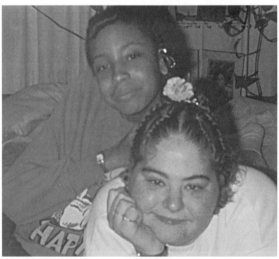

During a visit with Sammy and her mother,
Jenny requests a braided hairdo.

PART TWO

REMISSION
REVOKED

16. Just to be Normal

The first of August, 1991, Jenny joined the high school marching band after a summer of practicing on the marching French horn. She was thrilled to be a part of the band, and worked hard to keep up with the others. Her instructor told her to use her judgment and not to overdo it, but that was like talking to the Wall of China.

Jenny had missed out on so much. Since she felt good, she pushed and pushed and pushed. It was a hot summer and band camp ran long hours, but her goal had been set, and she did as much as the next student.

All was fine until I received a call from school asking me to come to the band room right away—something was terribly wrong with Jenny. When I arrived, Jenny Young was sick with worry. Our daughter had left the house healthy, confident and determined. Now she had no idea who she was, where she was or the day or date. It was obvious she was having tremendous head and joint pain.

Confusion overwhelmed me. I had thought we were finished with this ordeal. When I called the doctor's office in Indiana, the nurse told me to get Jenny to their office as soon as possible. I made arrangements for the children I was taking care of and rushed off with Jenny. It was August 6, 1991.

A rash had appeared, like the one she had earlier with her first Lyme symptoms. In addition to the head and joint pain, she was confused. She didn't act like the same girl.

I told her we were going to see Dr. Adams as we left the band room. By the time we got into the car, she asked again, "Where are we going?" I prayed she wouldn't backtrack. How could this be happening again?

When we arrived at Dr. Adams' office, Jenny was quickly taken into an examining room. After a thorough examination, the doctor expressed his concern about Jenny's decline and said

Jenny needed to go back on treatment for Lyme disease. I could not understand. I thought we had beaten it. Wasn't the disease dead? Wasn't her torment over?

It was then that I learned, that in most cases, if the disease is properly treated *before* it goes into the nervous tissue, the treatment is permanent. Once the disease enters the nervous tissue, however, the victim likely has it the rest of their life. The spirochete is always in the system. Sometimes it can be treated, sometimes the patient may get better, and if it goes into remission, all a patient can do is hope it stays that way.

However, depending upon what is happening in the immune system, the dormant *Borrelia burgdorferi* spirochete can be reactivated. This was the first time I realized I didn't know a lot of the science about Lyme disease. We were living with Lyme. I had never felt a need to research it.

It would be years later before I would learn that, when an antibiotic effectively reduces inflammation, it prevents joints from swelling and blocks the development of arthritic symptoms, thus masking one of the defining characteristics of Lyme.

Once Lyme has developed into the late stage, the bacteria changes the target sites that are recognized by the body's immune system (antigenic shifts) and it is able to stay a jump ahead of the immune system, making it difficult for the body's natural defenses to destroy the bacteria. It is like shooting at a moving target.

Also, bacteria frequently develop resistance to antibiotics. Even though a medicine may have been effective for a previous flare-up, treatment with that medicine may now be useless if the structure of the disease has changed at the cellular level. When Jenny was diagnosed in New Jersey, she was in the late stage of Lyme.

Dr. Adams made arrangements to insert another central line into Jenny's chest. He wanted it done by a doctor he knew who would do it that same day. It was hard to take. Jenny had relapsed so quickly. In this new madness there was one thing to be grateful for—we were fortunate to be with a doctor who believed she had Lyme and who didn't hesitate in providing treatment. He wouldn't let her decline into the condition she had been in before.

After getting directions to the hospital, we headed off for Jenny's surgery. An experienced heart surgeon inserted the catheter. Dr. Adams couldn't have selected a better doctor. The surgeon did a wonderful job and we were able to leave the hospital around eight that same evening. Arrangements were made with a pharmacy to bring the IV equipment and medicines directly to our home.

We settled into a familiar routine of nursing care but, during a procedure at home, a nurse accidentally flushed the tube for the central line and failed to release the clamp, causing a huge bubble in the line. When she realized what she had done, she opened the clamp suddenly and the pressure from the bubble moved the tube out of place.

After an X-ray at a local hospital and an exam at a satellite office by the heart surgeon, it was decided the tube needed to be replaced immediately.

Just three days after the central line had been inserted, we were back in Indiana having it replaced. Jenny's chest was sore from all the surgeries. Getting a central line in her wasn't an easy task, but the doctors did a good job. I was told to make sure that the medical people who worked on Jenny were more careful in the future. It seemed like a long trip home.

At first, Jenny was being treated without experiencing pain and burning from the central line. In fact, the line worked well, without any problems. Little did we know what was ahead. Those next weeks were a horror, but Dr. Adams was with us the whole way, even right after his wife gave birth. He believed in Jenny, but her condition went from bad to worse.

Her pain became uncontrollable and her seizures were more severe. Still, Dr. Adams continued to reduce the steroids.

It was a nightmare. Continuous tests kept track of how the medicines were working in her body. Dr. Adams didn't take any chances and we had complete trust in him, since he was determined Jenny would improve.

Jenny's pain became unbearable. To make sure he covered all the bases, Dr. Adams ordered an MRI because of her severe head pain. He was sure it was from the Lyme disease, but he didn't want to miss anything else. The trips back and forth to Indiana were hard on Jenny. She would lay in the back seat with pillows, and I would drive as fast as I could. She was on medication for her head pain, but it didn't seem to help. Finally, she would fall asleep in the car. At times, she would jerk hard, grab her head and scream in pain.

The MRI was okay, as were many other tests, but the pain continued. Each week turned into another week until six weeks had passed. It was an eternity. Then, Jenny began to come around. Just like in New Jersey, it took the IV antibiotic a while to do its job. She always got worse before she got better. But by September 20, Jenny was improving. After the doctor examined her, he decided to put her on oral antibiotics and see how she would do.

On October 4, Jenny began to decline again. The doctor didn't want her to have another painful relapse, so he quickly put her back on IV antibiotics. She wasn't good. It seemed that a very short time off the medication only caused more problems and she was backsliding. By November 7, she was seizing badly and I called an ambulance to transport her to the hospital in our county seat.

After the emergency room doctor examined her, he notified Dr. Adams of Jenny's condition and Jenny was life flighted to Indiana. This was the first time we had been separated when she was in a crisis. I felt helpless as the helicopter lifted off. Indiana wasn't that far from home, but I worried just the same.

When I arrived home, Pastor Dave and a friend picked me up and drove me to Indiana. I thought we would never get there. In the emergency room, we were told to have a seat and a chaplain would be down to speak with us. Fear surged through my veins. Pastor Dave was also uneasy. Why would the chaplain be meeting us? Something had to be very wrong. Jon had stayed back home at his job and I decided to wait before calling him.

Fighting All the Way
   The chaplain came and escorted us to the intensive care unit. Jenny was still alive! When Dr. Adams could talk to us, he told us there was a problem with Jenny's breathing and a tube had been inserted down her throat to help her breath. He told me Jenny wasn't happy with him, but he had to intubate to help her.
   When he took me back, Jenny was tied down by her wrists and the tube was in her mouth. Jenny gave Dr. Adams a furious look. She didn't want that tube down her and tried every possible way to pull it out.
   "If I untie you, will you take out the tube?" he asked.
   She responded "Yes!" by firmly shaking her head up and down. With the tube in her mouth, she couldn't speak.
   That was one thing about Jenny. She never lied. After the doctor sedated her, Jenny still tried to bite the tube. She was such a sad, sorry mess. She had fought when they inserted the tube and she was fighting it now. The doctor wouldn't do anything that wasn't necessary, so I kept telling myself Jenny would get over it. She would accept the tube because it was needed and that was the way it would be.
   When seizure activity continued, a neurologist ordered medicine to try and control it. After a couple of days, Jenny came around and agreed to leave the tube alone. And she did. From then on, she never touched the tube or tried to bite it.
   After a few days, Jenny was transferred to another room where her bed was padded to prevent injuries. During this hospitalization, she broke a front tooth while seizing. Her doctor

and nurses felt badly, but it wasn't any big deal to me after all of Jenny's struggles. By November 16, I was able to take Jenny home. A visiting nurse came and IV antibiotics and seizure medicines were continued.

Two New Hospitals before Christmas

On December 16, 1991, a home care nurse wrote a report to our insurance case manager, describing one of Jenny's seizures. The nurse said Jenny's right side was involved, not the left, and the nurse felt part of Jenny's brain had been damaged by Lyme disease.

She was also concerned that the seizure medicine was making Jenny lethargic. This astute nurse had been with Jenny long enough to quickly assess Jenny's changes, improvements and declines.

The next day Jan, another nurse, examined Jenny. While Jenny was on the couch, Jan began drawing blood through the central line.

Without any warning, Jenny jerked suddenly. Then she began jerking all over. It caught Jan so off guard, her name plate and glasses were knocked off. The neurologist who had been taking care of Jenny was out of town, and there was no way we would go back to Miseracordia when Dr. Sommers, her neurologist, wasn't available.

We decided to take Jenny to a community north of us. That hospital had a neurologist who had examined Jenny and knew all about her Lyme. He went along with the current treatment and agreed to work with Dr. Adams in Indiana.

After being transported by ambulance, Jenny was placed in one room, then another, and finally admitted to the intensive care unit. In no time Jenny was put into isolation. Everyone was kind and worked well with her, and I was thankful they allowed me to stay in the unit. In order for me to be in Jenny's room, I had to wear a gown, mask and gloves. The staff worked with her from December 17 to December 20.

When it was felt Jenny needed more help, she was transferred to an intensive care unit in Toledo. Both Jenny and I were forming an intense hatred of hospitals. I wanted to take her back to Indiana, but the doctors felt that was too far for her to travel in her condition.

We arrived at the Toledo hospital late at night, and the staff began working on Jenny immediately. Someone paid for a room for me in a motel by the hospital. My one hope was to get Jenny discharged as quickly as possible. She loved Christmas and it was just around the corner. If she could only get some strength back, she would start to feel better.

During her last hospitalization, she ran a fever, the rash returned, and she had seizures that seemed more like hard jerking. After each seize she was weak and complained of headaches and joint pain. It never failed. Whenever her steroids were changed, she would have jerking episodes. I had seen Jenny go through all this before. It was obvious there was a pattern, but no one seemed to listen much.

The hospitalization in Toledo was a total waste of time. Again we ended up with an infectious disease doctor who thought he knew *everything*. Unfair as it may have seemed, Jenny's experiences with doctors in this specialty led me to believe they had egos bigger than a bottomless ravine. It was like a returning nightmare. Suddenly, we found ourselves being asked psychiatric questions. There was no way I was going to subject Jenny to this again.

Cathy visited one day and couldn't believe what was going on. She called Dr. Adams in Indiana from Jenny's room. He told her Jenny wasn't there for treatment of Lyme disease. Rather, she was to be evaluated for the seizures, and he strongly felt we needed to get her out of there.

The Toledo doctor was gone for the day, and I took advantage of this when the doctor on duty agreed to discharge her. I knew that, if a patient just walked out, the insurance wouldn't pay anything. I had hardened. Learned how to play the game.

Within 15 minutes after the doctor left duty, I told the nurse, "If you want us to sign anything, do it in the next 10 minutes because we are going to be out the door." It worked like a charm.

Jenny was thrilled to be going home. All the way, she thanked me for getting her out of that hospital. I could have cared less what the doctor thought. We were gone!

Bluffton, a community between Toledo and our hometown, decorates from one end of the village to the other for the Christmas season. I drove there on the way home and Jenny was thrilled to see the bright Christmas lights and the festive trimmings. That night it felt like we were looking at the beauty of the first Christmas star.

It all happened so quickly—her discharge from the hospital, our trip home. Jon and Tommy didn't even know we were coming so our arrival was quite a shock. Without a doubt, the best present under our Christmas tree was Jenny.

During these hospital stays, Lyme titer tests were done. It was amazing how so many doctors felt that, if you didn't have a positive test, then you didn't have Lyme disease. One of the reports I read concerning Lyme titer was most revealing:

> Absence of antibody does not rule out Lyme disease.
> Some patients may never generate detectable antibody levels.

Jenny's Lyme titer was negative, but I really didn't care about test results. Jenny had improved. Since the test results were not conclusive in diagnosing, they didn't make any difference to us. After Jenny had suffered through misdiagnosis, we had become immune to what incompetent doctors thought. Being critically ill was bad enough. Dealing with the extra baggage of incorrect diagnosis was horrendous.

17. Rebirth at School—Baptized Anew with God

The next couple of months Jenny's health improved. Dr. Adams had taken Jenny off IV antibiotics and she was attending school. All seemed well. However, the nurses continued coming to the house because Jenny still had a Hickman catheter. Jenny thought it was "dumb" to have a nurse come, because she didn't need a nurse any longer.

When Jenny was feeling good, she thought she could conquer the world. The insurance carrier was firm. The nurse would come. Jenny wanted her life to be defined by more than an illness. "*Well people* do not need nurses," she said.

When the school bell rang, there was no other place Jenny wanted to be. Her nurse, Wanda, said that for Jenny, school meant *getting* to learn, not *having* to learn. It seemed everything she was introduced to she readily retained.

The day would come when Jenny got a good grade in French and Cindy didn't. Trying to explain away her "F" grade with humor, Cindy told Jenny, "My F grade stands for French."

Each fall that Jenny was able, she was out on the football field with the high school marching band. One year she stood at the sidelines playing the portable bells, always ready on the mark, in rhythm and looking sharp. Another year she was well enough to strut out for the band's entrance with a marching French horn held high, joining her friends in their fancy footwork before she jogged over to the bells waiting for her on the sideline.

For concert band and choir concerts she was groomed to a soft loveliness. In concert band, she wore a serious, concentrated look in the percussion section, where she played the bells, the chimes and other rhythm instruments. In choir, she'd smile or whisper occasionally to her neighbor, keeping time to the beat, whether slow and grand or bouncy and light.

She changed hair-dos faster than we changed light bulbs and she now wore dainty jewelry. Dresses were picked for flair. She loved feeling dressed up. Some years bandages covered the tubing in her chest.

At one concert, the long tube hung over the huge collar of her off-the-shoulder dress. People a few rows back likely did not know she was connected to her portable IV pump, having a treatment.

A Heavy Heart for the Class of '92

"I will never forget marching off the band field after pregame for my last time—the last home football game of my senior year," said Jenny's friend Jeana. "Seeing Jenny's face, so sad with tears, crying because she was going to miss us, the seniors. I always considered her still in our class, even though she was now two years behind.

"Before that moment I thought that evening was fairly insignificant until I started to cry, realizing how much I would miss her in marching band and everyday after graduation!"

Jenny's tears brought back to mind many memories for Jeana. The girls had known each other since they were little when Jeana was part of the cast in at least one of Jenny's original back yard drama productions. The one about a princess. As an adult, Jeana looked back and remembered that particular childhood memory as a truly wonderful summer day.

Friends, Friendships, Fast Friends

The teachers could see Jenny's efforts in school, on her homework, and to be with her friends. "Jenny tried to make herself available to people as much as she could," Mrs. Elliott, her science teacher said. "I think she had a real grasp on the fact that most things are not life and death situations. She *had been* in real life and death situations and that helped her to take a step back and not get so worked up about some of the little things."

Jenny Young also knew Jenny had a solid understanding of life. "She was special in her religious views and her kindness," Jenny Y. said. "She was my best friend. When you have a special friend from fourth grade into your junior year in college, that person is always going to mean the world to you. They have seen more of you than anyone else has seen," she reflected. "They know what you have gone through and they have gone through it with you.

"She was NEVER excess luggage. She was always the person I called when something really great happened. She was the first person I picked up the phone and wanted to talk to when I needed someone. Jenny was always a very big support beam for me and that doesn't happen very often outside of families...it was that amazing."

She Didn't know a Stranger

Jamie Sizemore had been amazed by Jenny for a long time. "I first met Jenny in kindergarten. I was having trouble playing my recorder and Jen said she was going to help me learn how to play this instrument. I followed her home like a little puppy dog."

When the kids arrived home that day, Jenny said, "Mom, this is Jamie. Jamie, this is my mom. Mom, we are going to practice our recorders." She wouldn't let Jamie quit until he got it right. "She always had that go get 'em attitude," Jamie said.

"Jenny pulled people out of being wallflowers. I was like that and I think she took me on as a challenge," Jamie said. "I was always the one who didn't want to be involved with anyone because I thought nobody liked me. People always got on me about my weight and I took that to heart. Jenny never did that. She accepted me for who I was and I loved her for loving me for just being Jamie."

He also admired Jenny for being interested in everyone. "I think she was on a mission to meet as many people as she could. She would just walk up to someone in the mall and say

'Hi!'" Jamie was amazed by her bold confidence. "Everybody just kind of caught onto Jenny's glow. She didn't know a stranger." Jamie saw that she did not define her life by Lyme.

"She didn't tell others about her Lyme. She never, never, never even mentioned that she had Lyme disease." When someone else would mention Lyme, she would respond, "No big deal," Jamie said. He observed Jenny in a lot of different settings and he knew "her sickness was not her social life. It was way, way back in her mind.

"Jenny cared about her family and friends and religion. She took everything seriously, but she was really a kind-hearted person. We knew she had firm religious beliefs, she shared things with us, but she wasn't a THUMPER. She didn't pressure you with it," Jamie said. "If you had questions, she would help you the best she could or she would find someone who could help you."

Since they had gone to Jamie's Junior Prom together in 1991, Jenny was like a sister and a best friend. "My last name is almost Umphress," Jamie would later laugh. He was at the house a lot, and when Jenny was well, they would go out to eat or to the movies.

"I felt comfortable with her. We didn't really go out on dates. Two people out having fun. That's just the way it was...no pressure." Jamie and Jenny both benefited by their friendship, even though Jamie liked to "hit her with a new blonde joke" every time he came.

When Jenny would shout "JAMES!", Jamie knew he was in trouble. One time they had a pillow fight in the living room. "We zapped a light bulb out of one of the lamps," Jamie said. "See what you did!" Jenny ratted. "I didn't do it," Jamie said as he threw another pillow. The war was on and I was sure my entire living room was going to be in ruin.

All went well until February 21, 1992. After Jenny had a bout with the flu, she started getting Lyme symptoms again. She also began having focal seizures—staring episodes and mental unclearness. I took her to Dr. Adams. After examining her and seeing her rash, confusion, joint pain and focal activity, he added a medication. She was to take another drug for inflammation. The debilitating headaches were back and she was extremely pale. When the doctor wanted her on IV antibiotic, I asked to try oral first.

By February 24, her condition was so bad I agreed it was time to go back on IV antibiotics. The doctor decided to try a different approach. He wanted her to take a very high dose of Claforan one day, then wait for the next six days, then repeat the dosage.

Dr. Adams had weaned her off all seize medicines since her ordeal in Toledo and he didn't want her back on them. We continued the IV therapy and Jenny began feeling better. The doctor planned on doing this treatment for nine weeks to see how she could handle it.

Disney World

All was fine until Jenny went to Florida in late March. The high school choir, band, and a song-and-dance group were to perform at Disney World. Jenny was a choir and band member. The school wanted her to go, but because of legal concerns the administration couldn't allow her to go by bus. A booster club covered the cost so Jenny and I could fly to Florida, and even gave us spending money. I was grateful Jenny was able to be included.

For the first time, Jenny felt like a normal student experiencing a school event. She blossomed, being part of the fun and foolishness, and everything seemed wonderfully well. One day Jenny even went to the ocean with friends. She didn't want to miss anything.

There were times Jenny didn't have enough energy to keep up, and a few people asked if I felt she should be so active. It was only fair to allow her to do the things she could do. There were so many things she had no memory of doing from earlier in her life. She was trying to make up for it all at once, and her smile made it all worthwhile in my eyes.

It wasn't until we were on the flight home that Jenny told me there was a problem with her chest tube. Little did I know, the dressing on her Hickman line couldn't keep salt water out when she waded in the ocean. By the time we got home, she was in severe pain, and pus was pouring from a large abscess at the entry site of her central line.

We knew she needed a new line and asked if a PICC line, which is placed in the arm, could be used? The nurse who put these in did not feel Jenny would be a good candidate due to her bad peripheral veins. Plans were set for March 30, when a new central venous line would be put in to allow Jenny to continue her treatments.

Baptized Anew

One day when Pastor Dave was visiting, Jenny asked if she could be baptized again. In December of 1985, Jenny, Tommy and I had been baptized together at the County Line Church of the Brethren. That was a special memory for me, being baptized with our two kids. Jon had already been baptized. After three and one-half years of illness, Jenny had a deep desire to be re-baptized.

Even though we had told her about her baptism, she had no memory of the event. Church and God continued to be important to her. Pastor Dave didn't have a problem with her request and asked her when she wanted to do it. They settled on March 22, since her tube was going to be changed on March 30. Our church practices baptism by immersion, so Jenny needed to do it before surgery.

Her re-baptism gave Jenny peace. She had a need to know, first hand, she was baptized. Now she knew it in her heart and not just because of a paper document. The real meaning of baptism for Jenny was captured in a photo taken during the service. Wearing a T-shirt that read *Indiana*, Jenny let her tears flow freely. It would be another two years, during her final hospitalization in Indiana, that I would think of the significance of her wearing an Indiana T-shirt for baptism.

In one of her notebooks she worked out different ideas on the subject of "My Present Lifestyle." She now wrote in cursive.

I don't believe in the use of alcohol, tobacco, or nonmedicated drugs.

I try to substain [sp] from gossip.

I attend church on Sunday and believe Sundays should be a scared [sp] day. I believe I'm an honest, trustworthy person. Someone who abstains from selfishness.

I respect others of greater authority.

Jenny got her new line as scheduled on March 30. Through all of her setbacks, Jenny had mixed feelings. There were times she became angry at God for allowing Lyme symptoms to reappear when she had so many goals to accomplish.

Overall, she wanted to be well. She wanted to get on with her life.

One nurse wrote in her chart: "Emotionally, Jennifer is accepting these setbacks rather well and shows tremendous desire to improve."

Talks to Lyme Support Groups

We also talked to Lyme support groups. These people were fortunate to have friends to share things, to help each other, to know others understood what they were experiencing. It was Jenny's goal that "doctors learn from this and no one else has to go through the same thing." Jenny approached these talks in a professional manner, preparing note cards with an introduction, her main points and a conclusion.

Have you ever wondered what it would be like to wake up one day unable to speak or walk or move?

...At one point in time, this was my life. A life I did not chose...I know how it feels when you're so tired you can't move and your head hurts so bad you think it's going to split in half...When I got so frustrated with doctors and couldn't stand going to the hospital again Mom was my punching bag. I'd get just plain mad.

Mom and I are so close some people think we are actually joined at the hip.

Hopefully, one day soon, more doctors will learn about Lyme disease and treat more aggressively. You see, this disease will never go away and there are a lot of things I will never be able to do...I've learned how much strength and faith I have and that every moment is precious...

18. A Family Doctor at Last

Jenny finished up the series on this treatment and did quite well. Our old Jenny was back. However, her monthly menstrual periods continued to cause her problems and be rough on her. If her Lyme was active, her periods made her symptoms even worse. It also seemed like getting the flu was a major illness and stirred everything up, aggravating her Lyme.

For the most part, the next few months went by well. Then we thought again about the need for a family doctor. After our first visit with Dr. Kane, a new doctor in town, our minds were made up. We had a family doctor. Peering out from his tiny, oval, wire-rimmed glasses, Dr. Kane looked severe, when he was actually open minded and concerned.

I made one thing very clear. Jenny only needed a family doctor for minor things. She had a doctor in Indiana for Lyme disease and she would continue to see him. We didn't have anything against this new doctor, but problems with many promising doctors from the past still haunted us.

A Mother's Day Blessing

For Mother's Day in 1992, Jenny wrote a piece for me. First, she gave it to Pastor Dave and then she read it during the church service. What a blessing, this child.

My Mom, My Inspiration

I wouldn't know where to begin to tell you what my "mom" means to me. Everyday people tell their mother's how much they love them, not always stopping to realize what those words mean.

For people who don't know my mom Sue very well, let me tell you a little bit about her. Mom has been married nearly 21 years, (to the same man!) and has raised 2 children. It's very hard for me to remember my life as a child, so I really only remember mom, the last 4 years.

I've come to love mom, not only as a mother, but she's also my best friend. No one said life was easy, and our lives certainly haven't been.

But I realize we have problems like everyone else; the difference being, not everyone has someone to stand by them and support them at any cost!

Mom is understanding, loving and strong; physically, emotionally and spiritually. I wouldn't be alive today if it wasen't for her faith in God, to pray continuelly for my healing.

Mom has a heart of gold, and she would sacrifice anything; if she knew it would help her family or benefit a friend.

I'm not going to say mom and I never argue or bicker, because that wouldn't even be normal. When we do disagree, it doesn't take me long to realize that no argument is that important, that I forget how special she is to me!

I just want mom to know [how] much I love and appreciate her. I want her to realize how important she is to me; and if she needs anything,

I will be here for her. HAPPY MOTHER'S DAY! I LOVE YOU!

Jennifer

A Personal Matter

Jenny's first appointment with Dr. Kane was made to remove a personal monthly item that she couldn't retrieve. She knew better than to go to Dr. Adams for this because he had told her to "never use that kind of sanitary item." Dr. Adams would be furious with her, so Jenny gave Dr. Kane a try.

"It was quite embarrassing to meet a doctor for the first time with a problem like that," she said. He was considerate of her predicament and took care of the situation. It was probably best Jenny had someone other than Dr. Adams for this problem. She had already shocked him silly once.

Anyone who knew Jenny well knew she could be bold. She never hesitated asking Dr. Adams personal questions. During a "wellness" visit one day, Dr. Adams was sitting on a stool with his back to her, writing out a prescription. Suddenly, out of the bright blue sky, Jenny asked him if she could have a baby. He swung around so quickly I thought he would fly right off of his stool.

"Are you sexually active?" he asked. Worried wrinkles formed on his forehead. She bubbled with laughter, making it quite clear she was only asking for the future.

The first time Dr. Kane talked to me about Jenny, he said he had been following her case with interest. One of Jenny's nurses had asked him if he would take care of her because she was so worried about Jenny. That was quite a while before we began seeing him. This nurse wanted us to have a good doctor near home that we could trust. Dr. Kane had informed her he couldn't tell me he wanted to take the case. I needed to initiate the contact with his office. I chalked one up for professionalism.

One month later, Jenny began feeling tough again. She had some swollen glands and was having a headache, fatigue and joint pain. I thought maybe it was just a sore throat, so I took her to Dr. Kane's office. He examined her thoroughly and said her Lyme had flared up. He wanted to begin treatment for

Lyme. I told him I held nothing against him, but I would rather take her back to Indiana where Dr. Adams knew her case. His office would be open the next day and I felt I could take her then. Dr. Kane didn't want her to leave his office without beginning treatment. I was reluctant, but finally agreed.

He put her on a medication and said we should let him know how she did. He asked me a lot of questions about her treatment with Dr. Adams. Dr. Kane really wanted to help Jenny. It was good to have a doctor at home, but part of me was still concerned.

Jenny continued to get worse and was eventually put back on IV. One problem was that Jenny had wanted the IV tube out, since it wasn't being used and was showing signs of infection. The doctors also didn't want to take any chances with infection. The nurses could not get a normal IV into her arm, and up to that point they were giving her Claforan shots in her buttock. No one can take that many shots without the tissues breaking down after a while.

On August 28, a Groshong catheter was inserted in her right chest wall. Jenny tolerated the surgery well and we returned home.

On Labor Day weekend, I was having a terrible time with the catheter. I even tried to draw back on the line to get blood, but nothing seem to work. I called Dr. Kane and he came down to the house. I was thankful for a doctor who makes house calls.

We couldn't get it to flush or draw back. He ordered more injections of Claforan until arrangements could be made to replace the catheter. Jenny was devastated. She knew how difficult it was to replace and she was tired of going through surgery.

A Six Hour Surgery

On September 8, Jenny was back in surgery with Dr. Lang. The people on his staff were always good to her and Dr. Lang was a unique doctor. "He always says a prayer before operating on me," Jenny said.

Our ministers were in the waiting room with me during the surgery. Jon and Tommy were busy having the pleasure of a visit to traffic court, since Tommy had gotten his first speeding ticket. After Tom's little talk with the judge, he and Jon came and waited with us. We waited and waited.

There was a hostess at the reception desk, and the room was jammed with people waiting for loved ones in surgery. The other people began to complain because something was holding up surgery. That something was Jenny.

After a few hours, the hostess left and asked me to just answer the phone because it was always for me. The doctor was thoughtful and had the surgical nurses call about every 45 minutes. Jenny's surgery lasted nearly six hours.

Jenny had not been put to sleep, but the doctor said she was incredibly good about the whole thing. He said she cooperated anyway she could. By the time she returned to her room, she had four incisions. One was almost five inches long. The problem was, the doctor did not have any place to cut. He tried everything and I knew he did his best.

He said if another catheter was needed, they might have to try to place it in her lower extremities, but that could cause problems with possible phlebitis. The endless surgeries took a toll on Jenny's recovery. She remained on IVs for a long time.

Trying to keep these lines in place became harder and harder. Everyone who worked on Jenny used sterile procedures, but her body just kept rejecting the tubes. Her chest was a mess. The cuts from the surgeries had caused adhesions and her veins were not healthy. Her earlier steroid treatments didn't help the situation.

After a tremendous amount of problems, it was decided to attempt a PICC line, which Jan and another nurse did on October 27. A PICC line looks like an IV on the outside, but it is fed into the heart through veins in the arm and chest. It worked wonderfully until the tube was pulled while removing a dressing. I was just glad I never touched that dressing. Another attempt was made to insert a PICC line, but it wasn't successful.

In October, Jenny wrote: "I'm thankful and praise God for my family—their love and support and openness. I'm so fortunate! [I am thankful] for Hope.

"I ask God to give me guidance and wisdom to see me through. I ask him for strength. (Lyme—discouraging.)

"I promise—I will always serve God. I will be a witness. I will keep reminding myself of all Jesus did for us!"

Throughout all this, her sessions continued with her therapists and her lessons continued through school. If working hard would gain her better health and catch her up in school, working hard is what she would do.

19. Prayers and Waiting

The first of 1993 brought a lot of changes. When the company Jon worked for switched insurance carriers to an HMO
plan, I felt Jenny's life and our security were in for a rude
awakening. I had heard horror stories about HMOs. From a list
of doctors, participants select a doctor. It had taken us so long
to finally go to Dr. Kane, and now, because he wasn't a partici-
pating physician in this plan, we needed another new doctor.

The insurance people informed us we could go to a different doctor in Ada. We didn't have anything against the doctor
in their plan, but none of us wanted to change. For a while the
new doctor and Dr. Kane agreed to work together. It was decided the new doctor would be our primary doctor, but we
were to go to Dr. Kane and the other doctor would order everything. That just didn't work out. We couldn't have been more
grateful when Dr. Kane joined the insurance company as a
provider. As a business decision, his heart wasn't in it, but he
did it for Jenny.

Jenny's last Hickman had been surgically placed in December 1992. All was going okay until February 8, 1993, when
her Hickman began malfunctioning. On that day, Dr. Kane arranged for a surgeon to put in a new one. Jenny had no desire
to go back to Miseracordia. I convinced her—we would go,
listen to no one except the surgeon, get the tube in and leave.
That was our plan, but the surgeon decided to keep Jenny
overnight for precaution. For once I had no fears of leaving
Jenny there, because a family friend was her nurse. She loved
Jenny, and wouldn't allow anyone to hurt her. I reassured
Jenny, she was in good hands. The catheter went in without
any problems, but the tube lasted only three days.

To help with the bills I was baby-sitting at home during the
day and working in the intensive care unit at a nursing home at
night while Jenny slept. Then I would hurry home to begin a

new day. At 6 a.m. on February 11, Jenny called me at work. She woke up feeling wet to discover she was hemorrhaging from her central line.

I told Jenny to hold a towel to her chest as tight as she could and I rushed home.

When I called the doctor, he wanted me to call an ambulance, but I decided to take her in myself. This is not what Jenny and I wanted. To return to the hospital.

Under fluoroscopic control the surgeon removed the old sutures, introduced a J guide wire, and removed the old catheter. Then a new triple lumen catheter was inserted through the guide wire, and the guide wire was removed.The surgery site was sutured, Jenny was given something for pain, and an hour later we were on our way back home. I gave endless thanks to God.

Later on, Jenny's platelet count dropped way down. Then it came back up. When the doctor had inserted the triple lumen, he didn't think it would last long. And it didn't. On March 9, he replaced it with a Groshong catheter. This tube was much better because it didn't need any heparin and there were less chances of bleeding problems.

The surgeon who performed these latest surgeries was blessed. He used general anesthetic, which made the surgeries so much easier for Jenny.

Her body had begun swelling, she had joint pain and severe headaches, but she was determined to get well. This tube lasted over six months.

When Jenny's headaches got extremely bad, her body would start jerking. The doctors told her it was mandatory for her to take her pain medicines so the pain would not get out of control. Jenny fought this.

She felt she didn't have control of her body or herself when she was on pain medication. Dr. Kane assured her she wouldn't become addicted. As soon as she was feeling better, he said she could go off them without having any problems.

As Stubborn As Me

All through her illness there was a constant battle between Jenny and her doctors. When she urged them to let her go to school, the doctors told her to pace herself. But that wasn't Jenny. If she felt even a little bit better, she went gung ho and paid the price.

Everyone in the medical field told me what I was supposed to do with Jenny, but they didn't live with her. They didn't realize how stubborn she could be. I knew what they told me was correct, but getting her to slow down, to pace herself and do things cautiously, was impossible.

Jenny continued to make up for lost time. She always had homework to catch up on. School still meant the world to her and she didn't want anything handed to her. She didn't want to take the easy way out and use her illness as a crutch. When she was selected for the National Honor Society, she told school officials she didn't want the honor because of pity. They had to prove to her that she deserved the honor.

Mrs. Elliott, her science teacher, didn't know Jenny before Lyme hit our home, but she had heard Jenny had been an honor roll student. "It was very important for Jenny to regain that honor roll. When she asked me, 'Do I deserve to be on the National Honor Society?' I told her it was based on her grade point average and her activities and accomplishments." Jenny fought that explanation. She didn't think she was in enough activities.

"You are in as much as you are able, and you have to be approved by teachers. You are such a trouble maker in class, I am amazed you got by on that one!" Mrs. Elliott pulled her chain a little.

"She was always afraid she was getting a break—that she was included because people felt sorry for her. She wanted it even—she wanted it fair—she wanted to earn it. She wanted no sympathy votes," Mrs. Elliott later said. Jenny finally came to terms with the decision and agreed to accept the award.

It was a proud, proud moment for our family—to see her standing there getting that honor. She had worked hard to re-learn and to be healthy. Someone who didn't know her situation would never have believed that just three years earlier Jenny couldn't walk, talk or eat. Her memory bank was blank except for what she had relearned since the onset of Lyme disease. The night of the National Honor Society induction ceremony Jenny wanted to be just one of the students being honored. She did not want to be the star of the evening, the recipient who had climbed over Lyme to get there.

Dear Diary

Very few people knew when Jenny's spirits were down. She started to write her feelings in diaries given to her as gifts by special friends, Kelly Connor, the vocalist, and Mrs. Sandy Waggoner, her high school guidance teacher.

Diary Entry—March 31, 1993

It's around 11:00 at night and mom has already left for work...I'm unable to sleep again. I just took some medicine with codine [sp] so hopefully I'll fall asleep soon.

Today has not been a good day for me. In fact the last 5 years haven't gone great. I cried most of the day. I also became very quiet, sheltered in my own shell. I figured talking about things really hadn't made any difference.

I am so tired. I have no energy. I feel so trapped. I'm not sure if the medicines working any longer. I feel so helpless. There's nothing I can do.

Mom and I talked and cried together.

I know she hurts as much as I do...

Sometimes I don't understand why God hasn't healed me. Maybe my faith isn't strong enough. Maybe I've done something wrong. The Bible tells us in God's time.

Well I'm sorry. I'm sick of holding on till another day. I've lost so much of my life already. Lately I really haven't felt like I'm living. I am so completely limited. I told mom tonight that if I was able to look into the future, I would have rather lived in a wheelchair—if I was able to have the energy and drive I need. At least I could live.

I would be able to enjoy life. I feel more handicapped now than before.

Mom and I prayed very hard—asking God for healing...I'm tired of waiting. Satin [sp] may have won the battle—but God and I are going to win the war!

20. A New Daughter

Lyme disease kept us unsettled and barely in focus. When Jenny felt good and was able to be active, we still remained battle-ready to fight symptoms when they ignited again. Among everything else that happened in early 1993, we got a new daughter, Meagan. Jon and I became her legal guardians in February.

When I first met Meagan as Jenny's friend, I never dreamt Jenny would come home one day and beg us to help Meagan by taking her into our home as another daughter. That quality Jenny had as a youngster—of investing in people—continued to be an essential part of her daily life. When ill and extremely weak, she managed to draw from some inner resource, expressing appreciation to her caretakers and eagerly inquiring about the activities and well-being of her family and friends.

When she was well, she went out of her way to do special things for others, putting all her love, generosity and feelings into birthdays, holidays and special occasions. Her greatest joy was to be gathered together with family and friends.

Meagan and her mother had been separated for many years following her parents divorce. Initially, I arranged for Meagan to travel south to visit her mother, but things just didn't work out. Driven by a deep desire to help Meagan, Jenny envisioned that happening only if Meagan became a part of our family.

Why did Meagan want to live with us? What had happened to bring this new challenge into our lives? Jenny begged me and the rest of the family to have some heart. She believed in Meagan and saw a lot of good in her. It was Jenny's goal to give Meagan a family, a comfortable home and that one great essential—unconditional love.

I thought of the mountain of bills and our humble resources. Then Jenny reminded me of the saying I often shared with her, "Everything happens for a reason." I've always loved kids and wanted to help, but this would be an extraordinary challenge. Could we muster up to it, given Jenny's unpredictable health and needs?

In no time, Meagan crossed our doorstep with her belongings and our lives made another dramatic change. Our new family of five had difficult moments for a long time. We had to deal with things we had never encountered before—alcohol and drug abuse, disrespect, lack of appreciation and a raw negative attitude. It was painful at times, but Jenny believed in our ability to open our family circle to one more, and in Meagan's ability to take on the concerns and values of a responsible young lady. At some point, Meagan began to make great efforts, and we held tight to patience on our part.

Not Winning Points

"When Jenny thought I had an attitude or I was being disrespectful, like when Tommy and I weren't getting along, there was a Bible verse about siblings and she would show that to me," Meagan said.

"You have to think, you have this nice little family and then you have someone as loud and as obnoxious and as rude as can be like me move in and live with you," Meagan reflected. "Everyone was trying to be so nice and I was just very moody when I first moved in. Jenny told me to stop it because I wasn't winning any points with Tommy and I didn't care. I didn't think I had to prove myself to Tommy."

Then there was the day of the "great shed cleaning." Tommy and Meagan weren't getting along, so I told them they had to go out and clean the shed in the garage. "We weren't allowed to come in until we could be nice to each other," Meagan laughed, recalling the event.

"Tommy was moving stuff and he would say, 'Watch out!' and throw something. Before the shed was cleaned out we were laughing with each other. We found stilts Grandpa Epley had made and I was trying to walk on them, and, of course, I couldn't. I think that day was good for us," Meagan said. "It bothered Jenny that Tommy and I didn't get along. And it bothered Sue." Jon worked so much, he wasn't involved in a lot of the tension.

"After the day we cleaned the shed, it felt more like we were all family. I had a place to call home. I had a family to come home to—a brother and a sister. And it made everybody feel better because family was always so important to Jenny," Meagan said.

Unconditional Love

The day would come when we considered it an honor to have Meagan as part of our family. No birth child ever came with guarantees and promises. It was proven once again that unconditional love can accomplish the world. As much as Jenny loved and treasured Tommy, she was thrilled to have a sister, one she had helped.

"Her greetings were real nice and chipper. 'Hi! How are you! How is your day! How is your life!' and she actually cared," Meagan later said. "Jenny really wanted to know how things were with you." We watched with wonder as God used Jenny to show Meagan that God's love is special.

"Jenny and I were such good friends," Meagan said. "I have a hard time opening up to people. I can talk to anybody about anything, but Jenny and I got into the deep stuff about how I really feel—because I don't trust people. I could always talk to Jenny. I think anybody could have trusted Jenny with anything.

"Jon and Sue raised me the best they could. Tommy and Jenny opened their arms to me as a sister the best way they knew how. That does change a family, to just let someone move in. And they did that in my junior year.

"When Tommy gets upset, he just doesn't talk. When I get upset, I just go off. I think Sue didn't know what to do because her kids weren't like that." But Meagan found Jenny's limits. "Jenny could, in the snap of a finger, put me back in my place.

I don't know what it was about Jenny. I don't know if it was because I had so much respect for her or because I loved her so much.

"Jenny and I were like sisters, but Jenny was my best friend and she could always tell when something was wrong. She always left it at, when you are ready to talk, come talk to me. I knew I always had an open invitation to talk to her. I could trust her. Things would stay between Jenny and me," Meagan said.

"When I first moved in here, Sue was still working third shift at the nursing home and Jenny and I would just walk and walk for three, four hours without going anywhere. Just in circles around Ada. We would just talk about everything. There were times we would get in her car and go and just drive and talk. Jenny was one of the very few people who could tell me to quit being self-centered. I am a very headstrong and stubborn person. I am very set in my ways, and Jenny could say, 'Quit being rude. Quit thinking of just yourself.' Those are some of my most important memories, just driving around."

While on IV antibiotics, Jenny improved and felt well again. By April of 1993, Jenny was losing toe nails right and left. She also had swelling in her ankles and feet. By May , she was pushing hard to finish up her junior year. She didn't feel it was necessary for the nurse to come. That would mean she was sick. She wanted people to see her as normal.

By the middle of May, Jenny admitted to a nurse that her energy level was poor. She was beginning to bruise easily and she showed the nurse a cut on her leg made when shaving. It was three inches long and bled for two days. Dr. Kane thought Jenny should go on the birth control pill because of problems she had with her periods. If Jenny didn't think she needed something, I couldn't get her to take it.

"She had days when she was so good you wouldn't know anything was wrong with her," Meagan said. "She would get up first thing in the morning and it would be sunshine and butterflies and birds and everything wonderful. She would be in just the best mood.

"Then she'd want her hair French braided and I don't like doing people's hair. Sometimes I would tell her no and Sue would say, 'Now, Meagan. What's it going to hurt for you to get up and braid her hair?' So I would do it.

"There were 'I Love Lucy' marathons on TV. Jenny recorded all of them. My favorite was where Lucy makes wine and pulls up her skirt to step on the grapes," Meagan said. "Honest to Pete, I could see Jenny doing that, hiking that skirt up and running through the grapes, squishing them through her toes. Jenny laughed and laughed and laughed.

"At night she would pop in those shows when she couldn't sleep. Never mind it woke me up. She couldn't sleep and they made her laugh," Meagan said.

Other times the girls chatted through the night. "There were nights Jenny would come into my bed and just talk. Sometimes she had a problem on her mind, sometimes she couldn't sleep, sometimes she didn't feel good and just wanted to talk to try to forget about it," Meagan said. "There are times she was in pain and wanted to keep her mind off of it and Sue was at work and Tom and Jon were asleep."

When Meagan moved in, she had an awful fear of needles. "Sue said, 'Get over it if you are going to help with Jenny.' All of those treatments were IV," Meagan said. Meagan only passed out once and that was during one of Jenny's hospital surgeries.

One time when I returned home, the girls were deep into a hair dressing experiment. "What are you doing?" I asked. "I'm *painting* her hair," Meagan casually replied.

"Jenny had gone uptown and bought some stuff. We didn't know it was bleach," Meagan said. "You were supposed to just brush it on and I was just a brushing away in big clumps. It looked really bad." Jenny had to have it professionally fixed. "It was painted in big clumps two inches away from the roots because I didn't want to burn her head," Meagan said, explaining her logic.

Tom and Meagan had first met in seventh grade. Meagan and Jenny connected the year Jenny joined Tom and Meagan in their class at school.

Even in school it was plain for everyone to see these were two very different girls. "Jenny fit back in school even with the age difference," Meagan said. "She was just one of the girls, although she got a little impatient with high school crap, girls sitting around talking about everybody. Jenny had important things to think about.

"Things like, 'So and so said I didn't match today,' she just didn't care about," Meagan said. "Jenny would sit and think and would find good—like with her family. Jenny and Tom were very close and Jenny and Sue had this unreal mother and daughter relationship. They were so close."

Meagan's jet black hair and hazel eyes suited her dynamic personality—coy, insecure and bold all rolled up into one. Tom's deep thinking and slow-to-speak characteristics were apparent with one glance at his serious brown eyes. His dark brown hair was always neat and worn in the latest guy style of the day.

In contrast, Jenny's generous, thoughtful and gentle soul was reflected in her sparkling blue eyes and soft-as-wheat hair. Three young people, all individuals with different personalities, resulted in a busy household.

Meagan picked up quickly that music meant everything to Jenny. "Jenny was always singing with tapes. Sometimes you could be downstairs in the bathroom with the door shut and you would still hear her singing," Meagan said. "She enjoyed that. She didn't care if she was off tune. She just sang. One time when she sang in church, she practiced and practiced and practiced and the big thing was she lost the back-up tape just before church. We couldn't find it anywhere. She was flipping out," Meagan said. "We were going through all these different tapes that had other songs on them. I don't remember where we finally found the right tape."

School Days

When the girls were in science, they did a project together. Here again, their very different personalities ruled the day. "We could only use so much tape, two paper clips, so much cardboard," Meagan said. "You could use a two-liter bottle. I decided I was going to make a waterfall. Jenny said, 'Meagan, you can't do that. You are using way too much tape and glue,' and I was using more than I was supposed to.

"Everyone said it wasn't going to work and headstrong Jenny also said, 'It isn't going to work.' Well, I said—yes it will, we just have to dump water down the cardboard. It will come right out." Even their teacher told them it wouldn't work.

"We had two weeks to design and build it. Everyone did theirs. Jenny and I did ours last. We poured our water. When the cardboard collapsed, water ran everywhere. We had dumped five huge cups at one time. I think we got an A because of Jenny—because she was more sensible," Meagan said.

Meagan was more casual about life and school, but she knew school meant a lot to Jenny. "I don't know if it was because she had missed a couple years. It meant a lot to both Tommy and Jenny that they were in the same class," Meagan said. "Jenny was always respectful to the teachers. She did her work. I think it was important because it was something she wanted to do. She wanted to graduate from high school and she was going to do it."

Attempts to Play

One snowy winter day Tom and Meagan enjoyed a snow fight. Meagan tried to toss the light snow as far as she could with her thick mittens. Tom, hiding around the side of the house, scooped his snow up by the shovel. Jenny and I laughed as we bumped into each other running from window to window, trying to capture them on film.

As a little girl, Jenny loved making angels in the snow, but she wasn't able to be out with Tom and Meagan as they enjoyed the fresh snowfall. Meagan dragged in looking like a mop with ear muffs and clothes all askew.

Another day Tom and Meagan held a 95-minute aerobic exercise challenge. Pushing the dining room table and chairs aside, they stretched and kicked, all the while both bragging, "I'm going to win." The prize was a $6 haircut. Sore muscles the next day were a sure bet for both of them.

One summer day when Jenny wasn't feeling good, Meagan wanted to show her a good time. I was visiting neighbors. It was the first time Meagan had a car and she asked, "Jenny, do you want to drive my car?" Jenny was on a lot of medication at the time. When Jenny said she'd love to drive, they headed off to see the town's Easter egg house, a brightly painted Victorian mansion that Jenny hadn't seen in its latest colors.

"She drove and she was fine, but she didn't have her glasses. We joked around and drove out by the park. Before we got back we switched drivers so Sue wouldn't know," Meagan said. "Well, Jenny told her mom and Sue was really mad at me."

"If something had happened, what would you have done?" I challenged Meagan. I gave Jenny as much independence as I could. Sometimes, when she visited Jenny Y. on campus, she wouldn't have her treatments for the duration of the visit. It was difficult to balance letting her experience life with maintaining her health. It always involved some risk taking.

One time Meagan and I picked Jenny up after a day with Jenny Y. "Jenny was very short and moody. She just looked tired, really terrible. All the way home she wouldn't talk to Sue because Sue wouldn't let her drive."

As soon as I saw her, I could tell she was in no condition to drive. I figured she got mad and she could just get over it.

21. Junior Year Homestretch

In March, 1993, Jenny had met a college sophomore, Alan, while visiting her friend Jenny Young at Bowling Green State University. Charmed to have a *college man* interested in her, Jenny wrote in her diary: "Recently God has brought someone else into my life." After a few dates, they agreed that Alan would take her to her high school junior prom.

Diary—March 30, 1993
I can't wait for prom. I want everything to be perfect. It makes me feel very lucky to have so many positive people influcing my life!

On April 4, Jenny was feeling well enough to spend a day with Alan on campus. Meagan and I drove her up and dropped her off.

Diary—April 4, 1993
Today was a great day! Alan and I spent the whole day together. We toured the whole campus. I got blisters. We talked a lot. I feel very comfortable around him...He can tend to be a small bit annoying, but isn't every man. I can be annoying also...But I think it looks promising.
I let him make all the first moves. He reached for my hand...He makes me feel special.
Today meant a lot to me. Alan told me he was more interested in a serious relationship—in time. We also kissed a couple times—nothing too deep—it was nice...I'm feeling so much better. Praise God. I think finally things are turning around for me. Spring has arrived!

Diary—April 5, 1993

Went back to school this morning. Had a great day! My tutor is trying very hard to get me caught up. I've decided at this point all I want to do is meet the requirements to get through the 11th grade. Grades don't matter as long as I do my best...I thank the Lord, I'm feeling great! How could I ever doubt him.

Diary—April 7, 1993

I'm so happy—I've had 3 good days in a row. I've felt so good and so alive...We went to the Easter Cantata at our church tonight.

It was so awesome! I was in tears. You could definitely feel the prescence of Jesus in the church.

This kept ministering to me—Jesus said before crucifiction, "There is no pain greater than the love I have for you." Isn't our Jesus incredible. All of the pain and humiliation he faced—for us—so we could always be safe.

I have to remember—that even though the problems and pain of this world are so immense at times. We are always safe and sheltered in the arms of Jesus.

Jenny was busy making plans with Alan so he could come for Easter. She recorded her heartbeat in her diary: "He is going to church with me. I'm lifting it up to the Lord. Only he has a perfect mate for me. I hope he's a lot like Alan. Maybe it is Alan. But I'm going to take one day at a time. And appreciate every day."

A Glorious Easter

Easter was a full and happy day. Alan was there for church and this was the crown jewels for Jenny. "I felt closer to him than ever before," she wrote in her diary. When it came to dinner, I was happy to turn the responsibilities over to Jenny and

Meagan. They made a wonderful meal, which included a delightful bunny cake made by Jenny. As usual our dinner table was a little wild and crazy.

Alan and Jenny started the day with a walk before church. They took another walk after dinner and by evening they were cuddled on the couch watching a movie. They also looked through scrapbooks and photo albums, and at the Lyme disease TV interview video.

It was obvious Alan was shocked, realizing the devastation of her illness and how difficult her recovery and therapies had been for her. On Easter Sunday she was able to write in her diary: "Praise God! I've had 8 straight good days that I felt terrific."

But by the Tuesday after Easter break she wasn't able to go to school. It was an unending cycle. Every time she had her period, she always had other problems too.

Diary—April 13, 1993

Oh, I've got something to tell you. Mom told me—but I have to act surprised. I was abducted [sp] into National Honor Society. It was unanimous!

I am so shocked. I cried.

I have to write a paper in English on how I fantasize my future. In my future Jesus will return for his children. And we will no longer have pain or suffering. What a glorious day it will be.

Jenny was excited about being invited to Alan's home to meet his family. Jenny's diary: "He is counting the days before prom—me too!"

By April 23, Jenny had missed two days of school again and Dr. Kane had taken her off her treatment. Jenny's diary: "Dr. Kane told me he thought the antibiotics were doing more harm than good. I do agree with him. I've been on IV's 6 weeks and I really haven't felt any better. I've had a few good days here and there. Which I'm very thankful...He is worried about the long term problems."

Her diary entries were sporadic. She wrote long, thoughtful, passionate entries—heartfelt conversations about people she loved and how and if she could help them, how Christ was actively working in her life, and how she worried whether a youth group at church would accept her testimony.

She worried about Pastor Dave each time he suffered with a kidney stone, and she cheered each time Tom participated in a track event. When she received responses to letters she sent to Christian musicians, it made her day, and any national crisis like Waco or a prison uprising concerned her. God was praised when she felt good. When days where bad, she questioned Him and asked for His guidance.

Broadcasting Volunteer

Interested in her dad's part-time work at WTGN, a Christian radio station, Jenny became a volunteer and worked days when Lyme symptoms weren't crashing her system. "She did everything. She was totally in control," Jon said. "Jen put programs on the air, weather, station identification, breaks and other things. I would be there, but she did it."

Jon found she was a little intimidated about the microphone and more content to work behind the scenes. "She liked to work the control board and did very well with that," Jon said.

The March following Jenny's death, Jon would be given permission to start a program featuring local Christian artists who have recorded professionally. The program—Northwest Ohio Music Connection—sprung from an idea Jenny had given to Jon.

"I don't understand why they don't promote Jim Boedicker and Kelly Connor and The Glory Bound Quartet and others more than they do," Jenny challenged her dad. Jon felt she had a legitimate point and, when the opportunity arose, presented the idea to management.

The Happiest Couple

Junior Prom was such an exceptional event for Jenny, it made a permanent impression on people who saw her there. Her science teacher, Mrs. Elliott commented, "I had never seen her so happy."

The theme was "Heaven" and Jenny volunteered to help decorate. The kids made a castle out of white foam core, trimming it in blue and silver. Zillions of stars were placed on the light blue ceiling accented with clouds, and favors were placed on each table. It was a dream world of teal blue, white and silver.

During a trip to the florist, Jenny found the *perfect* colors to match her blue prom dress and Alan's outfit. She asked Alan if it would be okay if she ordered flowers for both of them. Everything had to match perfectly, according to Miss Manners Umphress.

Jenny was radiant when she introduced her date to teachers at the prom. She simply beamed.

Mrs. Elliott observed, "It was a time she was doing what all the other kids were doing. Jenny and her date kissed during the evening and I thought—'Oh, I hope Sue talked to her.'"

Jenny was experiencing a first love and I couldn't have been happier for her.

Jenny and Alan were pictured in the yearbook as "the happiest couple at the prom."

Tom and his date doubled with them and Meagan and her date went separately. The girls looked sweet. The guys were handsome. I couldn't have been prouder.

Later, when she stopped seeing Alan, he continued to call for some time.

Jenny told him she didn't want to hurt him. She felt it just wasn't meant to be.

"Dad is upset that I broke up with Alan," Jenny told Jenny Y. "I told Dad, 'You date him then.'" When Jenny made up her mind, her mind was made up.

The Song and Dance Man's Song

All through school Jenny had a crush on Aaron, the "song and dance man" in the high school music program. Each time Aaron performed a solo for a concert, Jenny gave him a hug, telling him he was great.

She was impulsive and sincere with everyone, but her heart skipped an extra beat around Aaron. He was unaware of Jenny's special interest in him, but he loved her positive attitude and generous smile.

Years later, Aaron remembered Jenny having a grand time at her junior prom. "She had an IV connection tube, but it was like it just disappeared. It was just a great night of crazy fun...dancing...being with friends."

"The Dance," recorded by Garth Brooks, was a song Aaron loved to sing in school performances. "I had heard this song a thousand times while strolling in a mall, cruising in my car or relaxing at home," he said. Months after Jenny's funeral the association of that song with Jenny at junior prom threw him into an emotional collapse that Aaron would never have predicted.

Aaron was working at a large entertainment park in Ohio where he shared a room with 14 other people. "I was standing in my room. A buddy from home was with me. The music of 'The Dance' came echoing down the hallway and I fell to my bed. I didn't sit down. I fell to my bed. This song hit me so hard I just sat there in tears." I thought, "If I could go back, I would have sung that song at Jenny's funeral."

The Dance
By Tony Arata
Looking back on the memory of
The dance we shared 'neath the stars above
For a moment all the world was right
How could I have known that you'd
Ever say goodbye

Chorus
And now I'm glad I didn't know
The way it all would end the way
It all would go
Our lives are better left to chance
I could have missed the pain
But I'd of had to miss the dance

Aaron had not thought of Jenny as a girlfriend, but he trusted her completely and respected her. "As long as I live, I could live to be 110, I probably won't encounter a spirit like her spirit again," he reflected. Aaron found her to be a good listener.

"She didn't judge people. But she was honest. If she felt it needed to be said, she told people to get their butt in gear and reach for their goals. Jenny had such impact and will. She was never selfish."

I Do Get Well!

In July, Jenny was having problems with her wisdom teeth and the need to extract them became apparent. The surgeon was a little apprehensive, but went ahead with the surgery. Jenny tolerated the procedure well. She continued telling her nurse it wasn't necessary for her to come to the house all the time and she also told her she wanted the IV line out. "The tape is bothering me and I don't need it any longer." Dr. Kane cut her visits to monthly instead of weekly and Jenny got her other wish too. Her Groshong catheter was removed. Dr. Kane was pleased with her progress.

One time, on her own, Jenny barged into Dr. Kane's office and asked to see him. She wanted to show him how well she was doing. "I just wanted him to see, I do get well," she told me when she got home. Jenny felt the only time he saw her was when she was sick. He never saw how healthy she could be.

Fall, 1993, rolled around. It was her senior year and Jenny was delighted to be attending school again. As the class treasurer, a member of the band and choir, and a volunteer in the guidance office, she had full school days. She did everything she possibly could. That fall she went to homecoming with a long time family friend. Given how often her health crashed, it was amazing she was able to go to three homecomings and two proms. Jenny loved a party.

College—One Dream too Many
Different ideas were tossed around as Jenny dreamed of college. She wanted to be a doctor—a *good* doctor who helped people. But Dr. Adams had told her it would be too exhausting and she would never be able to complete the necessary college work. Then she thought about being a nurse. But she decided she didn't know how long she could work if she had to tolerate doctors like some she had encountered in her own illness.

Finally, she decided to go into the field of music business. Ever since she was little, she had always loved singing Christian music at church. After her throat became irritated from being intubated, her voice was never the same. She knew she would not be able to be a performer.

Her new dream was to go to Anderson University in Anderson, Indiana. She had watched the careers of many people advance after their experience at Anderson. The day Jenny and Jon visited the school, a deaf lady sang "Silent Night" during the chapel service.

Both Jenny and Jon were touched by her poignant selection. A dynamic speaker, she told of her early life reading lips for FBI criminal investigations of the Mafia. Later, she worked on Christian videos and in Christian witness. It was a powerful experience for Jenny to see someone take a disability and live dynamically.

Jon was made even more aware that Jenny believed God had given her abilities too, and she was going to take full advantage of what she had and do as much as she could as long as she could. "Jenny had more ministry on a one-to-one basis of encouragement in her few years than some people have in a whole lifetime," Jon would later say.

"Jenny was kind of a stabilizing factor in the family," Jon reflected. "She was always able to bring me back into a proper prospective. I would get off on a tangent about something and she would say, 'Oh, Dad.' She wasn't afraid to state her opinion. Many times we got into serious discussions about different musical groups and artists."

Love Letters from Home

Thrilled with how well she was doing in high school, and anticipating that her health would hold and her dream of going to college would come true, Jon, Tom, Jamie and I each wrote a note in her high school yearbook.

Jenny, This is harder than you may think. Last Friday, after the Anderson visit, it really hit me. You will be graduating soon, and then it's off to Anderson and the rest of your life. I have always known that your determination would be the factor to take you anywhere, and now I am seeing it come to pass. A parent can hope that the values they spent 20 years to instill will bear precious fruit, and I am so proud of you and the values you stand for. I will always be there for you no matter how far your career may take you. I will always love you, and you can be sure that I will always be as proud of you as I am today.

Love, Dad

Jennifer, (Sis) I must say I am so proud to have a sister, a friend of your character. I admire you more than anyone else. You have made me such a better person. I know the true values of life, what's important and what's not. It has been so great having you in school this year. You're a person I can really look up to. I wish you the best of luck in all you do. I just know you'll succeed with everything. Have fun in those college years! Please, I'm here if you need to talk.

I Love You. Tom

Jenny: You've been an inspiration and blessing from the day you were born. We've had so many happy and sad times, but through it all we have continued as a strong, loving family. I wish things had been different these last five and one-half years, but that's not possible, but just seeing your strength and love of Jesus shows people all is possible with God. I do feel some day this illness will be behind you and the strength and courage you've built up will take you where ever you desire to go. There is a light at the end of the tunnel, so keep on moving and keep your chin up. God has used you so much already but the best is yet to come.

Good luck at Anderson. You can make it.

I love you. Mom

Jen, Hey, Babe, Keep up the good work and great progress in all you do.

Later, Jamie

It was a hot-pepper day when Jenny was accepted by Anderson. As excited as she was about the possibility of going there, she knew Jon and I were concerned about what would happen if she went and had a health problem. If she was physically able to go, we were determined to let her do it. But by the spring of 1994, Jenny realized that if she did go to college, she would have to stay closer to home because of her relapses.

On that trip to Anderson, Jenny and Jon saw the Gaither Studio and Bill Gaither's home and where Sandi Patti lived.

Jenny thought so much of these Christian singers. Her two favorite male Christian singers were Mark Lowrey of the Gaithers, who made her smile when there wasn't much to smile about, and Ernie Hoss of the Cathedrals. Jenny sent birthday cards to artists and they would write back. She went to concerts and had her picture taken with her favorite performers.

Singing like Sandi Patti

Photos of Jenny's favorite Christian artists decorated the walls of her room. Once I wrote to the Christian recording artist, Sandi Patti, telling her Jenny's story and how much Sandi's music and mission meant to Jenny. In response, we received four concert tickets and an invitation to join her backstage after her show. Sarah Peltier, Jenny's elementary vocal teacher, and another friend went along with us. The concert was a magnificent high for all of us. Sarah particularly enjoyed Jenny's bright, beaming smile.

"As we entered the V.I.P. area after the concert, Sandi Patti and her secretary welcomed us," Sarah later remembered. "It was instant acceptance and recognition—very warm, like we knew them for a long time. They knew the story of Jenny's physical problems."

Sandi hugged Jenny and told her she appreciated knowing that her music had helped Jenny through the tough times. "It was such an honor to be asked to go," Sarah said.

I always felt Jenny and Sarah looked and acted more like mother and daughter than Jenny and I. They had the same blonde hair, genuine smiles, and soft, sincere way of talking.

Chatter filled the car all the way home. "How often do you get to spend quality time with someone so important?" Sarah reflected. Our evening out reminded Sarah of Jenny's stardom in one of her elementary Christmas plays. "The Curious Case of the Christmas Caper." The tension in the plot had centered around the characters worrying that there wouldn't be any snow for Christmas. Jenny, playing Susie Snowflake, came onto the school auditorium stage crying, "I'm doing my best..." And she had done her best. It snowed.

That was just one of many musical programs they had shared as young student and teacher. "She was very coachable, very animated. She would ask for help and always wanted to do more and do it better," Sarah said. "She was in many singing groups, did solos and played in the recorder club."

Although Sarah knew Jenny way back in elementary school, she visited often when Jenny was ill with Lyme. After Jenny learned to speak again, she asked Sarah to help her so she could sing in church. "Music was a very, very important part of both of our lives," Sarah said.

"As I started to work with her, it was mainly getting the proper breaths and the deep breathing, opening her mouth correctly, putting the consonants on the end. It didn't take many lessons." Sometimes they used Sandi Patti tapes. Sarah found Jenny just as easy to coach as she had been as a youngster. "Jenny was my *only* Susie Snowflake," Sarah said with a smile.

22. Senior Pictures and Parties

We had hoped all three kids could have their senior pictures taken together, but Meagan was visiting her birth mother. The photo session for Tom and Jenny took about four hours, including outside shots since it was a beautiful day.

Every minute of that four hours was worth the effort. They had pictures taken together in addition to their individual shots. It had been so much easier—and a whole lot more fun—than the photo shoot when she was 17, and the photographers worked until they were able to hide the fact she was sitting in a wheelchair with her head supported.

That Jenny girl was wild to get the finished pictures back. Each day when she rushed home from school her first question would be, "Are our senior pictures here?" As expected, the cost was considerable, but it was an investment never to be regretted. Formal, informal, bright and sassy, sweet and shy their personalities popped right out of those pictures.

Parties

Friends continued to be an important part of Jenny's life. She loved having them to the house, and "going out" was always the best thing. When her Lyme symptoms reappeared, her life flip-flopped by the day, by the hour or even by the minute. If she felt poorly and could hide it from those on the fringe of her inner circle, she did. One night, when she was out with a bunch of kids, her friends came face to face with the *incredibly sick* Jenny, the one she kept hidden from them.

"We were out at a party, dancing, having a good time," her friend Marcie said later. "Some of us went walking, got separated, and when we gathered together again we realized Jenny wasn't with us." They had just decided she must have gone back to the house where the party was being held when they came upon Jenny, collapsed on the ground.

"Seeing, first hand, what could happen to her scared me," Marcie said. "I realized, in a small way, what Jenny was dealing with."

Aaron was at our house another night for a party Tom and Jenny had for their friends. "When Jenny had a seizure, Tom and I carried her into her room on the main floor," Aaron said. "Everybody went about their business and she came out again later. We just lived with it." Jenny beginning to seize wasn't a shock to Aaron. He had witnessed it at school.

"When she was sick, she felt tired," Aaron said. "But she beat that down a little bit when she could and got on with her life again." The kids were always glad to see her back in school after she had been sick.

"She beat it again. She's here! All right!" Aaron would say, when she returned to school after a bad time.

"We didn't think about the next time she was going to be sick. We knew it would happen. She never talked about the pain. If she talked about the pain, people would feel bad and she didn't want that. She didn't want to be the center of attention.

"If she wasn't sick, her day was like everyone else's— taking notes, listening to the teachers, trying to get the teacher off the subject," Aaron smiled.

For some reason, Jenny shared "a real sweet letter she had written to Aaron" with Mrs. Elliott. "Jenny, you have to air this thing out before you give it to him," Mrs. Elliott told her. It was loaded down with perfume. "Do you think I should send it? Should I really give it to him?" Jenny worried.

Aaron would drop by the house and hang out with Tom. Jenny wrote: "When you are there [at the house] with Tommy, I think you are very special." She tried to compliment him further by saying something like he wasn't the "normal gross teenager." Mrs. Elliott, one of the few people who knew Jenny had a *large* crush on Aaron, didn't think Jenny ever sent the letter to Aaron.

That's My Daughter

I was working at the nursing home one night, charting a record, when I saw someone bouncing down the hall. This figure was almost springing off her feet. I thought, "Oh, she just looks so happy." I turned around, looked once more and then looked back again. "Oh my God! That's my daughter!" I cried out. Jenny's face looked so good and her long hair had been cut, cropped right off.

Jenny Y. is a tiny, brunette bundle of dynamite. While visiting Jenny Y. at her college, the two girls had decided to whack off our Jenny's hair. Our Jenny Umphress glowed. She was so pleased with her new look and wanted to make sure I saw her hair before she went to bed and messed it up. It was neat that she always shared things with me, whether they were big or little.

"Look Mom! I did a spur-of-the-moment thing!" she said proudly. "Oh, you did, you did!" I grinned. I was pleased. She did look wonderful, but I was a little surprised at her impulsive decision.

Jenny was always deliberate and thoughtful in her actions. Apparently, she had observed me doing spontaneous things one time too many, like the time I said, "Let's get make-overs," as we approached the cosmetic section of a department store. The clerk had fussed and fussed over Jenny, who often had problems with her complexion.

We had passed the fifth anniversary of Jenny's struggles with Lyme. In such a long ordeal, it became obvious who were foul-weather friends. Fritz, who delivered Jenny's medications for the pharmacy, played an important role in our lives. He was always there to help, even after the insurance carrier felt it was necessary to change IV companies.

Fritz left his beeper number, saying, "Call any time day or night, if you ever need anything." He cried with us when things were bad. He also had the ability to make me smile when I had nothing to smile about.

A Gaither Concert

Around Halloween 1993, Jenny and Meagan decided to take a trip to a Gaither's concert in Clark. They had gotten their tickets, saved money for the trip, and made plans to stay overnight. I told Meagan she had to drive. Jenny seemed to be slipping a little. Putting Meagan behind the wheel made me uncomfortable, but considering Jenny's health, it seemed the best choice.

After they packed *all* their things, it looked like they were planning to stay for a week instead of overnight. They got lost on their way, which was not totally unexpected. When they finally got to the motel, I got a call to reassure me. Then they got directions to the concert hall, and actually managed to get there. The girls had a great time, and were excited to have their pictures taken with Bill Gaither. They also saw the rest of the group back stage.

On the way back to their motel, they stopped and got salads at an all-night store, since the fast food places were closed. When they couldn't get the door to their room open, the manager begrudgingly got up, responding to their call for help. To top it off, one of the girls got the door open just before he came.

Once settled in their room, they realized they had forgotten about getting salad forks, so coat hangers were used for utensils. They never did explain how that worked or if it was anywhere near sanitary.

Throughout the night, Meagan observed that Jenny just didn't seem okay. Whenever she had asked Jenny how she was doing, Jenny said she was "fine."

It was 4:30 a.m. when Meagan called me. Jenny was really sick and Meagan was scared to be alone with her away from home. She asked if I would come right away. Jon and Tom had to go to work, so I called my friend, Lee, and asked her to drive with me. This woman never got up before 8:30 a.m. Waking her up at that hour was asking a lot.

The dear soul came along so Meagan wouldn't have to drive home by herself while Jenny rode with me. It didn't take us long to make the drive at that hour and we packed up the girls and headed for home. Jenny was too sick to even talk. I rushed all the way, worrying about possible seizures.

As soon as we got home, I put Jenny into bed and gave her some medicine. Once again, it looked like the beginning of the flu, which usually meant trouble.

By November, Jenny was very ill. She had been sick ever since the Gaither concert trip. Dr. Kane continued to see her, but she was getting worse instead of better. We hadn't been to Dr. Adams for quite a while. On November 9, Dr. Kane called, saying he didn't know what else to do. He knew Jenny was getting a lot worse and he just didn't know what to change in her treatment.

She had failed considerably since the day she had barged into his office, showing off her good health. I told him it was time for us to go back to Indiana and he agreed. I immediately called Dr. Adams and got Jenny an appointment that same day.

The minute Dr. Adams saw Jenny, he knew we had our work cut out for us again. Jenny had gone through this many times before and there could be no other interpretation. Something was really wrong. Earlier in her illness, when symptoms would begin again, Jenny and I would think it was just the flu. *This time* she would get over it without any problems.

To most people, the flu is something to ride out. To Jenny, it was a major setback. Even Jenny knew getting well wasn't going to be easy this time. She didn't have an IV line in her chest. Before treatment could begin, she realized yet another surgery would have to be performed.

23. Fighting Back

We went straight home and made arrangements for Jenny to have another Groshong catheter inserted. She was aware she had to go back to the hospital. Jenny didn't like it, but she knew her surgeon had been good to her. She was desperately sick. For once, she didn't fight the idea of surgery.

This particular surgeon always liked to keep her overnight to make sure there were no problems. The surgery went well, but this hospitalization wasn't any better than her previous experiences at Miseracordia.

Jenny was never given a chance by some of the medical staff. Instead of looking at her as a person with a serious health problem, they treated her like a *bad* person. It was so unfair. Competent, caring nurses softened the ugliness of the situation a little.

The traumatic incident that occurred this time had to do with the anesthesiologist. When Jenny got back from surgery, Jenny and her nurse told us the most appalling story. While Jenny was waiting for the surgeon, a nurse came over to her. "What is your name and what procedure is going to be done?" she asked.

As Jenny started to answer, the anesthesiologist blurted out, "Don't you know? She's got Lyme. She's fatal. Ha! Ha!" I couldn't believe a doctor who took an oath to help patients could make a remark like that, especially before the patient was asleep. What was that like for Jenny? To hear such a statement before surgery. It was enough to make a mother raving mad.

The nursing supervisor made attempts to reach the anesthesiologist to no avail. I wanted Jenny out of there as quickly as possible. Once she was settled at home, I wrote a letter to the doctor's medical group, informing them there was no way he would ever work on any member of my family again. It was predictable that I didn't get a reply.

I couldn't have been more dismayed. Jenny had a difficult, personal battle to fight. How could anyone who would make such a callous and crude remark qualify as a doctor?

After that surgery, Jenny was home again on IVs. It was another rough, discouraging time. Jenny had tremendous faith and rigid determination in spite of all her pain. She continued to give me a smile and thank me for being there and taking care of her.

Given the length and severity of her illness, it was amazing how she continued to appreciate every little thing done for her. Countless nights I stayed up with her, just holding her and talking. After drifting off to sleep, she would wake up gripping her head, crying or screaming from the pain. She suffered joint pain, and experienced confusion, rashes, dizziness and exhaustion.

People called asking how Jenny was doing. She continued getting cards and visits from friends. Our church friends lived the Biblical stories of *The Loaves and Fishes* and of *Love One Another*. Every few weeks church friends would gather up food for our family.

Letters arrived with money enclosed on a regular basis from a lady who remains anonymous. "I have a child the age of your kids, and just want to help," she wrote. I had the impression her husband didn't know she was doing this.

How I wanted to thank her. If it hadn't been for those unexpected money gifts there would have been many days we would not have been able to buy a gallon of milk or a loaf of bread.

Gradually, Jenny began coming around, a little more each day. It just seemed so much harder to come back each time. One thing that kept her going was a Helen Steiner Rice piece "Climb Till Your Dream Comes True," which she kept near her bedside.

Often your tasks will be many,
And more than you think you can do.
Often the road will be rugged
And the hills insurmountable, too.
But, always remember, the hills ahead
Are never as steep as they seem,
And with faith in your heart start upward
And climb till you reach your dream

Among others, she received tremendous encouragement from Jim Boedicker, a vocalist from our church. When his only child was born with multiple health problems, Jim and his wife depended on their faith in God. Through his dry humor and the way Jim lived his life, he encouraged Jenny to be strong in dealing with her problems.

Kelly Connor, her other singing friend, became Jenny's big sister in our support system. Ever present at the lowest points, she never allowed Jenny to look at her weaknesses. Rather, she emphasized all of her strengths, and when Jenny's health declined, Kelly stretched out a comforting hand.

Peer Pressure

There was one time during her ordeal when Jenny allowed peer pressure to get to her. She decided she wanted to be like other girls, as skinny as possible. Jenny had talked with a girl who suggested she make herself vomit.

This girl promised Jenny she could lose all the weight she wanted to this way. Jenny was naive enough to fall into the trap, but it didn't last long.

Within the week she started to force vomit, something told me to barge into the bathroom and check on her. Jenny was absolutely shocked.

"But, Mom, I'm so fat. If I do this maybe I won't be," she cried. I was so furious at the situation, I smashed a portable cassette player and headphone. And I yelled! That is the only time I remember really yelling at Jenny, but I didn't know how to deal with this new problem. I couldn't believe she would do something like that to herself, after all she had gone through to be healthy. I even threatened her.

"If you continue to do this, I will admit you to a psych ward." That wasn't a rational approach, but Jenny stopped purging right then and there.

She knew if I said I was going to do something, I would do it. I also think she realized how stupid it was and how much harm it could have on her health.

I told Jenny that Kelly knew about it. Jenny was embarrassed to face Kelly, but I gave her no choice. Kelly was incredibly understanding, telling Jenny that everyone does things they are ashamed of and embarrassed about. Then, Kelly did an exciting thing. She prayed with Jenny.

I also called Jenny's high school counselor, Mrs. Sandy Waggoner, and asked her to come and talk to my confused girl. When I needed her, Sandy lent her wisdom.

Testing Limits—Taking Risks

Sometimes, Jenny felt she was up on a pedestal and couldn't do anything bad. A normal teen, she ventured out and took some risks. Even though she knew she wasn't supposed to drink because of her medications, Jenny tried her first drink of alcohol.

Jenny Y. took her to a dance club and bar while Jenny was visiting on campus. Both girls were underage. "I could tell it made her feel attractive when some guy asked her to dance," Jenny Y. said later. "This didn't happen a lot with guys our age, and it was so important to her. She was having a good time, and I wouldn't let anything happen to her."

Then there was the time Jenny and Jenny Y. decided to investigate an adult leather and lace shop. Those two girls could be mischievous. As they looked bug-eyed around the shop, they told the clerk they had a friend getting married and just wanted to find something special for her. That shop was a whole new world to those young ladies.

When Jenny told Jamie about their adventure, he responded, "Jen, dang!" She hadn't told me yet, and Jamie thought, "Whew! All right!"

He admired her adventurous spirit and was more than a little curious about just what kind of a leather outfit she thought was so neat.

When Jenny got home, she chatted her head off, telling me all about it. I figured, all kids experiment and this was one of Jenny's few adventures. I rolled with laughter as she described the contraptions in that store. Jenny continued to be wonderfully funny and tremendously naive.

The two Jenny's remained close even though our Jenny was finishing high school and Jenny Y. was now in college. Their long history had begun in fourth grade. Vibrant, thoughtful Jenny Y. described our Jenny's charm. "It was her smile. It was wonderful, which has been said a hundred times. But more than that, it was what was behind the eyes. The way she looked at me and the way she loved me, unconditionally...that drew me in and kept me there." Jenny Y. felt other people saw that too.

"I knew that no matter what was going on in her life, she would take the time out for me. And it was the same for me. If I could take the time out, I would. If I couldn't, I would make time." Jenny Y. was nine when her mother died and around 13 when her father died. Jenny was sensitive to the feelings and needs of Jenny Y. They were outlets for each other, with complete trust being their common bond.

Jenny and I welcomed Jenny Y. into our intense mother-daughter relationship. "I always wanted to be a part of it, and they kind of let me, and that was nice," Jenny Y. said. When Jenny Y. or another best girlfriend would confide in our Jenny, it became a joke. The girlfriend would often add, "I know you are going to tell your mom, and that' s okay."

"After high school, Jenny was the only person I kept in contact with. But I didn't have a choice. I loved her too much," Jenny Y. said later. "She was more like a sister than a friend. It never occurred to me that I should cut off ties with her."

It took a while, but finally Jenny began improving with the continued use of IV antibiotics. The oral medications just didn't work for her. I was relieved something did work.

College Applications

While other mothers turned purple coaxing their high school juniors and seniors to give a little time and attention to filling out their college application forms, that wasn't necessary with Jenny. For her, college was a welcomed and necessary step to the career she hoped to attain.

In addition to Anderson, she sent an application off to a Bible college in Minnesota and to a few colleges within driving distance of home. Each application was filled out neatly and in great detail.

> Personal Statement: I have been told by many that I am a strong, determined, loving person. I have had an interesting but difficult life. Five years ago while our family was on vacation I contracted a chronic illness that still haunts me...As a result of my struggles, I feel I have greatly matured. I have learned life is not always fair or easy, but everything happens for a reason.

In another application packet:

> ..Because I had lost years of my life, my school work was pushed a side. But I was determined to return to school and graduate...my dream will become a reality...I feel I was given a second chance in life for a reason. It allowed me to make a more positive difference in society. I've given many interviews [about my story]

I want to be able to say to myself one day when it's my time to leave this world, "Good job."...We were always taught that sometimes you have to stick your neck out for others, and do what you think is right. And whatever you do, never look back.

About this same time, Jenny applied for a DAR scholarship. It was hard to take in her ability to approach the essay subject, "Our American Heritage and My Responsibility to Preserve It," given how long and how severely she had been side-tracked. Her personal struggles are reflected in the descriptions she gives of the struggles of her forefathers.

...brave and courageous pilgrims...must have realized, you have to seek out your dream and follow it wherever it might go...A new nation had begun, granting hope to everyone...America faced many times of sorrow...So you ask what can we do to preserve our American Heritage. People should learn all we can, respect our heritage, and learn to love one another, whatever creed or color.

We should be proud of one another and look to God for guidance and direction...Persons should live their lives to the fullest and show courage and honesty...We should be an example for all to see, showing confidence and love in all we do...America was built on hard work, a dream, ambition and hope for tomorrow.

She concludes her essay with an honest-to-Jenny personal statement: "Please, disreguard any mistakes I might have made. Living with a chronic illness you have good days and bad. This happens to be one of my bad days, and it took a lot of willpower to write this essay. I hope you look beyond the errors and find the true meaning of my composition. God Bless the U.S.A."

Defining a Life

"What will happen to me if the IVs stop working?" Jenny asked one day. I didn't know how to answer her. I told her she had to have a positive outlook and strive for goals. One of our philosophies was—there is always someone out there that is worse off than yourself. That was hard to picture when she was enduring unbearable pain.

Another important thing kept us going. A good sense of humor. Because of my own exhaustion and dealing with Jenny's problems, I was always falling down, running into walls, dropping things or just saying something stupid. To top it off, I would forget things all the time. Jenny loved to tease me about being a "klutz." I thought that was pretty good, coming from "Gracie."

Most of the time Jenny realized that no one is perfect, and that God put her here for some reason. She was determined to make the most of her life. Then there were times she would ask, "Mom, what do you think my purpose here on earth is? I wish God would let me know so I can do a good job."

She believed God gave everyone gifts, like Pastor Dave preaching, and Kelly and Jim ministering through their music, but she was still searching for her gift.

All the pain and turmoil and crises in her life seemingly defined who Jenny was—a sick young lady. But Jenny's special gift was being well used. It was the gift of inspiring others to keep going and showing them God's love. She climbed insurmountable mountains and when she fell down a steep slope, she got up and climbed again, pulling even harder.

Each accomplishment at the end of a difficult struggle made her effort worthwhile. There was the first time she was able to say "Mom" again, the first time she walked into church again to be greeted by Pastor Dave's welcoming smile and the congregation's response, the first time she sang with Kelly and Jim in concert, the first time she walked for the high school principal, her first prom, experiencing young love, learning to drive a car, her first grade card after returning to school, her selection to the National Honor Society, special "dates" with Tom, and the accomplishment of bringing home a new sister.

It was beginning to seem like it was not in God's plan for a complete healing for Jenny, but He allowed her to experience remarkable miracles during her fight with Lyme. She was meeting and accomplishing many of her goals.

24. A Musical Ministry

A wonderful, unexpected thing happened early in December, 1993. Something that made Jenny feel like she was accomplishing even more. A strong supporter of Kelly Connor's music ministry, Jenny repeatedly said, "Kelly you are going to make it in the big time." She also admired Kelly for putting her family ahead of everything.

After visiting Jenny, Kelly would leave thinking, "What talent is sitting there, wasting away in that body. Her mind is exciting and fresh. She is giving and caring."

Kelly knew Jenny had a computer and felt Jenny could work well with her hands and her mind. Jim Boedicker agreed. Jim had been promoting Kelly's music for over three years as her representative. He wanted follow-up contacts made with all the places where Kelly had given concerts, to see if they wanted her back.

Since Jim did not have time to go through all the files, Kelly and Jim decided Jenny would be the perfect person to help them. Jenny would fill a real need. It wouldn't be just busy work.

One day Kelly came down to the house and asked Jenny if she would be willing to help her out with her musical ministry. Jenny was a little confused at first. She wasn't sure what Kelly wanted.

"Jenny, we are so much alike because of the care and concern we both have for others," Kelly explained. "We have the same beliefs and feelings about things." Kelly said she wanted Jenny to do bookings for her concerts. Thrilled, Jenny wrote:

For the first time I have a purpose and I will be doing something I love, working for Jesus. This is the direction he is leading, and I will trust him...all the way home!

Jim guided Jenny, trained her, and wrote her a letter stating, "Here is what we want you to do, but if you cannot do it, if you are not up to it, if you are not feeling well, we want you to promise us you will take a break and not make yourself sick over it since this work can be rescheduled." Jenny agreed.

"We really didn't talk a lot about her disease," Jim said later. "I kind of sensed everybody did that with her. She didn't want to be pampered. She was tired of dealing with and being shackled to the disease. She wanted to do something different and fun.

"My, she jumped into this big time," Jim reflected later. "She did a great job and got Kelly a lot more places to sing than I had managed to arrange. Jenny was very enthusiastic."

When Jenny started to call churches, she would tell them, "Oh, you just have to have her." Jenny's enthusiasm for Kelly overflowed. People would tell Kelly later, "We had hundreds of packets on people, but the way Jennifer talked about you, we felt, if she is this excited, we have to at least listen to Kelly's tape." Once they listened to a tape, they were often sold.

It amazed Kelly to receive encouragement from Jenny, from someone so much younger. "Sometimes it would blow me out of the water to realize the wisdom that would come out of Jenny," Kelly said. "About life, death, God, friendships, things she believed in, things she didn't believe."

Kelly felt Jenny's wisdom came out of her pain and suffering. Jenny found happiness even on her worst days, which Kelly admired.

After going through all their business papers, Jim showed Jenny the contracts. They agreed Jim would see all correspondence. "It wasn't that I didn't trust her. Rather, we needed continuity in what the three of us were doing."

This new young business woman absolutely loved working for Kelly and put a lot of herself into every call and letter. It was decided Jenny would receive a commission for each book-ing. Jenny was a quick act. She had the ability to talk to people and win their hearts. She was genuine. Jenny never pretended to be something she wasn't, except for one thing. When representing Kelly, she didn't tell people she was still in high school. She identified herself as Jennifer instead of Jenny, hoping to sound older.

In no time, Jenny was busily representing Kelly. She would push herself hard, and then have a collapse, losing strength and the ability to function independently. Her pain would increase. Kelly felt terrible, worried the work was too much for Jenny. There was no doubt Jenny was doing a super job, but Kelly didn't want Jenny's health to suffer.

It was a fulfilling, but demanding time. Kelly's total trust and faith in Jenny made Jenny feel capable—able to do something good for others. Organized to perfection, Jenny kept immaculate files and loved purchasing office supplies.

During this time, Jenny tossed around the idea of going to college. Jim encouraged. Kelly said it wasn't necessary for this job. Still, she wanted what was best for Jenny. At times it was hard for Jenny to do her high school work and the bookings, but she stubbornly gave it her all.

Another sideline in Jim's life was selling Gospel shows to county fairs. To make contacts, he attended the Fair Management Convention where 95 fairs and 25 festivals were represented.

Jim thought Jenny might be interested in learning about this business and got her a room at the Hyatt Hotel where the convention was held. It suited her taste for beautiful, elegant things, especially the crystal chandeliers in the lobby.

Over lunch Jim explained how to talk to the fair people. "You don't want to oversell. You don't want to undersell. Some people are interested in ministry, some in entertainment only." He explained how to be sensitive to the client and sort that out. "She was sharp. She understood everything even though it was all new to her," Jim said.

One night they went to a showcase entertainment, six free big acts a night where they had front row seats. "It was like they were doing a concert just for us even though there were perhaps 3,000 people behind us. It was fun and Jenny enjoyed it." Again, it was a totally new, unique experience. Something her classmates were not ready for.

When Jim got home he called and asked her how she was doing. She said in a wavering voice, "Oh, I'm okay." She would never say, "I don't feel very good." This time, though, she did say, "I'm pretty tired."

"Well, Jenny," Jim said, "I'm tired too." It had been an exhausting time and he was wiped out, without carrying the burden of Lyme. He was trying to let her know it was okay to be tired. "I think she thought that if she whined or talked about her disease we would think she couldn't do the job and we would bail out on her," he later reflected.

Jim appreciated the fact that Jenny believed in his Christian ministry too. "She was a big fan and we developed a fast friendship. Over time we developed a closeness and talked more about music things. I considered her a friend and an associate.

"She wanted to see Kelly record, so one afternoon I drove her over to Pinebrook Studios in Indiana, a state-of-the-art, top drawer studio. A bunch of interesting people came through and Jenny enjoyed watching Kelly record," Jim said.

"It was another experience when Jenny was away from home. No one was fussing with her to take her medicine and she was doing something the high school kids weren't doing," Jim said.

"As long as she was okay I never said anything or asked anything about her health. If she looked like she was tired or struggling, I would slow down.

"I puzzled Jenny a lot because she never knew if I was serious or not," Jim grinned remembering. "We would talk business and I would deliberately say something wrong like...and then you send a bill for a million dollars and if they send you $70,000, that is okay. And she would go, 'Oh, okay.' Later on, she would question, 'Did you really mean that?'" It tickled Jim.

"She seemed to delight in our teasing. She told me I played, sang and listened to songs that were dumb or corny," Jim said. "I just go nuts on purpose with this stuff. She would say, 'If Jim sings that stupid flying pig song one more time...' But she did have fun with them."

A Picture Book Christmas

December 25, 1993, was a picture book Christmas. It reminded me of the fun we had when the kids were little and Jon would play Santa Claus at Sugar Grove United Methodist Church.

"I was always glad to do it for my kids," Jon said. "It was fun to fool them. I would make an excuse about why I couldn't go to church and Susan would take the kids."

When Jon arrived at church later he would park out back and I would keep the kids away from the church windows so they wouldn't see him or his car.

"I changed my voice when I talked to Jen and Tommy," Jon said. "They were pretty awed when I talked about things special to them. They would think and wonder, 'How did Santa know that?'"

Since we had purchased the video camera to record Jenny's therapies for her New Jersey doctor, we were pleased to have it around for special occasions and used it non-stop Christmas 1993. God's grace continued to bless our lives. We did not know it would be our last Christmas with Jenny. My best Christmas present was a handwritten letter from her.

Dear Mom, I thought I would write you a short note and express how grateful I feel at this moment. I am surrounded by so much love and warmth and I am so lucky to say you are my parents.

Christmas of '93 was a wonderful and special time for me, with or without the gifts. Just knowing I am a part of a family who loves one another and realizes how important the Lord is. I can't imagine life without you.

When I look around and see so many broken homes, it only makes me realize how fortunate I am. Whenever anyone mentions to me how much we are alike, I feel very proud that you have instilled in me some of your values. You are a wonderful wife, mother and overall person, and you deserve the best life has to offer. Thank you for being my mom. Next to the Lord, Dad and you are the most important people in my life and I promise wherever life takes me, I will always make all of you proud.

All My Love, Jennifer

Meagan stayed with us instead of traveling to be with her mom. It was her first Christmas with us. Christmas had always been a special time in Jenny's life. When we could, we would go to a candlelight Christmas eve service, then go home and the kids would dig into their stockings. The three kids had a ball that year. At one point, Jenny looked at me and asked, "Is this a hint, Mom, or what?" *Santa* had hidden *two* toothbrushes in her stocking by mistake. Tom and Meagan let her know they only received *one each.*

All four grandparents were with us Christmas day, and Jenny made sure our big Christmas breakfast started with grace. "Jenny always reminded us what Christmas was about even though she liked parties," Tom said.

Each year Jon accepted as status quo that I would go wild buying the kids a lot of Christmas gifts. "We always went way out for Christmas," Jon reflected later. "Even before Jenny was sick. The kids never gave us any serious problems. Nothing that wasn't easily overcome. We weren't overly strict with them, and we weren't overly permissive with them either."

The gift that thrilled Jenny the most that year was a phone answering machine. "Now I can be a *real* business lady," she said, glowing with pride.

Jenny was groomed to a "T" in a Christmas sweatshirt decorated with a jolly Santa surrounded by a splash of gold stars. Santa's hat had a real bell on the top. It was a given, Jenny hummed or sang to Christmas music playing in the background.

Since she had graduated from speech therapy and Metta's influence of loud trinkets, Jenny was now into understated jewelry—dainty chains and earrings. She wore them constantly and thrilled receiving them as gifts. "Ohhhh, (breathless) my ring!"

Opening a chain and cross, "Oh, that is so pretty. Thank you Mom and Dad. I really like that." Jon and I were rewarded tenfold as Jenny and Tom promptly and sincerely expressed thanks for each gift.

Tom had always wanted a cowboy hat and Jenny gave him a really handsome one for Christmas. "Jenny was so excited watching me open that box," Tom said later. "It was the best gift I ever got from her. She put a lot of thought into it and it really meant a lot."

In the madness of packing, wrapping and labeling gifts, a few mistakes were made which made for more fun. Once in a while after opening a package, Jenny would say, "This one isn't mine, Mom. I wrapped it for you for someone else." And tape, Lordy, we should have invested in tape stock. It seemed like those presents would never come undone.

By afternoon, Jenny was exhausted and needed to rest. She didn't get up again until much later. When I went up to her room to check on her and give her an IV treatment, she said, "Thanks, Mom, for such a nice Christmas."

Christmas with Jenny was cookie baking, lots of thoughtful shopping together, and special gift wrapping. If anyone ever lived the true spirit of Christmas, it was Jenny.

Tutoring and Treatments as the Year Turns

After being treated again, Jenny continued to improve. She was working hard at home with a tutor, Sandy Waggoner, the high school counselor, who said she didn't have much to do because Jenny was such a go-getter she just more or less guided her and gave her tests. Jenny was always going to her teachers and getting work so she could catch up from the times she missed. Her teachers told me they never had to worry about Jenny skipping her work. She usually did more than was required. It was against her nature to take the easy way out.

Arrangements were being made for graduation. Eric, my brother Scott's son, was also graduating. Since the cousins would graduate together, Scott wanted us to have one big family graduation party. We figured we would invite a lot of the same people and it would be nice to be together. Plans were made to have a party at a club near our home.

On January 17, 1994, Jenny had to go to outpatient to have her Groshong repaired. The catheter was leaking near the hub. Once it was repaired, we were out of there. Other than that, things went along fairly smoothly. I had quit my job at the nursing home back in December. It had become too exhausting with the care Jenny required. Since we no longer had a nurse coming to the house, I was responsible for her total care again.

Fran Dean, our case manager, assumed we still had a nurse since the IVs had started up, but I did everything. All the pharmacy did was bring the supplies I requested. When the bills continued to submerge us, I began working weekend nights with a bedridden lady friend. I also baby-sat at home during the day while working with Jenny. Fortunately, the grandmas would help with the little ones if we had to go to the doctor's office.

I leaned on Fran a lot and she solved many complicated problems. But Fran and I disagreed at times, usually over taking Jenny to the hospital. What she didn't always understand was that Jenny had a mind of her own. Sometimes Jenny just didn't want to go back to the hospital. There was no doubt that Fran had Jenny's best interests at heart, but Jenny was sick of hospitals.

If I really needed someone, Jane, a close friend, would come or call. It took Jenny a while to get to know Jane, probably because she now worked at the hospital. Jenny couldn't trust hospital people very much. Later, when they developed a strong bond, Jenny wanted to stop the nurse/patient relationship and just relate friend to friend.

Friends were one of the great rallying points in Jenny's world. She treasured each friendship and the talks she shared with each friend. There was Amy Poe. Born with cerebral palsy, Amy had been critically injured in a car accident shortly after she was out of high school. Amy and Jenny experienced a lot of the same head injury symptoms, so they could relate to each other's recovery process. Amy's mom and I had some heartfelt talks over the phone. We understood what the other was experiencing.

In February, local musicians, The Glory Bound Quartet, along with Kelly and Jim, gave a concert for Amy. Physically, Jenny was feeling awful, but there was no way she would stay away from Amy's concert. "I have to go for Amy. Nothing is going to stop me." She understood first hand the accomplishments Amy had made, and Jenny wanted to be there to let Amy know she cared. Life had dealt them both some tough challenges. Amy's improvement and effort to live a happy, productive life were an inspiration to our girl. Jenny put on her make-up, fixed her hair in an attractive style, and no one at the concert knew how poorly she was feeling. Not even Amy, when Jenny gave her a big, generous hug.

In March, Jenny was elected Teen of the Month. She was honored to represent our local high school at a county-wide event. On the day of the luncheon, she was very sick. But once again, she fixed up her face, put on her smile, and no one knew how difficult it was for her to be in attendance.

As a senior, Jenny participated in the National Honor Society induction for the junior class, presenting candles to two special friends. That evening she was terribly ill, but she pushed herself. People had no idea how badly she felt much of the time. Some of the kids thought she would take time off from school for no reason.

"Some kids think I'm taking a lot of vacation, Mom," Jenny said. People didn't hear her complain, and pity was not allowed. Often, she suffered alone and in silence.

Sometimes people from the school called and asked if Jenny should be pushing herself so hard. In January, 1994, the high school principal told her she had enough credits to graduate in May. He said she could stop attending school, and take care of herself so she would be able to attend graduation.

"Absolutely not," was Jenny's response. No one else was allowed to do that, and she wasn't going to be treated any differently. The principal told her if he had to carry her onto the graduation platform, she would attend graduation. The whole school was pulling for her.

"She wanted people to think of her as Jenny Umphress, one of our friends, a senior this year. Not Jenny Umphress, the one with Lyme disease," a girlfriend said.

25. More Madness

On March 11, 1994, I took Jenny to the outpatient treatment center to meet the surgeon who had put Jenny's Groshong catheter in the previous November. We felt it was infected. Jenny could always tell when it was starting to be a problem—it would either burn badly or get red and swollen. The doctor did a culture and said it was scar related and we should go home.

Even so, I felt there was a serious problem. I knew it was infected whether he said it was or not. We had had problems in the past with tubes that doctors said were okay. Too often we were told nothing was wrong, and it ended up to be serious.

A few days later, the doctor's nurse called and told us the lab culture showed Jenny needed to be on antibiotics on top of the IV antibiotics. We had already known there was a problem, but who were we? Just a sick patient and her exhausted mom. It was tiresome being treated like we were ignorant.

I had been giving Jenny medicine to keep her fever down. If the nurse hadn't called, I would have done something more for her. When another medication was added to her treatment, the infection cleared up.

A Bag of Medicine

Jenny continued working hard in school, looking forward to graduation. Many times she carried her portable IV machine and bag with her and the school nurse would help with any problems. This compact machine was nice compared to her bigger one. Most people just thought it was a purse strapped around her waist, until it started to beep. We didn't have any problems with this CADD pump. It was easy to operate.

Once our dear pharmacy friend, Fritz, tried to make me use another pump. I just couldn't operate the machine. He kept saying it was much simpler and there was no reason I couldn't operate it if I had done okay on the CADD pump. I begged him to get me a CADD pump again and he couldn't. Then I told Fran Dean. Well, that was like turning a wild bull out of a pen. When she wanted something done, it was done.

In no time at all Fritz called and asked me why I had got that woman on his back. He assured me I didn't need to go that far. The next day I had a CADD pump. Fritz remained my friend even after I turned wild woman Fran lose on him. It was an experience we would laugh about much later.

On April 8, Jenny's tube began acting up again. She was hurting and felt a burning sensation. We called the doctor who had inserted the tube, and he told us to meet him at the outpatient clinic again. The nurse could tell something was really wrong, and was puzzled when the doctor said everything was okay and we should leave the tube alone. The nurse explained there was redness, tenderness and seepage by the tube. "I can't get another tube in so just leave this one alone," the doctor said.

Well, I was smart enough to know that when a Groshong catheter site is infected, the catheter has to come out. I called Dr. Adams. He was out of state and his nurse said she would see what she could do. She called me back for Dr. Adams. He wanted that tube out and another put in, NOW. If the area surgeon didn't wish to do it, then I had to find another doctor who would perform the surgery.

I called Fran Dean. Naturally, it was a Friday when it was difficult to get in to see a doctor. Everything seemed to happen on Fridays. After making some calls, she told me to take Jenny to the town of Meeker to a Dr. Gardner, who would see her in the emergency room.

God Sent a Surgeon

Meeker was about an hour drive east of Ada. I didn't know the town very well, but I managed to find the hospital. It was immediately obvious the hospital personnel were compassionate and more concerned than most of the staff at Miseracordia. They told me the doctor had been paged and he would be in as soon as possible. I knew this was asking a lot of a doctor who had never seen Jenny. To see her late on a Friday night wasn't fair to him, but there wasn't any other choice for us. We waited quite a while, and every time we saw a doctor we wondered if it was Dr. Gardner.

Finally, a barrel chested, broad shouldered gentleman came in, apologizing for making us wait. He told us he had been talking with his pastor, and it had been a long time since he had been able to meet with him. This man made a great impression from the first hello. He talked freely about his beliefs in God, and Jenny immediately bonded with him.

I gave him Jenny's background and described what had happened recently. He looked at the site and said it was infected. The tube needed to be removed and another put in. Taking a cautious approach, he didn't think the emergency room was the place to do something that complicated.

He felt it should be done in surgery. But he did put in a temporary triple lumen catheter, which might work for ten days, until he could schedule her for surgery. I warned him of all the problems Jenny had had in the past getting tubes in, and the amount of tubes that had been placed. He didn't have a minute of trouble inserting the temporary catheter. Then he removed the infected tube.

The first of the week, I received a call from the other surgeon's office. The one who said he couldn't replace the tube. His nurse said the culture had come back positive and Jenny needed to be on antibiotics for the infection. I didn't tell her that old tube was already out and a new temporary one inserted. Instead, I thanked her and hung up.

They had called in a prescription for the infection and told me to pick it up. I never did. Once again, Fran had saved the day by making arrangements for us that no one else could make. Jenny had peaked with temperatures over 105 in the past, and had developed serious problems from infected tubes. That wasn't about to happen again. At this point, I was certain I could teach a medical course called "Utilization of Common Sense while Treating a Patient."

On Monday, April 11, I took Jenny to the new surgeon's office to have a physical before surgery. Jenny was being treated for Lyme with 2 grams of ampicillin every six hours via IV. On April 15, Jenny went in for surgery. Everyone was pleasant and thoughtful. What a difference in attitude from some of her other hospitalizations. I made up my mind then and there, we were *never* going back to Miseracordia.

The doctors allowed me back in surgery with Jenny until they were ready to operate, which made Jenny feel much more comfortable. She wasn't left in a cold hallway by herself, staring at a blank wall for an eternity until they were good and ready in the operating room.

They couldn't have treated her with more respect. Everything was explained to us, and a nurse was assigned to our family to keep us informed of what was going on in surgery. It was wonderful to have Jenny treated with dignity.

The surgeon didn't have any problems during the hour long surgery. Jenny was put under anesthetic, so she didn't feel anything. Dr. Gardner came and explained he had put a port-a-cath in Jenny's chest and told me I could take her home. He asked if we had help at home and I had to admit I was doing all of her care.

He decided, until I felt comfortable with accessing the port of her new cath, I should bring Jenny to the chemo department at his hospital. He said they were the experts and he trusted their work.

The port-a-cath is placed under the skin. To access it, a needle is stuck through the skin into the center of the catheter. Meagan and Tom were there for the surgery and Meagan got sick in Jenny's room while they were trying to access the port. Meagan had helped me with many of Jenny's procedures and had never gotten sick, however, this particular procedure really bothered her that day.

A special nurse had been requested to insert the needle before we left. She was running late, needing to make arrangements for her kids getting out of school. Once she arrived and everything was ready, she pulled her hair back and began to work.

After she stuck Jenny, she said she wished they had done the procedure while Jenny was still asleep in surgery. The needle wasn't working properly. She called in another nurse and finally they got it working. The first nurse was feeling uneasy when we left.

The needle inserted into the catheter would be used for the IV treatments. It would remain in for one week. Then we would return to the chemo department, where they would insert a new needle and apply new dressing. The routine seemed to work okay. But Fran found out we didn't have home health nurses coming to the house. Since that was our agreement, some changes would need to be made—soon.

26. The Dove Awards

Jenny had been invited by Kelly and Jim to go to Nashville, Tennessee, for the Gospel Music Association Dove Awards. What an opportunity that was for her! She would meet people involved with Christian music, and, hopefully, learn things that would help her with Kelly's musical ministry. It was also important for her to just get away. Jenny had never been able to pack up and leave for more than a day or two. This trip promised to be a great opportunity to spend quality time with special friends.

I had to let Fran know about the trip being planned. The thought had entered my mind to just let Jenny have her grand adventure and not mention it to Fran. Jenny was hoping this is what I would do. But I knew if I didn't tell our insurance consultant about a trip Jenny wanted to take, something would go wrong for sure and then we would have major problems.

An Angel in a Chiffon Dress

I decided I would do anything I could to help her go to Nashville. Excitement filled the air as she made plans for the trip. I bought her some clothes, including a new coat, and she had been given luggage for Christmas so that wasn't a problem. The frosting on the cake was a white chiffon evening dress.

"Look what I bought! Look what I bought!" Jenny floated into the house the night Tom and Jenny brought a beautiful new dress home. "Tommy bought it for me!"

"Wait until you see her in it. She looks just like an angel," Tom said. He looked like he had just won the Indy 500.

Jenny got busy making lists upon lists similar to her packing lists for our Georgia trip in 1988. However, this time it would be a working holiday, and Kelly and Jim were just the perfect people to lift up her spirits.

Passport from Fran

I told Fritz that we would need extra IVs for Jenny to take to Nashville. The problem was that the IVs only lasted a couple of days, since they were pre-mixed, so I told Jenny I had to call Fran and tell her what was going on. Jenny protested. She just knew Fran wouldn't permit her to go to Nashville for most of a week.

"Mom, just keep your mouth shut. We are just going to sneak out."

"Jenny, I will have that wild woman after me," I said. Eventually, I called Fran and asked her if they had IV service companies down in Nashville.

"Why, Susan?" she asked.

I had promised Jenny I wouldn't tell Fran about the trip even though I knew that was wrong and could be bad for Jenny's health.

My indirect question was my way of not breaking a promise to Jenny. Fran was smart. I knew she would pick up on it as quickly as a hunting dog on scent.

"What the hell do you think you are doing?" Fran bellowed. "Susan?!?"

Once I explained the situation, Fran could not have been more understanding. But she said she would only allow the trip if a nurse was hired down in Tennessee, since I would not be going. She arranged for an IV company in Nashville to go to Jenny's hotel and take care of everything

Jim had decided that Jenny had to be told, "You can go if you agree to some criteria. If you assure us of this, this and this." Jim sensed Jenny's indignation. An uncommon attitude for her, but he understood.

"I really don't know what the big deal is. I'm almost 21-years-old. I've had this disease a long time. I know what is going on. I know how to take care of myself. I know when I am sick. I know how to take my medicine. I know all about it," Jenny protested.

"Jenny, all of that is accurate," Jim told her. "No one is denying that one bit, but what if something would happen to you and you wouldn't be able to tell us? What would you do if you put yourself in our place? What if you took me down there and I got really ill and you didn't know what to do for me? How would you feel?" Jim put the monkey on her back. She didn't like that, but she understood their concerns.

Nursing Duties

Kelly came to the house and practiced the required medical regime. She was a little nervous, but she did well. If they had problems, they knew I would be at home. Jenny was thrilled everything had been worked out and was truly shocked that Fran had agreed. Even Fran knew Jenny needed this special experience away from home.

Before she left, Jenny wrote us a note:

Mom thank you for helping me to go to Nashville. If it wasen't for you, I probably wouldn't be going. Thank you for believing in me, loving me, and I know you will always be here for me.

How could I ever ask for more. Say a prayer that every thing will go *fine*! Dad - I Love You and I'll bring you something special back.

I Love You Both!   Jenny (smiley face)

They left Ada early on Sunday morning, April 24, 1994, and were to come back the following weekend. Kelly was amazed to discover they were hauling more packages of medicine than suitcases full of clothes. Jim was shocked.

There were two large boxes of medicines and a cooler full of things for Jenny. "How can anyone be on that much medicine for that length of time and not have an adverse affect on them?" Jim questioned. But Jim knew, if it wasn't for the drugs, Jenny wouldn't have made it this long.

While they were gone, we planned to paint some rooms in the house and do a lot of things we normally couldn't do when Jenny was there. Jenny called, telling us she was having a great time. She loved dressing up like a professional business woman.

Always a Price to Pay

One time when she called, I could tell by the tone of her voice she wasn't feeling well. But I didn't question her. By the second or third night she was really dragging.

Finally, Jenny called me when no one else was in her room. "Mom, I am so sick, but I don't want them to know.

"I don't want to ruin this. I want to have fun. I want to do this no matter what."

I told her she had to tell Kelly and Jim.

"Mama, please don't make me come home. Please. They aren't like you, Mom. They can't read through me. I can get away with it." When I heard her call me "Mama," I knew how sick she was. She only called me Mama when she was really, really sick.

If I had been with her, I would have known right away how she was feeling. When Jenny was sick, she lost the twinkle in her eyes. Nurses who were with her for any length of time even picked up on this.

According to Kelly, Jenny had overdone it. But Jenny refused to slow down until she didn't have a choice. Finally, Jim suggested he and Jenny skip a concert they wanted to see, go back to the room, and order in some food. "We had a nice meal and rested and reflected about what was going on," Jim said. "She was always trying to dream up good ideas for Kelly."

"Kelly is so good, Jim," Jenny said. "I just don't know why someone doesn't pick her up and make her a star. I know. We'll have her open for a big star."

"No problem," Jim told her. "You just give some group $20,000 to $30,000 and you can open up their concerts all across the country. Now where can we get $20,000 or $30,000?"

"Oh well, then..." Jenny scratched her head. Jim realized Jenny was caught up in the excitement of it all. She wanted to devise a way to do a big thing for Kelly. The seminars and concerts had diverted her mind away from her disease. For a while she was a special person in a special world. Jim could see how much Jenny loved the business of Gospel music.

Jenny loved the whole scene. She told Kelly, "This is *like* a dream come true. This *is* a dream come true, Kelly." It was a thrill to get her nails done and her hair fixed, and she told others how pretty they looked. Jenny felt blessed she had friends who would include her in such a special event.

"Maybe I could go around and talk to people about my disease," Jenny said after one of her seminars. "I could have a traveling ministry and help people. Maybe I could write a book. How would I do that? How do I write it? How do I get it published?"

"Our room looked like a drug dealer's headquarters," Kelly said. "There were so many IV needles and supplies and coolers for her medicine. People laugh about baby bottles and diapers, but this was like nothing I had ever dealt with my boys. Every bit of it was worth it to see her face and to see how she reacted and responded to those seminars. It was amazing."

Fran's Fury

On Thursday, the nurse called from Tennessee. There were serious problems with the tube. Fran and the nurse in Tennessee called me again and again. Finally, Fran asked me, "What did Dr. Gardner say?"

"Weeeellllll," I weakly responded.

"Oh, my God! Susan! You didn't tell him she was going?"

"Weeeellllll, wasn't that your job, Fran?"

"No! It wasn't my job," Fran stormed. The wild woman was loose again.

Since Dr. Gardner wasn't aware Jenny was in Nashville, we had to tell him now. The nurse in Tennessee worked and worked on the port-a-cath, but couldn't get it to function. Surprisingly enough, she did manage to get a peripheral IV into Jenny's arm. I was shocked. Most of Jenny's veins were in very poor condition, they collapsed easily, and normally it was impossible to get an IV in.

Dr. Gardner wanted her home right away. Jenny begged me to let her stay for the Dove awards that night. Kelly promised she would drive all night after the awards ceremony if they had to, in order to get Jenny back for surgery the next day. Her surgery was scheduled for 7:30 a.m. on Friday, April 29.

Dress Code: Formal Wear and an IV

For the Dove awards Jenny wore her new white dress from Tom. It was low cut and you could see the bandage which covered her chest tube for her treatments.

"She didn't care. We didn't care. We were just so determined she would get to see the Dove awards," Kelly said. "We were in our seats in the auditorium at this formal gown/tux event when Jenny needed a treatment. We just gave her a shot right there.

"Here we were with our fancy dresses, little beaded purses, pulling out IV needles and shooting her right there as the Dove awards were being televised. It was kind of comical in a way. A few people around us were getting nervous, but we didn't care. We had gotten her this far. Jenny was living a dream come true. Even though she was terribly sick, with her makeup and hair done she looked pretty and bright. We felt blessed having her with us."

After the awards, they changed and loaded up, putting Jenny into the back of the van, where she slept through the night as they rushed straight home. They arrived home in Ada at 6 a.m., unloaded, and Jenny and I immediately headed down the road to the surgeon in Meeker, an hour away.

27. Surgeries, Never-Ending

After arriving at the hospital, Jenny was admitted to the oncology department where she had been treated previously. It was April 29, 1994. Her primary nurse made sure everything was taken care of so Jenny could be transferred to surgery immediately.

The anesthesiologist used a Velcro strap to keep pressure points on her wrist to prevent nausea and vomiting. Some of the staff razzed him about this, but it did wonders for Jenny. Hardened to what others thought, all I cared about was what helped Jenny. In future surgeries, we would ask to have the Velcro strap used, since it worked so well for her.

It was always difficult getting the IV into her arm, but eventually that worked. Jenny was put to sleep and Dr. Gardner did a revision on the port-a-cath. Once they got the tube working, a sterile dressing was applied. Dr. Gardner was concerned.

He felt the tube's life expectancy was limited and he would probably have to revise it at another time, perhaps with a direct access into the internal jugular. For now, he decided to get it to work as long as possible. After Jenny came around, she was allowed to be taken home. Since the surgery was a revision instead of a new tube insertion, it wasn't her worst experience.

A Seesaw of Surgeries

We continued to use the tube, but it still didn't work like it was designed to operate. On Friday, May 6, Jenny had to return to surgery. Why were Fridays so tough on her? The doctor knew there were problems, and after doing a test to monitor her blood flow, he found the needle was in good position but solution was being flushed back along the line of the port-a-cath.

It was decided to remove the old port-a-cath and insert a new one in her right internal jugular vein. All went well in surgery, and Jenny was returned to the oncology department. She should have been on the same day surgery floor, but the oncology staff knew her well and Dr. Gardner felt it best for Jenny to be in familiar hands. The nurses did a superb job.

"Her surgeries were difficult because of scar tissues and chest muscles," Grace observed, "but she always met the world with a smile, enthusiasm and a will to make the most of what was dealt her."

More Hassle than Help

Before we left the hospital, Fran Dean arranged for a different IV company to come to our home and be involved in Jenny's case.

It would be nice to have someone else to lean on a little and take over some of the responsibility. Still, Jenny wasn't happy to have anyone else involved.

When we were settled at home, the nurse from the new IV company arrived. We were supposed to have another nurse, but since it was late on a Friday night we got the weekend nurse. She had IV bags with her, but wasn't sure how to use them, and she was supposed to teach me!

This woman didn't look like a nurse on duty and her perfume didn't sit well with Jenny who was still queasy from surgery. The last thing Jenny needed was to be disturbed unnecessarily. This nurse made me feel extremely uneasy. Finally, I told her I understood everything, just so she would leave.

Sunday, I had problems with the machine and tube. Since it was late at night and I didn't want to deal with that same weekend nurse, I decided to wait and call first thing Monday. When I called in Monday morning, I was asked why I hadn't called earlier. I explained how I felt about the nurse on Friday—she wasn't on the ball like the nurse they had sent before surgery.

They apologized and said they would send a nurse out immediately. What a relief. I hung up and waited and waited. When the doorbell rang, I answered and nearly fainted. They had sent that same nincompoop nurse.

There was swelling around the site of the tube, and the nurse decided to change the needle. Jenny did not like being touched or examined by her. When the nurse pulled the needle out, she didn't secure the port with her hand. Instead, she used only one hand for the procedure while her other hand hung down at the side of Jenny's bed. She pulled and pulled until Jenny's skin began to arch over the port. We heard a snap as Jenny let out a howl and turned pale.

Finally, the nurse inserted a new needle and redressed the port. I was so relieved when that woman left. Neither of us wanted to see her again, ever! Jenny was really suffering.

Later, when I asked Fran how to take out a Huber needle, she said, "You hold the port securely with one hand and pull straight up with the other." When I took Jenny to Dr. Gardner's to have it checked, he was outraged. Dr. Gardner insisted Jenny come to his chemo department for every needle change. He didn't want a nurse working on her like that again.

When I called Fran about the incompetent nurse, she said she would take care of the situation. We were to be serviced by yet another new IV company. This did not make Dr. Gardner feel any better. He didn't want anything to happen to that tube again, and he totally trusted his hospital nurses.

Profile on WGTN

During her senior year in high school, 1993 to 1994, Jenny gave an interview for WGTN radio's "On Profile" show. That was the station where she had volunteered and where Jon worked part-time, so the staff was aware of her long struggles with Lyme disease.

After reviewing her symptoms and treatments—how she had gotten from there to here—the interviewer asked Jenny to compare who she was before Lyme to "Who you are now..."

"We didn't have a video camera when I was little, before I had Lyme," she explained. "It would have been nice to be able to see who I was and what I did, but we don't have that.

"*I'm me now*," she said, expressing her acceptance of the person she had become because of her challenges—because of her stubborn, determined work in therapies—because of support from family, friends and strangers alike—and because of her faith.

"I don't know what I was like before this," she said. But that was okay, even though it was still frustrating at times not to have a memory of her life before Lyme took it over.

Jenny recalled a testimony she had given at a church of 50 - 70 people in which the members were experiencing many real tragedies and problems in their lives. "It was awkward for me to get up there and try to tell them words of encouragement and stuff because when people are going through something rough, they don't want to hear encouragement. People get depressed and sometimes you feel sorry for yourself and that is allowed."

Jenny was able to share her belief that "everything happens for a reason." She said it was the only thing that had gotten her through over five years of struggle "because there are many things that I will never understand."

If it had not been for her illness, Jenny felt a unique set of circumstances would not have occurred which brought her to work with Kelly. Also, she would have had no life experience from which to give a testimony or a ministry "if I hadn't gone through my illness.

"I really believe," she concluded, "even in those down times, you have to look to the future and what it can lead you to."

True Blue Tammy

The new IV company sent a nurse called Tammy. Immediately, I felt sorry for her. Tammy was aware of the doctor's apprehension about taking care of Jenny's tube at home. She said she understood his concerns and would do her best. Jenny was leery of her at first, but she soon became very trusting of Tammy's work.

After examining Jenny and her floating port-a-cath, Tammy knew it wasn't going to be easy to access, even though the swelling and edema had decreased. Jenny was taking 2 grams of penicillin G every four hours by IV, 800 milligrams of Motrin four times a day, Darvocet for pain as needed, and flushes for the port-a-cath.

It was difficult for Jenny to do all of her IV treatments because she became confused and had memory loss and would mess things up, so I did all of her care. Tammy was to come every week and draw blood every two weeks to make sure there were no surprises. She seemed sincerely interested in Jenny's case.

On May 13, 1994, Jenny began experiencing more neurological problems. I contacted Dr. Adams, who made a change in her medication. The change was given every four hours. Over the phone, Tammy walked me through the reprogramming of the CADD pump. By May 16, Jenny was improving and having fewer symptoms.

We all knew Jenny was pushing herself to the limit. She was so close to graduating. Her goal was just at the end of her finger tips. She had to be well. Tammy warned Jenny that it was important for her recovery to take time to rest. It was like Jenny wore blinders when it came to school. Nothing else was on her mind.

Tammy made another visit on May 16, and replaced the Huber needle. It took her three attempts before it was properly inserted. She had me hold the port-a-cath in place while she placed the new needle. Jenny tolerated the ordeal well, but Tammy felt terrible that she had to try it three times.

Previously, she had always gotten it the first time. And Jenny felt sorry for Tammy. She knew Tammy was doing her best and that the doctor was uneasy about this being done at home. On May 23, Tammy replaced the Huber needle on the first try. Jenny was happier for Tammy than she was for herself.

No Family of her Own

"Near the end," Pastor Dave said later, "Jenny talked to me, expressing regret that she would never know what sex was and that she would never know what it was like to give birth to a baby. It was the only time I felt there was a cloud hanging over her—when she thought about not being able to marry and have a child. She felt a sense of loss, missing out on being a wife and experiencing motherhood." She spoke as bluntly to Pastor Dave as she did to me.

"I don't think there was one hidden thought that they would not say to one another as mother and daughter," Pastor Dave told a mutual friend. "There was no judgment from Sue. Jenny could have said absolutely anything and it would be taken as it was given." Pastor had seen her love the kids we baby-sat. When they sat on her lap in her wheelchair, she grinned from ear to ear, simply thrilled she was able to hold them.

This subject was on her mind a lot. She shared these same regrets with different girlfriends from time to time. "I want to get married to a wonderful man, who will love and take care of me and build a family together with me," she told one friend.

With Kelly she expressed her desire to "find a special love and to be a mother." It was a dream she also shared with her Grandma Epley—to get married and someday adopt children.

Looking back at the beginning of her fight with Lyme, I thought of all the ways Jenny and Tom filled my heart. They were truly the greatest gifts God had given to me.

As sad as things were now, I could look back at a fulfilling motherhood. What glory I experienced because of our kids. Notes from Jenny had accumulated through the years. I especially loved one she wrote December 1, 1988, when her Lyme first brought her down.

Mom, Your such a special person.
In all you say and do.
What would my life be like

Without you.
Probably chicken stew.
GOD BLESS YOU. Thanks for being there.

Love Always "JENN"

28. Senior Pride, Tears and Graduation

As graduation approached, Jenny was able to participate in most of the special events at school. However, she didn't make plans for her last prom. She had three surgeries in three weeks and was very ill. The night of the senior prom, Meagan went into Jenny's room just before she left for school with her date.

"I sat on her bed and Jenny said, 'You look real nice. I hope you have fun,' and she started crying." Meagan told Jenny, "I'll stay here with you if you want me to."

"No. You and Tommy go and have fun," Jenny said. And Meagan knew she really meant it. "I think if that had happened to me I would have felt so sorry for myself, I would have said, 'Yes, stay home,' but Jenny was concerned with me and Tommy having fun."

There was a sparkle in the air the night both girls got ready for the spring concert when the seniors are honored. Tom had given up choir, but Jenny and Meagan were still members. Jenny decided to wear the white angel-fluff dress Tom had bought her for the Dove awards. Meagan and some of the other girls wore their prom dresses. Meagan's was a simple navy blue slip style with spaghetti straps.

The night of the spring concert, Meagan fussed with Jenny's sunshine-bright hair, twisting it into a French braid as she had many times before. "Beyond Beautiful" was the unspoken dress code for the evening. With a touch of make-up here, a little jewelry there, and lovely gowns smoothed into place, their inner beauty glowed.

Emotions were high and tears rolled. During the senior honors, the choir sang while pictures of the seniors—as young kids—were flashed onto a large screen. When Jenny's photo appeared, bigger than life, little Tommy was pictured at her side.

The choir director gave each senior a rose after the slide show, which they took to their mother. As the seniors sought out their parents in the front rows, both Jenny and Meagan approached me. I was blessed with two flowers and two kisses. From family group to family group tears flowed throughout the school auditorium. That evening took us one step closer to the day of Jenny's dreams.

After handing out their roses, the students were to return to the stage and stand with their section, altos with altos, etc. Jenny had other plans. When they returned to the stage, she intended to stand next to Meagan.

"When we got back on stage," Meagan said later, "Jenny, a soprano, was supposed to stand on the opposite side of the stage from me. But she took my hand, walking me right across the stage to my alto section, where she remained."

These two very different girls, now sisters, had supported each other through tough times. As their senior year was coming to an end, Jenny smiled warmly, reaching out to Meagan until their foreheads touched. Then she gave Meagan a comforting squeeze. It was a bittersweet moment. Tears glistened in Meagan's eyes as they sang the last song together, hand in hand.

The night of the music awards Jenny received a standing ovation when she was recognized for her participation in band and choir. Meagan told me Jenny cried. I was ill and unable to attend. How I wanted to be there for her as she celebrated the rewards of her heroic work. In addition to her National Honor Society membership, she was listed in Who's Who Among American High School Students, and represented our school as Teen of the Month.

Other activities included Shangri-la, Secret Admirers, work on the prom committee, senior class treasurer, and volunteer in the high school and guidance offices. She was also offered a $1,000 college business scholarship. On a college application form Jenny wrote, "I wish everyone could be healthy and have enough spunk to make their dreams come true." What Jenny didn't have in health she sure made up for in spunk.

A Scrapbook for Tom

Meagan had been Tom's Secret Admirer during their freshman year, and had made him a scrapbook and other Go-Tom-Go stuff during that football season. As seniors, Jenny and Meagan worked together on a scrapbook for Tom for graduation, highlighting his track career.

"It took forever because Jenny had all these ideas of how to do it," Meagan said. "I thought we should just throw newspaper articles in a photo album. I bet it took us two months to put together a simple little scrapbook. We had to go back and get all the old newspapers because we included his junior year too. That was fun. It was quality time," Meagan said.

Senior Memory Book

Ever since she was little, Jenny had been obsessed with details. No matter what she touched, it came out orderly and attractive.

This meticulous part of her personality, along with her knack for creativity, continued during her years with Lyme. Her bedroom shelves were full of scrapbooks, albums and other systems of organization. She took this love of collecting and preserving to the pages of her Senior Memory Book.

Was there ever another senior anywhere who worked as hard on their book? Jenny's memory book bulged from cover to cover with snapshots, invitations, newspaper clippings, concert ticket stubs and other treasures overflowing from the pages.

Her senior book also turned into a diary of sorts as she completed each section, expressing her feelings. Most seniors take it for granted that graduation day will come at the end of their 12th year in school. Jenny had never been promised a 12th year in school and her Senior Memory Book enabled her to celebrate the fact—she was, indeed, a senior, a member of the graduating class. Some of her responses follow:

> Our school generates a feeling of—compassion and understanding for one another. Our school is small, so everyone watches out for one another. Although we may argue and disagree, we are like a family. We take the good with the bad!
> Our class is different—it is very small, 53 students...when the going gets tough we all work together to get things done. We're one big family.
> The best thing about being a senior is—a sense of freedom and independence. A sense of great accomplishment, a new chapter in your life.
> Hobbies—making tapes, dubbing and recording, watching movies and listening to music.
> As a senior I feel—excited. I have waited for this year for so long. I am so ready to go on with my life, and open up new doors!
> I feel at home in—sweats and a large sweatshirt, no make-up.
> I like to wear—dress clothes, my cream colored suit, jewelry, perfume, knitted vests and colored socks.
> I admire—people who are willing to speak up and do what they feel is right. Ignoring peer pressure, letting Jesus be your influence.
> I'm first to—take one of my brain storm ideas and try to make it work. Give someone special, someone I love, a hug. Push myself as far as I can go.
> My proudest moment—induction into the National Honor Society.
> My most embarrassing moment—picking up a small basket from the trash at a church I visited. When a woman came back looking for it, I had to dig it out of my purse.

My funniest moment—wearing two different shoes to class before Meagan pointed it out to me.

My scariest moment—knowing where I should continue my education. Will my health stop me from attending? Trying to break into the music industry. Wondering if I'll make it!

My bravest moment—returning to school after being gone for two and one half years. Proving to everyone that I could make it.

My rowdiest moment—when Jenny Y. and I took off for Findlay, but ended up in another town. Trying to go dancing at "Harry's Hideaway." I drove on the wrong side of the road. We chased guys all over and visited an adult video store.

My family—there are five people in my family. My dad is someone I'll always remember with the same part in his hair and glasses, walks on his pants. Mom is not only my best friend, but she can read my mind and always knows what I'm going to say. Tommy, my brother, hard worker, great in track. Wears the preppiest clothes. Meagan, my sister, my friend, taught me a lot about life!

Advice I give frequently—everything happens for a reason. The darkest hour is before the dawn. There's joy in the morning. Another day—another dollar. This too shall pass.

Things I do that drive my family crazy—when I eat cereal and I can't feel the milk hanging from my chin. When I take dad's stamps out of his desk drawer. Driving dad bananas when he is my passenger. Making long distance telephone calls—frequently! Making organized lists about everything. Constantly rearranging my bedroom.

Things we do together—Dad and I spend time at the radio station working together. Mom and I escape by shopping. We love to spend $$. Rearrange furniture. Go to concerts of the Gaithers and the Cathedrals.

Funniest moment—when the seat in dad's old Mazda rusted through and he fell to the floor.

Non-so-funny moment—when Meagan came to live with us. Trying to comfort and help her through her feelings. Knowing the right things to say.

Feelings about my family—I have the most supportive, understanding, loving family. I don't know what my life would be without them! I thank God for each one of them.

She goes on to claim Jenny Y. and Meagan as best friends, details some of their antics, and explains that honesty, kindness and encouragement are important in friendships.

I'd like to learn to—drive the speed limit. [She drove too fast rather than too slow!] Have more confidence in my abilities. Stay healthy, slow down and pace myself.

Locker inventory—a small mirror, a heart frame with a picture of Jenny Y. and a small plaque with the poem "Take One Step at a Time" and a picture of Vince Gill.

Favorite music—Christian Contemporary, Country, Sandi Patti, Michael English, Cathedrals, Vince Gill, Reba, and Alan Jackson.

Time wasters—watching TV and videos, making a list of something, going shopping, cleaning my room.

Jenny filled in all the blanks for who was the most popular, smartest, most likely to succeed, etc. in her class. Jenny and the principal's son were listed as "Teacher's Pets."

Several more pages listed every teacher she had for every single class. Sports events for the different seasons were given attention and the autograph section was full of notes from friends:

"To a nice person." "You're a very sweet caring person." "You're a very special person in my life." "To a very sweet friend ." "Your determination and enthusiasm have been a real inspiration." "I'll always remember your sweet smile and caring attitude." "To a great friend with one hell of a drive..."

From cousin Eric. "It's your favorite cuz. If you don't believe by now that you deserve the best of things, I don't know what it will take. You are very sweet and I hope to stay close."

A long note from Meagan ends "God made us sisters, but love made us friends."

The Graduating Class of 1994

Graduation night, Friday, May 27, 1994, finally arrived. Meagan's birth mom came, and plans for graduation and the party were coming together. My heart was full. Our three kids were graduating together.

In the midst of all the excitement and celebration, Jenny had one worry. She wanted people to remember she was only one of four people graduating in our family. All three of our kids plus her cousin, Eric, would walk across that stage representing our family. And they were just four members of a class of 53.

She didn't want any more attention than anyone else received. Graduation was incredibly important to each senior, and she was proud and thankful for her classmates. After all, they had made her feel welcomed when she joined the class of 1994.

As the seniors lined up in a hallway before the ceremony, Jenny teased Tom that she wanted to trade her plain, ugly robe for his.

The girls had silver gowns, and she thought his purple robe would set off the regal gold stole she wore representing her membership in the National Honor Society. Tom teased her back, but he couldn't have been happier for her. He knew what it had taken for Jenny to reach her goal.

Tom had carried her into the house when she was too weak to walk. He had flown out to New Jersey and donated blood while he was there. He had sat patiently at her side, timing her as she learned to talk again. Tom had helped her out of class-rooms during seizures and lifted her from bed to toilet and back again, all the while respecting her dignity and pride. He had glanced at her in wonder as she sat in the grandstand shouting, "Go! Tom! Go!" at his track meets, knowing she was often not well enough to be there.

And when Jenny and Tom had dates to eat out and take in a movie, Tom glowed when Jenny bragged, "I am going out with the best looking date."

Close as young kids, Jenny had been a proud, overprotective little mother hen to Tom. When Lyme reversed their roles, their friendship became even more intense. "Every time something important happens in my life, I have to talk to Jenny and share it with her," Tom said. He knew she could be blunt in her opinions, but she was never critical. He trusted her. Often, they talked late into the night in her bedroom.

"If these walls could talk," Tom would say, glancing around her room. Most people treated Jenny as if she was younger. Tom never did that. He teased and joked and laughed with her.

"It was an opportunity for me," Tom said, when he took on the role of older brother. "We had a bond that could never be broken." Tom loved and nurtured Jenny, he helped with her most basic needs, but he never, never babied her.

Tom and Jenny sat side by side during graduation. They were so close it almost looked like they were holding hands. All you had to do was look at them to tell how much they meant to each other. When Jenny whispered to Tom, he smiled and nodded his head.

As I surveyed the graduating class, I was filled with thanksgiving and pride. All three of our kids had been through tough times. Meagan was trying to make a new life. Tom had grown up quickly, riding a roller coaster. When he woke up each morning, he never knew if Jenny and I would be there or at a hospital.

And Jenny had fought battles no young person should have to fight. In spite of it all, here they were. It was an evening of star light, star bright. We had no idea how soon the brilliance of those stars would become clouded. In God's great wisdom He hid the end of the summer from us, allowing us this time of celebration.

When Jenny crossed the graduation stage, she raised her right hand in triumph, pumping it like the wheels of that little train engine as if to say, "I knew I could. I knew I could." Beaming from ear to ear, she went out of her way to shake hands with the principal before receiving her diploma. She seemed to walk on air. Her dream had been fulfilled.

Later, outside, flashbulbs went off like strobe lights. We had to get pictures of every possible family grouping, and friends and teachers were captured congratulating the kids. Jenny skipped into the scene as we gathered my mom and dad with their four graduating grandchildren for a picture.

Grandpa Epley was scolded by Grandma Epley for being frisky with a giant-sized squirt gun. The kids, dressed in their caps and gowns, got a kick out of that.

Not until much later, as I looked over the pictures from that night, did I see the exhaustion on Jenny's face. At the time, I was so involved in the ceremony and celebration I didn't realize how tired Jenny was or how hard she was pushing herself.

Party Time

The next day before the party, Dr. Adams and Pat from his office drove up. We were delighted to see them. It meant the world to Jenny that they had come over from Indiana. Dr. Adams walked all over Ada with Jenny. She asked him a lot of questions and he answered all of them. It gave me time to have a rare, relaxed visit with Pat.

We were all pleased when Dr. Kane came to the party with his family. And Jenny received a phone call from the head of our insurance company, who told Jenny everyone was proud of her and happy for her. How refreshing. An insurance company with a heart. Fran Dean and another employee from the insurance carrier brought their families, joining our families and people from our hometown and surrounding areas to make the day complete.

The party was a flurry of flowers, balloons, hugs and happy chatter, little kids playing and wrestling on the floor, rocking music, presents and cards and graduation cakes.

Jenny wore her hair up in a French braid with soft ringlets on her neck and Mamie Eisenhower bangs. In contrast to the huge, bold jewelry she wore early in her therapies with Metta, she now settled on understatement, setting off her outfits with dainty pieces. For the party she wore a delicate necklace.

Her typical response upon opening a gift was to look around for the gift giver and sincerely say, "That's really nice."

"Their graduation party was so neat," Kelly said. "It was like Jenny was torn. Who should she talk to first? Who should she talk to next? There were many, many people there who cared about her and she wanted to be with them all at once and she couldn't. It was so sweet to see her excited about all the people who came. She wasn't the type of person who expected things, gifts. To her, friendship was such a gift that she enjoyed every little bit about the day."

A teacher from grade school, Ann McKinley, looked with pride at Jenny at the kid's graduation party. It brought to mind a quote she had heard once: The same heat that melts the wax—hardens the clay. Ann was thankful that "the young sweet-natured girl I once knew had retained her bright mind and her cheerful, friendly personality. She had something inside her that others needed. They were attracted to her."

The first couple of days after graduation were up and down. The kids wrote thank you notes, put gifts away, and college was on everyone's mind. Meagan and Tom planned to go to the Ohio State branch near our home. Jenny was arranging to do college work through correspondence. This depressed her, but she realized her health would not allow her to go off to school yet. I kept telling her, someday.

When she felt good, she did more. One day Jenny and Meagan put on roller blades and skated through town. They ended up flying into their high school counselor's office for a visit. As they were taking off that day, I ran out the door, chasing them with a camera.

The neighbors laughed as I attempted to snap a picture. That was one of Jenny's last carefree, impulsive adventures. She was doing something spur-of-the-moment!

Another crazy thing she did was spend the night at a county fairgrounds with Meagan to be first in line for Alan Jackson concert tickets. Jenny came home laughing. "When I had to whip out a syringe for my treatment, girls waiting in line beside us thought I was a dope addict with a lot of guts."

Meagan said the smell of pot and alcohol made her sick, but Jenny was just fine. "Jenny put her portable IV down on the floor beside her while we were playing cards, then crawled across the floor and these girls just watched her little machine sliding along with her hooked to the tube," Meagan laughed.

When Jenny's nurse, Tammy, came on May 31, just four days after graduation, she observed Jenny's Lyme symptoms had returned. She felt this was probably due to Jenny's increased activity during graduation.

29. Short-Lived Celebrations

On June 2,1994, Jenny was so ill she had to see Dr. Adams. He increased her penicillin to 4 million units every four hours and, with the increase in medicine, Jenny's health improved. When Tammy visited on June 7, Jenny was dressed and wanted to go out with a friend. "Jenny looks better, the seizures have lessened and her neurological status is better," Tammy observed. When Tammy needed to change the Huber needle in the port-a-cath, she got the gripper needle in on the first attempt.

On her June 14, visit, Tammy drew blood and inserted another Huber needle. It was the same horror we had gone through on May 16, when it took three attempts before she was successful. Although the procedure was always terribly painful, Jenny never complained. She continued to trust Tammy and only worried about the doctor getting upset with Tammy if the needle wasn't put in just right.

Seven days later Tammy could not get the Huber needle inserted into the port-a-cath. She had me hold the port-a-cath in place while she tried to do the procedure as swiftly as possible for Jenny's sake. Tammy became terribly nervous as she made several attempts. She didn't want to have to call the doctor, but there was no other choice.

Prayer Time

"Tammy, do you think it's about time to say a little prayer, maybe?" Jenny whispered.

"I just did," Tammy sighed.

We ended up taking Jenny to the hospital where the needle was inserted using fluoroscopy. Jenny had missed two doses of penicillin due to problems with the port-a-cath. Fran suggested I be more assertive and tell them I wanted the port-a-cath changed. It had been floating since it had been torn loose by the incompetent nurse. Still, the doctor was reluctant to change it. He wanted to see how long the tube could be used.

Dr. Gardner finally changed the port-a-cath in surgery on June 27. The surgery went well, but the doctors were concerned. Dr. Adams felt Jenny's condition had worsened because of the malfunctioning port-a-cath. The surgeon felt Jenny should be hospitalized in Indiana, since her health had deteriorated so rapidly. After the two doctors reached an agreement, Fran Dean was called and told to re-admit her to Indiana.

Fran wanted me to transport Jenny by ambulance. Concerned about all the expenses, I decided to drive her myself. Jenny was groggy from surgery and pain medication. Her head pain was raw and all-encompassing, and all her other Lyme symptoms were in full bloom. Before we left, I tucked Jenny into the back seat with pillows and blankets.

On the way to Indiana, I stopped at home where a message was waiting—Dr. Adams wanted me to call. When I reached him, he asked for my time of arrival so he could be at the hospital. It was a difficult ride for Jenny. The pain medication didn't last very long and I drove as fast as I could. Of course, Fran had been right about calling an ambulance, but Jenny preferred to go with me.

Dr. Adams got to the hospital as we arrived, we skipped admitting and he took us directly to Jenny's room. Dr. Adams couldn't believe the severity of Jenny's condition. Wanting to rule out any other problems, he ordered extra tests to make sure he didn't miss anything. He also ordered pain injections. Jenny had no appetite, she was extremely lethargic, her rash had recurred, and she had joint pain and swelling. Her buttocks were black and blue from all the pain shots. After a few days, I asked to have the dressing on the port-a-cath changed. I was concerned about infection.

Jenny desperately wanted to go home. On July 3, 1994, I asked Dr. Adams if I could take Jenny home. He had made some changes in her medication and added Zithromax along with the IV antibiotics. I thought maybe if she was home her appetite would come back. She loved homemade potato soup and I promised I would make her some as soon as we got home.

Dr. Adams agreed to discharge her, but it was difficult getting home, and making arrangements with the IV company because of the July 4, holiday weekend. Once again, Fran worked out everything and the hospital made up antibiotic IV bags for us until the IV company could come to the house.

The weather was extremely warm and our house was uncomfortable. Someone had given us money to help Jenny, so we purchased an air conditioner for her room. We brought her VCR down from her bedroom and she watched her favorite Christian artists and "I Love Lucy" episodes. Lucy's antics helped her escape the pain for short periods of time. Helium balloons and greeting cards still filled her room.

She was glad to be home, but she was terribly vulnerable. Her pain became incapacitating and Dr. Adams ordered Anexia, but it didn't help. When I called him again, he decided it was time to try morphine. After the morphine liquid was started, Jenny began to vomit. When her condition continued to decline, morphine suppositories were prescribed.

Breathing Crisis

Jenny began having breathing problems on July 5. When I called the nursing staff, I was told Tammy would come as soon as possible. Fran suggested I take Jenny to the emergency room, but Jenny still bucked going to any hospital. If I waited a little, I thought, surely things would improve. By now her pain was so severe the morphine didn't offer any relief. Her respirations were going from bad to worse and her neurological status declined. It was as if her brain was shutting down.

Terrified, I called a nursing friend who came and worked on Jenny. Fran kept calling, and finally she told me she didn't know if Jenny was going to make it. Nothing existed for me but Jenny and her agonizing pain and her slow respirations. I called the ambulance right then and there. Jenny would breathe and then stop for 55 seconds and breathe again. When I called Dr. Kane's office, the receptionist said he was busy.

"Jenny has stopped breathing," I blurted out before slamming down the phone. They knew I never called unless something was really wrong.

Within seconds Dr. Kane called, telling me to order the squad. When I told him I had already done that, he ordered Narcan to counteract the morphine. He said the Narcan would improve her breathing right away. The ambulance crew worked quickly and rushed Jenny off to the closest hospital. We passed Tammy on the way. After two doses of Narcan, Jenny vomited twice, initiating the brand new ambulance on its first run. Our hometown ambulance squad was a blur of familiar faces, busy hands and big hearts.

Tammy came to the hospital and checked Jenny out along with the doctor. He felt Jenny would be okay and even told Dr. Adams in Indiana that she was fine. But her breathing never totally improved. Before we left the hospital, Tammy and I both talked to Dr. Adams. He changed Jenny's antibiotic to Claforan and also changed her pain medication.

When we returned home, her respirations were still low. I know Dr. Adams felt badly about the reaction to the morphine, but no one could understand why her respirations didn't improve as soon as the Narcan was administered. I couldn't take my eyes off of her. We pulled a recliner into her bedroom so we could take turns watching her closely.

Jenny began running a low grade fever and her symptoms continued getting worse. Tammy had a hard time with Jenny's port-a-cath and had to use urokinase to help break up the clots blocking the tube. On July 12, Tammy was able to insert another Huber needle after two attempts, but she also called Dr. Adams about Jenny's deteriorating status. Lab work showed Jenny's nourishment was extremely poor. Dr. Adams felt Jenny needed a NG tube placed, in order to begin a feeding supplement immediately, and he talked this over with me. When I told Jenny, she got upset, but I convinced her it was necessary or Dr. Adams would not have suggested it.

NG Tube Anguish

The next day Tammy came and inserted a NG tube down Jenny's nose. It took two attempts, but she finally got it in. We called a home X-ray company in order to check for placement of the tube. After it was determined to be okay, we began slow feedings. Jenny was in tremendous pain. She experienced nausea, vomiting and dehydration. Tammy determined Jenny was no longer in stable condition, and told me to check her vital signs every four hours. Jenny was also started on Buprenex, an IV push for pain. Hydration was also started through her port-a-cath. The doctor felt she needed to have IV fluids.

It seemed as if Jenny was no longer living. She was simply existing in a dark, endless pain. There was no moment of comfort, and her respirations were still low. Jenny wasn't bouncing back and I didn't know what else to do. On top of all her other pain, the NG tube in her nose was unbearable. Even though I was sure she knew how to pull it out, she didn't. Our relationship remained special and she always did what I asked of her.

Finally, one day, she was so upset with the irritation of the tube, she begged me to remove it, promising she would try really hard to eat. It got to the point where I just couldn't stand to see her in such misery and I pulled the tube out of her nose. She hugged me hard and thanked me. She tried to eat, but she was too sick and too weak. I knew the consequences. Eventually, *the authorities* would know the truth.

"Tell me you didn't pull that tube out," Fran said one day.

"I wish I could tell you that," I said.

"Did you take out her NG tube?" Fran asked me directly.

She was extremely upset and disappointed in me, but I could live with myself. She wasn't in my shoes. She didn't have to look at Jenny's pain-ridden face. When Tammy found out, she understood, but said we had to notify Dr. Adams. He understood, but told me I had to try really hard to get nourishment into her. Deep down, Fran understood too.

30. A Missed Birthday

During days of madness, July 16, 1994, Jenny's 21st birthday, came and went unacknowledged. She was so ill she wanted to wait and celebrate her birthday when she felt better. Everyone knew Jenny always got better. No matter how rough the road, she always struggled back, so we waited, even though birthdays were still special events in our house.

On July 16, it had been six years since Aunt Connie had made Jenny's Georgia birthday cake, the one with melted frosting. That seemed very long ago. For her 21st birthday not one of us got Jenny so much as a card. This would later haunt us.

A Tortuous Surgery

When Jenny's reports continued to be poor, Dr. Adams insisted it was vital for her to have nourishment. It was decided that Dr. Gardner would insert a gastro-intestinal tube into Jenny's stomach. Pastor Dave said he wanted to take Jenny and me to the hospital for her surgery.

Due to her respirations, which ranged from six to eight per minute, her doctors didn't feel it would be safe to put her to sleep. It was the worst surgery I remember Jenny going through, even worse than the six hour surgery to place a Groshong tube.

Considering the surgery wasn't supposed to take long, we couldn't understand the exhausting wait. There wasn't a lounge for family members, which meant we waited in the hall just down from surgery. Pastor Dave, who always prayed with Jenny before surgery, paced back and forth.

Jenny's prayers were direct and to the point. "May this be the last surgery. May this one work. May this one not close off. May they get the medication in."

Pitiful, inhuman howls echoed down the hall. I could not comprehend Jenny's pain. Tom had planned to come, but changed his mind. I was thankful he wasn't there to hear her heartbreaking cries. Part of me wanted to grab Jenny up and run out of there, but she needed the stomach tube. She couldn't improve without nourishment.

Dr. Gardner was a fine Christian man. We had never heard him raise his voice. But that day he rushed out of surgery, yelled at the nurses to get such and such, and rushed back in. Staff ran in and out continually. Jenny must have been suffering terribly for her to scream in such horror. She had always tried to be stoic and cooperative.

As we waited, I felt whiplashed. It was like the calendar was flipping backwards through all the months and years, through all the surgeries and all the suffering Lyme had ground into Jenny's body.

Finally, Dr. Gardner came out. He was drenched in sweat and apologized for the length of the surgery and all the problems.

He was use to inserting this type of tube in the thin stomach walls of older ladies, not in a young girl's stomach. When I finally joined Jenny, she told me how badly she felt for the doctor. After all she had been through, she was concerned for Dr. Gardner because he was upset at what he had had to put her through.

In Surgery more than Home

We left for home the same day, with orders to start with water, gradually begin the food supplement, and change dressings. The tube looked huge. Pastor Dave helped me with Jenny and we headed for home. I gave thanks to God it was over.

When Tammy could not access the port on July 21, she had to call Dr. Gardner. He said he would meet us at the hospital. Jenny cried. She was scared and didn't want to go back. She never knew for sure what would have to be done. Jenny didn't dwell on it, but when she was told she had to go back to a hospital, she dreaded it.

This time I didn't have the strength to convince her we had to go. Thankfully, Tammy finally convinced her. Tammy was upset that Jenny had to go to the hospital because she, the nurse on duty, could not access the port. When Jenny realized how badly Tammy felt, she didn't want to add to Tammy's problems and agreed to go.

Dr. Gardner worked and worked on the tube, but could not get it to function. He knew Jenny was bad and decided he only had one choice. She had to go back to surgery. This time he would insert a Groshong catheter instead of a new port-a-cath. The surgery went well and I was able to bring Jenny home again, the only place she wanted to be.

On July 26, I had to call and ask Tammy to come. Jenny was vomiting and seemed to be getting even worse. Upon seeing Jenny, Tammy agreed. Jenny's respirations were only four to six per minute, she had continued to lose weight, and the pain in her head and joints was beyond comprehension.

Dr. Adams suggested I see if Dr. Gardner would be willing to start Jenny on Total Parenteral Nutrition (TPN) through the IV. This potent nourishment was considered a liquid gold of necessary minerals, proteins, carbohydrates and fats. It would be given through the vein, since Jenny was vomiting so much. Dr. Gardner agreed and told me to bring her to the hospital by ambulance. At this point she was so sick she didn't fight going.

When the doctor saw her, he decided she needed to be stabilized first, then transported to Indiana. Jenny was placed in intensive care in Meeker from July 26 to July 28. She began another nutritional supplement and the nurses took blood sugars. When Jenny's blood sugar kept going up, she had to be treated with insulin.

She was now diagnosed with Lyme disease, probably with brain stem and cerebellar involvement, persistent headache, vomiting, dehydration, respiratory rate depression, and persistent Lyme disease of the central nervous system. A heart specialist and a neurologist were called. They were concerned about Jenny's condition and felt she had to be moved quickly to someplace where they better knew how to work with her.

A Very Long Trip

Our ambulance crew from home came and an intensive care nurse traveled along with Jenny to Indiana. It was a very, very long trip for her.

Jenny was admitted to the floor that monitored heart patients. She was put in a room with a patient whose family members flowed in and out, depositing food and all kinds of stuff everywhere.

This hurricane of confusion and noise was too much for Jenny.

When the other patient complained of pain, Jenny said, "If she hurts as bad as she says she does, I would think she would need it a little quieter."

Jenny always spoke her mind. There was no way Jenny's condition would improve in this room. When Dr. Adams came in, he immediately ordered the nurse to transfer Jenny to another floor. I was thankful. If something hadn't been done soon, I probably would have taken her out of there myself.

Dr. Adams worked hard to get her better. Her vomiting was wrenching, she was running a fever, had a rash, sore joints, severe head pain, and was extremely lethargic. He sent her to X-ray and tried to advance a tube through the G-tube into the proximal intestine without any success.

During this hospitalization, Jenny never improved. Dr. Adams said he had let her leave the hospital too soon the last time, and he needed to keep her in longer this time. Jenny was hungry, but she continually vomited green bile.

When the G-tube leaked green pus, I was told this could be a result of the size of the tube. Jenny had not had a bowel movement since before the G-tube had been placed. When she would go 12 days without any bowel movement, I gave her enemas. This time without much success.

Cathy came with her husband. Later, Cathy told me that when she saw how much Jenny was vomiting and how poorly she looked, she felt Jenny wasn't going to make it.

Dr. Adams had increased her Claforan to 3 grams every eight hours and added Zithromax again. He also continued 250 milligrams of steroids through her IV every eight hours. The only medicine he stopped was the Dilantin because he didn't feel her seizures were epileptic.

On August 3, Dr. Adams told me he had to leave town for a meeting and Jenny would be in another doctor's care. When I asked him if I could just take her home, he said absolutely not. Later in the day, he called and said he would allow us to go home if I could get the surgeon in Ohio to take responsibility for Jenny until he got back. The other condition was that I keep her on all her medicines, including the TPN.

At first, Dr. Gardner was a little reluctant. Then he agreed, and arrangements were made with an ambulance to transport Jenny home. The IV company was notified and received orders from Dr. Gardner.

We arrived home around 6:30 p.m. on August 3, 1994. Tammy came around 7:30 p.m., loaded down with supplies. Jenny was so exhausted she was only able to give one word answers. Tammy was concerned about me taking on all the responsibility when Jenny was in such poor condition. She was also uncomfortable with her nursing situation. Tammy had never been called upon to give such intensive care to a patient in a home environment.

"If you really try, with your past experience with Jenny, you can possibly care for her," Tammy finally said. It would be a lot of work, but I had no better person to put my efforts into. I prayed I would be able to do a good job for Jenny. Even though I was stubborn at times, Jenny came first. I didn't want to mess things up because of my stubbornness. For more than four hours Tammy went over everything, writing each thing down.

At that time Jenny was taking:

- Claforan 3 mg. every eight hours
- TPN by IV 24 hours a day
- TraumaCal 20cc per hour around the clock
- Zithromax 500 mg. two caps via G-tube once a day
- Docusate three tablespoons via G-tube once a day
- Bruprenex 1cc every three hours IV push
- Reglan 2cc every eight hours IV push
- Solu-Medrol 250 mg. every eight hours IV push
- Motrin 600 mg. suspension every six hours via G-tube
- Extra strength Tylenol two tablets every six hours
- Bumex 1 mg. each 12 hours or two times a day IV push
- Lanacaine cream applied four times a day
- Benadryl given three times a day
- Insulin using a sliding scale four times a day

1990—Photographers manage to hide Jenny's wheelchair and she escapes her head support by resting her chin on her hand.

Nadine Wagner

December 2, 1990—Jenny sings in concert with Jim Boedicker and Kelly Conner.

Christmas 1990 Jenny surprises Tom with a letter jacket. That fall, she had scooted her wheelchair to town to specify each detail.

Jon joins Jenny on a TV interview.

Mike Quinn

Jamie and Jenny leaving for his Junior Prom.

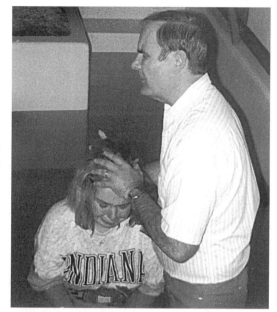

Jenny sobs with joy as Pastor Dave re-baptizes her. She has no memory of her first baptism.

Sandi Patti sends Jenny guest concert tickets and treats her like a VIP.

Jenny at her Junior
Prom. She loves music,
dancing
and being free.

Ada Schools

"Just one of the Kids"
in the band.

Fall 1993
Senior Smiles.

Christmas 1993
Meagan joins Tom and Jenny in our family circle.

Tom buys Jenny a white chiffon dress for
the Dove Awards. She is not
embarrassed by bandages
on her chest from her treatments.

Meagan and Jenny dress "Beyond Beautiful"
for their senior spring concert.

Cathy Nelson is the first to diagnose Jenny's Lyme.
She proves to be a steady friend.

Cindy Nelson, a childhood friend, congratulates
Jenny the night of high school graduation.

May 1994
Three graduating seniors. Two proud parents.

Summer 1994—A sad decline since graduation.
My silent prayer—that loving her would be
enough to make her well.

PART THREE

THE FINAL
JOURNEY

31. On Our Own

Excruciating headaches and swollen joints made the next 19 days difficult for Jenny. To keep track of her care I made a notebook with sections for vitals, medicines, blood sugars, insulin given and other notes.

Record keeping took time, but it helped me keep everything straight. I didn't want to screw up. My strength came from the only thing Jenny wasn't losing...her faith in God.

When it was time to have a new G-tube put in, Jenny was not well enough to tolerate the surgery. Even though she felt miserable, she didn't complain.

Rather, she continued to express appreciation for everything done for her. Jenny was easy to care for. Her personality didn't fight me. Her body did.

She was swelling with retained fluids, her temperature continued to rise, there were problems with her bowels, and I seemed to be the only person concerned about the pus coming from her G-tube. The typical response was—it happens.

Fran Calls

Fran called, saying she would be making a house call. Someone had once told me, "Don't be surprised if your insurance carrier pulls the carpet out from under you all at once." I was apprehensive. Later, when Fran was unable to come, I felt bad, misjudging the purpose of her visit. She had always been a strong supporter of Jenny's rights and ingenious in finding care for her. And she had always been honest with me.

One time it was suggested it might be cheaper to put Jenny into a nursing home because of the amount of skilled services she required and all the equipment. Fran and I had long talks, but she never insisted we do that. Fran knew—as long as I lived—Jenny would not go into a nursing home. When Fran called that day, she talked to Jenny, encouraging her to hang in there. It was the first time they had talked since things were critical.

Fluid Build Up—Weight Gain

Jenny was started on a medicine to draw off fluid build up. When it became difficult for her to get to the bedside commode, we used a bedpan. Forever conscientious about her appearance, Jenny was upset that she looked puffy and had gained weight. I assured her that once the steroids were stopped, she would lose weight again. It was necessary to buy her larger underwear and sweat suits. When I gave her baths and washed her hair, it totally exhausted her. To give her a little change, I would put her in the recliner. It bothered her when Meagan and Tom discussed college plans. She wanted to go more than they did.

It seemed ages ago when her nurse, Nancy, had delighted Jenny by dancing around the bathroom to Elvis music while Jenny was in the tub. Nancy knew Jenny hated to be a burden or any trouble, so she had tried to make the daily tasks fun.

A Crochet Hook and a Coloring Book

During long, painful days, Jenny got bored watching TV, so I tried to show her how to crochet. Neurologically, she was so messed up she couldn't control the crochet hook. That was the first day I felt sorry for her. Was this my darling girl who had worn her cap and gown with such pride just months earlier? I died inside thinking about how she felt, not being able to accomplish anything.

While on an errand, I bought her a Beauty and the Beast coloring book and some crayons. As a youngster, she had loved to color. She tried. She wasn't a quitter. But she had little strength and couldn't finish a picture.

One day I got a call from a hospital. Tom had been hurt at work. Would I come? Tom didn't even want me to know about his injury. He wanted me to stay home with Jenny, but I had to go for Tom. I finished Jenny's medicines and got her settled before a friend came to stay with her. In case I was needed quickly at home, I took my beeper.

More days than not, I felt stretched as if I carried the weight of a suspension bridge. The circumstances of each day determined the activities of that day.

"Mom, my brain doesn't seem to be working," Jenny said one day. "I'm mixed up on things." She would get so confused. It really bothered her to feel out of control in her thinking, but it occurred every time her Lyme flared up.

Preparing to Leave Us

In hindsight, it seems Jenny was trying to prepare us. One day my friend Joyce came to visit. Jenny had dated Joyce's son, Jeff. "Where's Jeff?" Jenny asked. When Joyce told her he was waiting in the car, Jenny said she was glad, because she didn't want to see Jeff the way she looked. "You are beautiful to me," Joyce said. As Jenny shed a tear, she told Joyce, "Don't worry, because very soon I'm going to be beautiful and feel good."

At the door, Joyce asked me if I thought Jenny was going to die. It hit me so hard. Joyce's oldest son had been killed in a traffic accident when he was a college student. Did Joyce sense the end of Jenny's journey?

My every thought had been, "How can I help Jenny be well again?" We had been fighting Lyme for over five and one-half years and she had always managed to get better. Always.

The last time Pastor Dave talked with Jenny in her bedroom he must have sensed the destination of her journey was changing. Her work on earth was almost done. "Jenny had no fear of dying, but this thought came to me—I don't want her to die. We were such good friends. She was so unique that I just wanted to see what life had in store for her.

"She had that gift of ministering to a lot of people. I wanted to know what else she might be able to achieve, what other things she might do. With her incredible glorious smile, she seemed to exist at a higher level than most people." She had accompanied Pastor Dave on calls to nursing homes and hospitals. She had to be careful, she couldn't be exposed to germs, but people enjoyed talking to her because they trusted her.

"I think, towards the end, Jenny just got tired going back and forth, tired of fighting so hard," Meagan said later. "She had days when she was down in the dumps, but I would too. I could not imagine being strong enough to live through what Jenny had for so long. There were times when she would just lay in bed and cry and cry."

One day when Meagan's birth mom had been with us for graduation, Jenny said she was going upstairs to rest. Meagan's mother asked if Jenny was okay. "Jenny sat right up and said, 'I'm fine. I'm fine.' It was like she didn't want people to know. She didn't want anybody's pity. She didn't want anyone to feel sorry for her. I think she just got tired of it," Meagan said.

The two Jennys were supposed to go to an Alan Jackson concert on August 19. When Jenny was too sick to go, Jenny Y. came home anyway to spend a little time with her.

"At that point, she knew she was dying," Jenny Y. said later. "We had been dealing with it throughout the summer. She would call me when she was really hurting and scared and we would talk it through, spending an hour on the phone crying. She knew it wasn't going to be a whole lot longer.

"The best gift she gave me is that we hugged and I kissed her cheek and we said we loved each other and always would." Jenny Y. had not had closure with any of the other deaths in her life, but she did with our Jenny. "I would have done anything to hang on to her, to keep her, but she had suffered enough.

"She knew she was going to Heaven, there is no doubt about that," Jenny Y. said. "And she didn't want to put pressure on her mother anymore. She wanted her mother to have a normal life again. In that sense, she was ready for the suffering to be over."

The kids' cousin, Eric, had watched his mother, Connie, help me push Jenny's wheelchair down the street many times. "It made me realize what my family would do for each other," he said.

In August, when Jenny was so desperately ill, Eric came down with a card for Jenny. "Sue was trying to make Jenny comfortable with pillows and giving her medications. When I gave Jenny my card, she peeked out at me from heavy eyelids."

"Thank you. It means a lot to me," Jenny said in a soft voice. Eric thought with wonder, "Even with physical weakness she has emotional power and strength."

An Unexpected Outing

One day Jenny surprised me, saying, "I feel better than I have in a long time, Mom." I dragged out her old wheelchair—the chair she swore she would never get into again—and asked her if she wanted to go for a walk. She was a little concerned about people seeing how she looked, but said, "Yes, maybe the sunshine will be good for me."

It was difficult taking Jenny in her wheelchair because of all the equipment with IVs dangling. We looked like a cartoon played in reverse. With Meagan's help, we managed and Jenny loved being out. We walked and talked all over Ada and laughed when we got things tangled up. Then Jenny decided she wanted an ice cream cone. Her spirits were high and it seemed as if she could have eaten a gallon of that cool ice cream.

It was a delight to see her outside and responsive. We stopped to visit my bedridden friend. On the street, people yelled "Hi!" to her or came up and talked. When we walked by Dr. Kane's house, he came out and talked with Jenny. After we walked off, I was dumbfounded when Jenny asked me, "Who was that?" Later, Dr. Kane would tell me he had no idea how terribly Jenny had failed until he saw her the day we went walking.

Another Call to Battle

As good as Jenny had been feeling that day, the bottom dropped out suddenly. By the time we arrived home and got her into bed, she was shaking all over, saying how sick and cold she felt.

Then she said, "I'm scared." Was it the first time she had said that? Before her surgeries she was always fearful, but this was different somehow.

Her temperature began rising rapidly. It seemed to happen instantly.

Could Jenny be losing her battle? Aunt Connie and Meagan helped me through an extremely rough weekend. Dr. Adams and I talked a couple of times, and he ordered pediatric Motrin in liquid form.

At this point, she was taking 2 grams of Claforan three times a day, 800 milligrams of Motrin four times a day, Buprenex every three to four hours for pain, an IV push, Bumex every day by IV push, Compazine every four to six hours for nausea and vomiting, 250 milligrams of Solu-Medrol three times a day by IV push, and insulin when her blood sugars were over 200.

I had purchased a new scale to get a more accurate weight record and more bed pillows to prop Jenny up and ease her pain.

When I wasn't holding her, I propped her up in the recliner with pillows or gave her a bath in the tub to soak her joints. Tom would carry her to the bathroom for me or two of us would lift and drag her. Her entire body was swollen.

When she saw herself in the mirror, she looked sad and said, "Mama, I look so ugly and big." Later she told me she didn't care what she looked like, she just wanted to feel better. But I knew she cared.

All day Sunday I held her in her bed, running my hand through her pretty blonde hair. She loved people and wanted to help them. She had so many goals and dreams. We talked about everything. I tried to reassure her, "We need to give the medications time. Getting well won't happen overnight."

"If I get better this time, how long will it last?" Jenny asked, pointing out that her bouts of illness seemed to be happening closer and closer together.

The Big Question

"If you get worse, what do you want to do about the machines?" That was the hardest question I had ever asked Jenny, but I had to give her the choice. It was her life, not mine. She had rights and I needed her to tell me what she wanted.

She was by far my best friend. We could tell each other anything, but this was not a question a mother ever thinks she will need to ask her daughter.

"I want to live more than anything," Jenny quickly responded. "Everything possible should be done to save my life." Then she added, "If I am brain dead, nothing more should be done. Let me die and be with God."

I was uneasy about every little thing. While I knew something was extremely wrong this time, I did not have a sense that this would be Jenny's last weekend at home.

Should I call Dr. Adams again? I had already called him twice. He was always pleasant and anxious to help Jenny, but I felt I should wait until Monday. At eight Monday morning, as soon as the IV company opened, I called. I told the head nurse something was very wrong and I needed Tammy to come. It seemed forever until I heard Tammy at our door.

"Something is really wrong," was my desperate greeting. When I did Jenny's blood sugar, I couldn't get her to stop bleeding. Blood sugars were done every six hours around the clock. It was just a finger stick, but the bleeding continued. Finally, I had to put a dressing on Jenny's hand to stop the bleeding.

Before Tammy left, she called Dr. Adams in Indiana only to discover he was terribly angry with her. I had never heard him like this. He was unhappy about how late he had received the results of a blood draw the previous week. Jenny's platelet count was down to 57,000.

Why did Jenny have to suffer like this? Why couldn't it be me? She was so loving and giving and could do so much for people. She deserved to have a healthy life.

Dr. Adams told me to back off on the Motrin because she was vomiting so much. I was to keep up everything until he got the latest test results. He instructed Tammy to get the tests done *stat* and call him immediately.

I worked on Jenny continually, all afternoon, doing IVs, injections, turning her, moving pillows to try and relieve the pain, doing IV pushes, and just holding her in an attempt to comfort her. Or was I only comforting myself?

How I wanted to take her pain onto me, but all I could do was be there. Every nerve in my body was on edge, and at the same time I was stripped of any sensibility, of any feeling. It was as if my soul died a little each time I looked at her.

In addition to the swelling from the steroids, Jenny's left foot began drawing inward as it had when she ended up with "drop foot." This worried me.

Pastor Dave came, as he had for almost six years. What a dear friend. He was truly a second father to Jenny. He listened and tried to comfort her.

Surely he had shed as many tears as we had over our daughter's suffering. Jenny and Pastor Dave leaned on and encouraged each other. While he ministered to her, she prayed for him. He had over 200 kidney stones during the time Jenny was sick. Together they sought out their Lord.

Turning Point

At half past three, Jenny suddenly got a black swollen right eye and black under the left eye. She was hemorrhaging. I wanted to pick up the phone right then and call Dr. Adams, but he was waiting on lab work.

I didn't need lab work anymore. I knew things were desperate. If I called the doctor, he would trust my judgment, but I decided to wait until he heard about the lab work. The hands on the clock must have stopped. How long would it take for Tammy to return to Clark and get the test results?

Finally, at 5:30 p.m. Ohio time, the phone rang. I got off Jenny's bed and answered in the kitchen. It was Dr. Adams in Indiana. I said, "Hello," and he responded with his first name.

"Sue, we've got problems. Jenny's platelet count is only 7,000." Such a low platelet count severely impaired the ability for her blood to clot. Dr. Adams told me to get her to the nearest hospital in order to get her stable before transferring her to Indiana.

A long time before this I had vowed she would never have to return to Miseracordia. Dr. Gardner's hospital was 50 miles east of Ada, the opposite direction from Indiana. Dr. Gardner wanted her with Dr. Adams, and Dr. Adams knew Jenny could easily bleed to death without immediate care.

A lot of her other lab results were also extremely bad. Dr. Adams talked about getting air transport. If I arranged a ground transport, he said I was to make sure qualified medics were on board.

After I hung up the phone, I told Jenny about the lab tests. She was scared and did not want anymore surgeries, but she trusted Dr. Adams. She believed in him. Finally, through her tears, she agreed to be transported. We cried and hugged each other. After explaining to Tom and Meagan what was happening, I called Jon, who decided to stay at work.

Using the kitchen phone so Jenny couldn't hear me, I called Fran, our insurance rep. She started her calls. I talked to a member of our local emergency squad, requesting a paramedic for a ground transport. He told me he would see what he could do.

Dr. Kane urged me to air lift Jenny, feeling she was critical and needed to get to Indiana immediately. The phone rang non-stop as I threw things into a suitcase. Meagan tried to help me pack. Tom stayed with Jenny.

Dr. Adams called again. I was to discontinue the Claforan, Bumex and Solu-Medrol and just give her a pain injection and hyperal IV. Her bone marrow was shutting down. Our friend on the squad called back, assuring me, "A full crew will be right there." I called Dr. Adams and told him we would be in Indiana in less than two hours. He was supposed to be gone, but he set it up so he would be paged.

My mother came and helped the kids get things together. In minutes, the squad arrived. Connie was there too. I was with Jenny, unhooking and flushing tubes and giving pain shots. Dr. Kane called back and told me to hook Jenny up to some normal saline IV. While the squad got the saline bag, I continued unhooking tubes and hooking up other things. My heart was racing and I tried hard not to let Jenny see how badly my hands were shaking.

I don't know what Jenny was thinking, but she reached up, touched my hand, and said, "Mom. I love you."

Dr. Adams told me to pack her in pillows, and I loaded an extra Buprenex injection. Jenny's pain was intense. Tom and Meagan both gave Jenny a kiss and a hug while I threw my suitcase into the ambulance. As the crew loaded Jenny, I stressed, "We need to roll." Somewhere, in some past year, I had lost control of my life.

32. God Be With Us

As we neared the hospital, Jenny was given another shot for pain. She was hurting terribly, and I didn't want to take any chance on how long it might take to get medicine ordered for her pain once she was admitted. Dr. Adams had told me Jenny would be admitted directly to ICU, so we headed there. When we got to ICU, we were sent to Coronary Care. The nurses in CCU were ready for her, got her right into bed and notified Dr. Adams of our arrival.

Jenny had been coughing since early afternoon and I told the nurses I felt it was getting a little worse. As the emergency crew loaded up to return home, I thanked each and every one of them. Kind, gentle, knowledgeable people, welcomed faces from home. Once again, they were a godsend.

The nurses asked me for medical information. Jenny tried to help them, but she was too ill to respond. After I described Jenny's situation, a RN questioned, "Are you a nurse?"

"No," I answered. "This has gone on for quite sometime and I am familiar with Jenny's medical care."

A nurse asked me to go to admissions so the staff could get started on the orders from the doctor. I explained to the admission's clerk that Jenny was in CCU and had been in their hospital just three weeks earlier. All the paper work would be the same.

"Can't I just sign the papers and go back to my daughter?"

The clerk wasn't busy, but it took the longest time. The irony was that *after we returned home* from the *previous* admission, the hospital called saying *they had forgotten to do an admission and would I "give approval for admission" over the phone and answer all the "admission" questions?* I was ready to revamp the whole system.

Jon stayed in Ohio, buried in his work for the most part. And I understood. It was his way of handling the terrible stress.

Pastor Dave and his wife, Dixie, came. We went to the CCU floor where my mother and father were waiting. My folks had brought an extra car in case I needed it. They both cared so much. Pastor Dave and Dixie sat with my folks while I went back to be with Jenny. She was in unbearable pain.

I overheard the nurses talking. They hadn't realized how bad Jenny was until they talked with Dr. Adams. When Dr. Adams arrived, things suddenly started moving. He had changed his schedule so he could come to the hospital.

Deep Concern

When Dr. Adams saw Jenny, his expression told me the depth of his concern. He ordered numerous tests and began her on platelets and whole blood. Then he talked to both of us. For some reason her cough really bothered me, although he didn't seem too alarmed about it. Her breathing seemed different too.

He ordered pain medication every three hours. It took time to get the medicine order into the computer, down to the pharmacy, and back to the unit. Jenny kept saying her head hurt so bad. The nurse assured her that as soon as the pharmacy sent up her medicine, it would be given to her.

"I'm sorry for being so rude and impatient. I just hurt so bad," Jenny said, looking at the nurse. Tears rolled down her cheeks. Gently, the nurse told Jenny there was no reason to apologize. They could tell her pain was overwhelming, and the nurses were good to their word.

As soon as the pain medications arrived, they were given to Jenny. It seemed her pain had gotten out of hand and it was difficult to get it under control. I encouraged Jenny to try to relax and give it time, but I was uneasy. Her coughing seemed worse.

From 9 p.m. to 11 p.m. I leaned over her bedside, running my hands through her beautiful soft hair, trying to comfort her. Pastor Dave and his wife came back to see Jenny for a minute. He said a prayer for her, kissed her forehead, and they left. My parents didn't come back. It was too hard on them. If I needed Jon, I knew I could reach him by phone.

In the afternoon Jenny's cough had sounded dry and nagging. Now it sounded different. Finally, at 11 p.m., I demanded that someone listen to her again. I knew she was rattling in her chest and struggling to breathe. The nurse listened and called the doctor immediately.

Since we had arrived at the hospital, Dr. Adams had either been at the hospital or on the phone responding to Jenny's needs. Now he ordered her put on a respirator. "Jenny, it will aid your breathing and ease your pain," I explained.

They contacted an anesthesiologist to put a tube down Jenny's throat. Jenny said she was scared, but wanted to get it over with.

They put the machine outside her room until the rest of the equipment and the doctor arrived. Then they came in to hook her up. I thought for sure they would kick me out, but I was told I could stay if I could handle watching the procedure.

The doctor gave her something to help relax her and explained the procedure he would be doing. I held Jenny's hand and continued to run my fingers through her hair. I wanted her to feel me close to her.

Last Words

Jenny looked me in the eyes. "Mama, these nurses are so nice to me. I just want to get well." Those were the last words Jenny said to me. She was right twice. She did want to get well and her nurses were kind and caring.

They put her bed back so she was flat, and gave her a medicine to make her go limp. If the doctor hadn't explained to me ahead of time what would happen, I would have thought she had died.

Working from behind her head, the doctor lifted up her chin, and placed a tube down her throat between her vocal cords. It was difficult. Apparently, Jenny had hemorrhaged the length of her throat. The staff was efficient and professional, and I trusted Jenny in their hands.

After everything was hooked up, the machine was turned on to get her breathing and the tube was taped to her face so it wouldn't come out of her mouth. Nurses continued giving her medication to paralyze her body so she couldn't move.

When the medicine started to wear off, Jenny would try to bite the tube in half and struggled to move. They also gave her a medication for anxiety. Unable to move, the patient normally gets scared. The meds were timed so they wouldn't wear off, allowing Jenny to thrash around.

The rest of the night was filled with a doctor and nurses working non-stop. Dr. Adams probably didn't get any sleep either. If the nurse wasn't calling him, he was calling into the hospital. Someone brought in a recliner for me and offered me food. I took them up on coffee.

Jenny's nurse was on a 3 p.m. - 11 p.m. shift, but she never left until 4:30 a.m. the following morning. Both that nurse and the night nurse worked on Jenny continually. They put in a catheter, since she could no longer use a bedpan.

Dr. Adams arrived by 5 a.m.. He was concerned about her low urine output, and called in a specialist in dialysis and kidney problems. He wanted to make him aware of Jenny's situation. Dr. Adams also notified a doctor to help with Jenny's blood work.

When Dr. Adams came back at 8 a.m., he called in a lung specialist. By 10:30 a.m. the situation required another emergency decision. Dr. Adams felt Jenny was in kidney failure.

As the dialysis team assembled, Dr. Adams took me aside and explained what was ahead. He said, given the amount of fluid in the patient, sometimes when they first do dialysis, it is such a shock to the heart the patient goes into heart failure.

If this happened, Dr. Adams said he did not want to code Jenny because during CPR her ribs could break and go straight into her heart. He said he couldn't do that to her. He couldn't say for sure what would happen, but he wanted me to be prepared for the worst. The dialysis had to be done. We had no other choice. I was scared and haunted. Jenny had worked hard to come back from the doorstep of death many times. What was happening to her now? Why did she have to suffer like this?

While they performed the procedure in her room, I waited at the nurses' station. People raced back and forth getting things. I felt so alone. God was with me, but sometimes I was angry with Him. I knew that was wrong, but my pain for Jenny and frustration at her situation could not be eased. I thought of how many times Jenny had pulled through when doctors didn't know if she would.

I questioned God. "Why did you bring her through so much just to end it this way?" I challenged God. "Jenny is a good Christian girl. She does so much for others and is an inspiration. There are bad people in the world and others who abuse their bodies and don't care about their lives. Why, God? Why take Jenny? She could do so much of your work. Why not continue to use her?" The medical staff wrestled with her body and I wrestled with God.

When the doctors came out, they said Jenny had come through the procedure fine and they had taken off 15 pounds of fluid already. Each dialysis would take about four hours. Jenny still had such a strong will to live. When I went back into her room she was barely swollen. Even the swelling in her chest had gone down some.

The dialysis nurse watched Jenny's vital signs continually, because her blood pressure bounced around. The nurse seemed to draw blood constantly.

They had given her so many bags of platelets and blood that they were having a difficult time getting what they needed from the blood bank. Tom was there and offered to donate. He needed to do something to help. The nurses said they didn't have enough time and they needed far too many units for her.

As they brought in more and more IV pumps and equipment, Jenny's room seemed to get smaller and smaller. I stayed with her almost all the time. Once in a while I would go out to the waiting room or down to the bathroom or out to grab a snack. Connie, Tom, Pastor Dave and Meagan stayed nearby in the waiting room.

Tom and Meagan were hurting and I tried to talk to them, but I felt pulled to be with Jenny. More friends and family came. Only a few people were allowed to see Jenny.

A Prayer for Strength

Dr. Gardner, who had done many of Jenny's surgeries, called me in CCU that day. He was at a seminar when his office called him about Jenny. He wanted to know what was going on. When I told him, he was concerned and told me it didn't sound good. I knew he was right.

Dr. Gardner asked if he could pray with me over the phone. It was not a prayer for a healing of Jenny. Rather, he prayed for God to give us strength. He had lost a child of his own and understood our heartache. With his comforting prayer he was acknowledging medical skills could no longer help her. He tried to help me place Jenny in the care of the Great Physician.

By night time, another dialysis was required. Jenny was filling up more and more with fluids. Even her left breast area was swollen. Again, the staff worked on her through the night. She was surrounded by high-tech monitors and machines. Other people—professionals, specialists—were now needed. I felt helpless. I had always been able to do things for Jenny to help make her better. Now all I could do was be there, talk to her and pray.

I remembered a time she had been in a coma, and I had talked to her constantly. When she came out of it, she knew what I had told her. That experience made me feel that perhaps I could help her through my voice, with my words, deep in my prayers. I loved her so much.

Each time I stepped into the waiting room, I saw the strained faces of Tom and Meagan. The couple times Jon came to the hospital, he didn't stay long. But we talked every day. Tom and Meagan had always been involved in Jenny's care. They were at the hospital as much as possible, traveling home each night. Tom was able to be at the hospital more while Meagan helped with things at home.

That night when Dr. Adams came back he brought his office manager, Pat, along. Jenny thought so much of Pat. She had always been there for us. Now she came on her own time, after working all day. She had a daughter Jenny's age and it upset her to see Jenny this way.

Still, I leaned on Pat. The three of us, Dr. Adams, Pat and I, stood outside Jenny's room and talked. What words could tell them how much it meant to me to have them come as supportive friends?

That night, Dr. Adams told me he had changed his mind about coding Jenny. He said, since she had pulled through everything so far, when they didn't expect her to, he was going to go all the way and fight like all get out.

Throughout the night, I sat in a straight chair next to Jenny's bed, holding her hand. The lights were dimmed. The monitors played out a melancholy symphonic poem. Jenny and I were together and still, each of us, was very much alone. Caretakers in white shuffled in and out through the night like fleeting ghosts. What else waited just outside her door?

An Angry Infection

Wednesday morning, August 24, 1994, got off to a hectic start. Jenny wasn't responding well. Dr. Adams had received the results of a test showing she was fighting a Gram Negative Bacilli infection. He was on his way in.

The good news was that Dr. Adams had already put Jenny on the proper antibiotic beforehand. I noticed a nurse with tears in her eyes. She was fighting so hard for Jenny. Later, she told me she had lost a child to leukemia a short time before, and it was tough for her to work on a young person like Jenny.

After reviewing Jenny's condition, her doctors determined they had to drain fluid off her lungs. Tubes would have to be placed in her sides. It had to be done. I had no choice. I kept remembering what Jenny had said about machines and procedures.

"Do everything, unless I'm brain dead." Jenny wasn't brain dead!

I left the room so they could begin. It was overwhelming to wait while they cut into my sweet child again. While experts invaded her fragile body with yet another critical procedure, my mind was a whirlwind of worry and remembrances. Friends and family had helped me stay strong. Jenny had fought so hard to live. She couldn't die now.

People in the waiting room tried to make me feel better. They talked about other things and tried to joke. I didn't feel like joking. I could think of nothing but Jenny and what she was going through.

Was she hurting? Was she scared? Did she approve of the medical procedures? She couldn't answer for herself. Her words throbbed in my head. "Do everything, Mama, unless I'm brain dead."

Jenny loved wearing Tom's jeans and tops—she seemed to think they shared dual ownership of the contents of his closet. At first, he wasn't pleased about her interest in his wardrobe. Later, he decided it didn't much matter. We had been fortunate parents. Their friendship was rare.

As I looked at Tommy's face, tears began rolling down his cheeks. He came over and asked me to never—not ever—let them bring Jenny back if she coded. He said he couldn't stand for her to be put through anymore pain. He begged me to promise him. I told him I would see. How could I answer? What was ahead? I gave him a kiss and a hug. Then the nurse called me back to Jenny's room. The procedure was over.

Aggressive Treatment

Jenny lay helpless in a room of disarray while a nurse tried to clean things up. Everything was bloody and Jenny was now wearing a hospital gown. They had to cut off her Vince Gill nightshirt. She loved his country singing and thought, "He has the prettiest blue eyes." She had bought tickets to his concert at the Ohio State Fair for her and Meagan. When she was too sick to go, Jenny sent Meagan off with a boyfriend. Meagan bought Jenny the Vince Gill nightshirt at the fair.

The nurse felt badly and kept apologizing about having to cut her shirt right down the front, and she worried that our pillows from home were all bloody. I could have cared less. I didn't want reminders of all this pain and trauma.

I walked over to Jenny, kissed her, and held her hand. The lung specialist was a large gruff-looking man, but he treated her with tenderness. He showed me the tubes—one coming out of each side of her body—draining bloody fluid.

The kidney specialist explained a procedure done on newborns, which he said he would check into for Jenny. They continued to pour units of blood and platelets into her. She was on eight IV pumps with two or three things on each pump. The respiratory therapy department brought in a new machine capable of doing more for her.

At first, Jenny had difficulty with it. Finally, her body accepted it. They wanted to pull her off the paralyzing medications and respirator as soon as possible. They were treating her aggressively, but I trusted Dr. Adams.

A specialist told me Jenny might not make it through the night. "Who was this cold doctor? Was he God?" Later, a nurse told me that that doctor knew medicine, but he only dealt with diseases, not people. He did not allow himself to become involved. She told me to pray and hand the situation over to God...to never stop believing.

Before she left, she gave me a hug, telling me to keep my spirits up, saying she would pray for Jenny that night. For the most part, God had given us fantastic, caring nurses and doctors.

That night, everyone was uneasy about leaving, and Connie ended up staying. I didn't see her much, but I knew she was near. Pastor Dave had told Jenny he was leaving and that she didn't have to keep fighting to live for us. It was okay for her to stop fighting and to rest. He said good-bye and kissed her.

It was another long night of constant treatments. I helped the nurses give Jenny a bath and change her bed. Jenny had always felt better after being cleaned up.

When I mentioned to the nurses that Jenny's feet and hands were bluish and cold and I wanted to put socks on her feet, they told me to do anything I wanted. The ends of her toes were getting black from poor circulation. Her limbs were being starved of blood and oxygen.

I asked if I could do range of motion exercises to try to get some circulation back. Again, they told me to do whatever I desired.

Cleansed by Tears

A bath always refreshed me when I was exhausted. Each time I showered in the nurse's lounge, I completely lost control and sobbed and sobbed. I could have kept the faucet off and showered in my own tears. After each shower and good cry, I returned to Jenny's room thinking I could be strong for her. But nothing relieved my own pain and anguish and the pain I felt for Jenny.

"God, let it be me instead of Jenny. She hasn't lived yet," I prayed. Since the Lyme had stripped her of her memory, all she remembered was being ill. She had been robbed of her young life. I was angry at the unfairness of it all.

Throughout that night, I massaged Jenny's hands and feet. Even her finger tips were turning black. My thinking was simplistic. If I massaged them, the circulation would come back and the blackness would fade. I also continued range of motion of her arms and legs, bending them at the joints to keep them from getting stiff. She had worked too hard to get back the use of her limbs.

I wrapped up her arms and legs and feet so my baby wouldn't be cold. Throughout the night the nurses hung more and more IV bags and units of blood and platelets.

33. All I could Recognize

As morning approached, a new nurse came on duty. When she needed to get a blood sample, instead of sticking Jenny, she was able to get a sample from the dialysis nurse. Jenny's blood pressure continued to bounce around and her eyes were looking bad. Because of the paralyzing medicines, she couldn't open and close them. Dr. Adams ordered ointment to ease the dryness of her eyes. They were so terribly swollen the bottom of her eyeballs were bulging out.

Dr. Adams said her platelets and blood count were a little better, and told me they were considering an artificial lung. But it was a waiting game. I showed Dr. Adams the blackness in her extremities and a long area under her neck that was splitting open because she was so swollen. What had happened to her so quickly? The only thing I recognized was her beautiful, blonde hair.

Then Dr. Adams expressed concern about the monitors. Jenny's vital signs were way off. The nurse said the readings weren't accurate because they couldn't find an area to get her pulse. Jenny's body continued to break down. The doctors came in together, giving their best word—the blood work showed improvement. Jenny was still fighting.

All day long people from home stopped by. We also had friends in Indiana, from years before when they lived in Ada and I had baby-sat their little girl. Now they worked in offices across the street from the hospital and were available for anything we needed.

Fran Dean continued her support via the phone, and other friends called. I couldn't imagine going through such a difficult time without the support of family and friends. We had our church, fine medical professionals and the support of our home community.

An A-line Added

Later in the afternoon, the nurse needed to get more blood gases from an artery. A nurse stuck Jenny a couple times with no luck. I asked her to please stop and try something else. Wasn't there another way? Because of Jenny's poor circulation, it was impossible to get a blood pressure reading or pulse.

One of the specialists asked if it would be okay to do an A-line into the left groin area. They could hook IVs into it and take her blood gases with ease. I agreed, and it didn't take the doctor long to do the procedure. Even Jenny's nurse felt better. She hated having to stick Jenny so often.

Pitiful. Jenny looked pitiful. Countless invasive procedures had been done. How much pain was she in? What was she feeling? What was she thinking? It tore me up.

I needed her to talk with me as we had in the past. What I would give for one of her special hugs, but she was helpless. I wiped away fluid draining from her eyes. When she was put on medicine for seizures, I wasn't alarmed. Seizures happened every time they pulled her off steroids, especially when she came off them fast.

Diagnosis Poor

The staff was honest about her condition. Her major organs were breaking down and her arms and legs continued to get blacker and blacker. A thousand things passed through my mind.

What could I have done differently? For weeks I had felt something was wrong with her stomach. She had described burning and terrible pain. If only I had pushed the issue more and followed my instincts. Perhaps, if I had done things differently, she wouldn't be full of this terrible infection.

Dr. Adams trusted me. Why hadn't I told him earlier I felt things weren't going right? I should have expressed my feelings and opinions more. Did I fail? Was I responsible for Jenny being critical? Self doubt haunted me. When X-rays were ordered of Jenny's stomach area, several attempts were made, but it was impossible to get any results.

Tom came back to the room and we worked on Jenny's arms and legs, doing range of motion exercises the entire day. It was one way Tom could do something for Jenny. After a while Tom left.

When he came back, he tenderly placed a tiny gold guardian angel pin on Jenny's chest. He had also found a scroll decorated with roses for her bedside table in the hospital gift shop. "Faith is Believing" was written on it. Surely Jenny was aware of his gifts and his love.

Tom's gigantic, tender heart was being torn to shreds. All the time he massaged her limbs, he talked to her non-stop. His words were meant for Jenny, but they helped us too. Later, a friend took Tom for a walk. I was thankful he had someone else he could talk to.

Other patients also had family members waiting for them. There was an elderly gentleman whose wife was in CCU. Alone and nervous, he paced non-stop, talking a mile a minute. He just needed someone to listen. We were fortunate to have so much support, both at the hospital and home.

Cathy's Good-bye

My friend Cathy came to be with me again. In May, 1989, she was the one who had suggested that Jenny might have Lyme disease. Cathy, my steady friend, always there to help or support. She asked to see Jenny.

I love Cathy and her generous heart and Cathy, in turn, treasured Jenny's love and friendship, feeling it transcended all age limits. But Cathy could never show that to Jenny. Instead, she played the bad guy/tough nurse with her.

No matter how poorly Jenny felt when Cathy came to visit, Cathy always challenged her, "Get your butt out of bed." Jenny had told me once, "If Cathy ever comes in and is nice to me, I will know I am dying."

As Cathy and I walked to Jenny's room, I told her, "If you tell Jenny to get her butt out of bed, I will be furious with you forever." Cathy agreed to cool it. When we walked into the room, Cathy fought back tears as she took in Jenny's condition and appearance. After a 25 year nursing career, my tough cookie friend wasn't so tough after all.

While we were in the room, a nurse aspirated huge amounts of bile and blood through Jenny's tubes. Her stomach was so swollen it was shiny. Quietly, Cathy said good-bye to Jenny. Cathy had helped me through the years as Jenny fought Lyme again and again. I was sure she was thinking, "What else could I have done for her?" We didn't stay long.

Back in the waiting room, another doctor came and asked to talk with me. He was concerned about the seizure medicine. While he explained Jenny's grim situation, he grinned from ear to ear. I didn't need that. When he said he wanted to do an EEG, a brain wave tracing, I said that was an unnecessary test at this time.

Words could not describe the torture Jenny's body was going through and how bad she looked. I told him, "If tests need to be done later on, maybe then." I went back to be with Jenny. I had to be near her.

An Expression of Love

Jenny had always had the most beautiful blue eyes. They would sparkle when she felt good. Something came over me. I had to talk with her and I had to know she was listening. Dr. Adams had decreased the medicine that paralyzed her body. I had to know she could hear me. I missed her so much. I missed our long talks. I missed my best friend.

Tears flowed as I told her how much I missed her and that I had to know she heard me. I told her I knew she was giving all she could. As I hugged her, tears streamed down my face. Up to then I had always tried to be in control around Jenny, but it was impossible now.

Somehow I had to make contact with her. I had to know she was still there. I asked her, "Is there some way, anyway, you can let me know you hear me?" I told her I knew how hard it was, but I pleaded with her. I badly needed some response from her. She hadn't moved her eyes for so long. I told her, "If you could twitch your eyes—it would be wonderful."

I looked deeply into her eyes for a long time and nothing happened. Then, all of a sudden—through all of the mucous—I watched as her eyeballs moved from side to side. I was overcome. Jenny was letting me know she heard me. That was the only time I saw her eyes move the entire time she was on the respirator.

My tears flowed without ceasing as I shared personal thoughts with her. In my heart I always felt Jenny heard me, but I needed her to let me know. It must have taken every bit of her energy to move her eyes back and forth for me. Her effort brought me peace. My girl was aware of me. She knew I was there for her. I could talk to her and she heard me. I was moved by the power of her response.

Taking a Stand

Around 10:30 that night a technician came in pushing EEG equipment. She said she was there to do a 24-hour EEG. "No," was my emphatic reply. This test was not being done on my daughter. I told her I had informed the doctor I didn't want it done and I meant it. Jenny's seizures were from steroid withdrawal.

In my view, an EEG reading of her brain was not a life and death matter. Jenny's nurse understood and agreed and called the doctor, telling him I had refused the test. He was simmering and asked to talk to me.

When I went to the phone, he tried to tell me I understood we were going to do the EEG but no other test at this time. I said, "No. No EEG!" He was very upset and tried to make me feel like the world's worse mother. He said the test was no big deal. Jenny was in a coma and didn't even know I was there. He was rude with a capital R. He told me I was exhausted and wasn't making rational decisions.

"Have you ever been in a coma?" I asked.

"No," he answered.

I informed him that Jenny had been in a coma before and while she was in that coma I told her things only she and I knew and when she woke up she told me about some of those things. He told me if she wasn't on the proper medicine she would die. If I refused this test, I would be killing her.

Then he said he was going to sleep well that night and hoped I could, knowing my daughter would probably die and it would be my fault. I couldn't believe his arrogance. But then I remembered other encounters with arrogant doctors. This bully placed such a guilt trip on me, I finally broke down and agreed to the EEG.

It took a long time to get all the equipment into Jenny's room because of all her other machines. When they tipped Jenny's head forward to hook up the electrodes, Jenny's swollen head and neck shut off her breathing.

She struggled for air. The technician only had two wires on, but I couldn't handle anymore. I couldn't stand to watch Jenny gasp.

Turning to the nurse, I told him to call Dr. Adams. I pulled away the towel, which held Jenny's neck forward, and told the technician, "That is it! No more." She agreed. As soon as I laid Jenny's head back, she began to breath easier.

I told Jenny I was sorry I had agreed to the EEG, knowing it wasn't the right thing to do. When I talked to Dr. Adams on the phone, I explained the situation. He agreed. As Jenny's primary doctor, he told the nurse to cancel the EEG order.

Back at Jenny's bedside, I kissed her and told her I was sorry. I repeated a promise I had made to her earlier. That I would never allow anyone to hurt her again. Never again would a doctor make me feel like I was a bad mother.

Why did God let someone like that near us at a time like this? Hadn't we experienced enough rudeness and poor treatment?

As I thought it through, I realized maybe it was God's way of helping us appreciate the truly great doctors we did have. Dr. Adams and his associates could not be giving her more tender, thoughtful care. Back in Ohio, she had Dr. Kane, our family doctor, and Dr. Gardner and Dr. Scott and Dr. Miller and Dr. Lang, excellent surgeons and caring people, who always treated her with dignity.

Dr. Paige and Dr. Nkomo in New Jersey, professional through and through, were there when we needed them in 1989. The first to determine a diagnosis of Lyme, they established our battle strategy.

That night a nurse told me, "By taking a stand, you did something that most of us would love to do at certain times, but professionally, we have to follow orders. Our hands are tied." They know some procedures are uncalled for, but they have no authority to stop them. Only a patient or the patient's family can do that. We had learned the hard way. The patient does have rights.

After everything settled down, I took a shower, checked Jenny, and went out to the waiting room. Connie and her daughter, Gail, and Meagan were sound asleep. It was around 3 a.m. and I visited with a lady whose husband was in ICU. She had a soft, soothing voice and it was peaceful being with her. She made me appreciate even more that I had family near.

After a while, I went back to Jenny. Dr. Adams had made it possible for me to be with Jenny at anytime. I was careful not to abuse the privilege, and other families in the waiting area were unaware of the amount of time I spent with her.

34. A Child on Loan

A new nurse arrived with the morning. It was Friday, August 26, 1994. From the windows in the waiting room, I could see it was a beautiful late summer day. Tom surprised me by getting up early and arriving at the hospital around seven. He had left the hospital so late the previous night, we had agreed he shouldn't rush over in the morning. But I was so glad to see him, my leaning post, my rock. Our family's fight with Lyme disease had forced Tom to grow up quickly. I was thankful for and proud of this wonderful son.

Dr. Adams came in early, waved, and walked down to the nurse's station. A Dr. Lukins stopped in and told me he was covering for another doctor. As I continued doing range of motion on Jenny's arms, he looked at her through glasses resting on the tip of his nose. Concern registered on his face as he told me he would be back. He was quiet and respectful and I trusted him instantly.

Dr. Lukins walked clear down to the end of the unit with Dr. Adams where they talked for quite a while. Then Dr. Adams flew by Jenny's room, saying he would be right back. He shot out of the unit like lightning. I continued massaging Jenny's legs to try to warm them.

In a few minutes Dr. Lukins returned, asking if he could talk to me. He touched Jenny's arm, then asked a nurse where we could talk. After we settled into a conference room, he told me things weren't good. Jenny was filled with a horrible infection. He described her condition in detail, organ by organ.

Her heart was bad, her liver was not functioning, both kidneys had shut down, her lungs had holes and Jenny's arms and legs would likely need to be amputated. He had treated people with this infection in the service and they didn't survive, even though they hadn't been in Jenny's critical situation. Dr. Lukins didn't feel Jenny would survive much longer.

When Dr. Adams arrived, I was trying to talk through my tears. There had to be a way to make sense of everything I had been told. Even though I had never met Dr. Lukins before, I felt his compassion. He had kids. He understood this was a hard message for a parent to hear.

I told them I didn't ever want the doctor who had ordered the EEG in Jenny's room again. Both doctors assured me, he wouldn't get near her. They would see to it. Dr. Lukins explained he felt the infection had either come from the line in her chest or from the G-tube. I had always felt something was wrong with the G-tube.

He said they weren't going to stop completely. He wanted the lung doctor to pull the central line in her chest and see if that was the source of infection. He told me he knew this was hard news, and said if there was anything he could do, he would.

Dr. Adams stayed with me after Dr. Lukins left. This was tearing him up. He said he wished he could do more for her, and gave me a hug. Panic filled me—I had to be with Jenny.

Tom and Pastor Dave had observed the activity and wondered what was going on. I wanted to talk with them, but I had to spend a few minutes with Jenny first. Then I called Fran Dean. Rough, solid, the "I can arrange anything for you" gal seemed to crumble.

She assured me that I had done everything possible. Knowing Fran, she would have told me if she thought otherwise. Through our long ordeal, she had been a dependable friend. We would have never gotten through our many trials without her.

I went out to the waiting room to get Meagan and Tom, but only Tom was there. I didn't want to have to explain my swollen eyes to anyone, so Tom and I went back to the conference room. A secretary from CCU asked if she could get us anything. She knew just the right things to say. She told us Jenny's nurse was a person of compassion, and Jenny was being well taken care of. The secretary got us a phone and pillows. The room was ours for as long as we needed it. She didn't want us bothered.

Tom sat in a haze as I explained what the doctors had said. He told me he knew right then Jenny's life on earth was over. He begged me to not let them bring her back when she died. I had so many things rushing through my mind. I never thought I would lose her. She had pulled through so much. She had such a will to live. She had so much to live for and to give.

I talked to Tom about Meagan and how special our family was to Jenny. Tom was polite with Meagan, but he had held back a deep commitment. It was like an invisible wall, keeping Meagan at a safe distance. Tom felt Meagan didn't appreciate what Jon and I were doing for her, that Meagan took things for granted. While this was often true, I knew we had to grow beyond that. We discussed this for a little while.

Meagan had made positive changes in her life. By the way Jenny lived, she had taught Meagan a lot about values and family love. I reminded Tom that it was an important goal in Jenny's life to give Meagan a new home, a new life. We could handle this one of two ways. Keep the wall up and have tension or drop the guard and fulfill Jenny's dream.

I told him Meagan wasn't there to ever replace Jenny. She was there to have a home and be loved. Tears filled his eyes as he said he really cared about Meagan too.

Tending to Tasks

We agreed we would not allow any life saving efforts if Jenny coded. We had no idea how soon it would be. Today? Tomorrow? In a week? In a month? Jon was at work. Since we talked every day, he knew the decision we had ahead of us. In a few minutes, Meagan and Pastor Dave joined us.

It was hard talking about losing Jenny. We all agreed we would not have an open casket. Jenny had such pride. She would never want others to see her this way.

There were many things to consider. It was something we didn't want to do, but we had to make some decisions. I never dreamed I would have to make funeral arrangements for one of our children. It's not supposed to be that way. Hard as it was, we had this to do for Jenny.

After Connie joined us, Pastor Dave made a list of pallbearers. The first person we thought of was Jenny's friend, Jamie. Pastor Dave listed newspapers and people to contact. We talked about her funeral.

My heart was breaking, I hurt so bad. Never again would I get a hug or a kiss from Jenny. How could I live without her? She had taught us so much about life. God was number one. Would she be with Him soon? I would never know what she was doing or feeling.

How could I handle life without her? A numbness settled over us.

All of a sudden, I said I would be back. I had to spend as much time as possible with Jenny. Tom and Meagan left to call friends while Pastor Dave called the church. Connie went to find her daughter. "I am your favorite aunt," Connie had always told Jenny.

Jenny's room was crowded. Her nurse was working on her and the dialysis nurse was getting machines ready. As I looked at Jenny, my heart shattered. She had gone through so much. People had hurt her, but she never carried hate. How could God let her go through so much suffering to have it end like this?

In her short life, she had touched so many and done much good. How much longer would I have her? Part of me wanted to keep her forever, no matter in what condition, but I knew that was selfish. About 10:40 a.m. the nurse asked me to sign a paper giving permission to remove the central line. She asked if she could do anything.

"What I want more than anything, you can't do," I whispered. Every cell of my body was in pain. My soul was barren.

When I gave Jenny life, I never thought I would have to watch her die.

After the nurse left, I ran my hand through Jenny's hair again. Her lovely fair hair was messed up and sticky where they had started the two EEG connections. I kissed her hand and looked into her eyes. They were blown out on the bottom.

Anyone who knew Jenny would no longer recognize her. She looked so much worse than the day before. Rubbing her arms, I looked at her beautiful nails. Jenny loved pretty nails and could never grow them very long. She was dying and now her fingernails were growing.

Her body drew me to her. There was the little hole in her right knee from a roller skating fall when she was 10. When she was one, she had taken a fall at Aunt Helen's house. A scar remained from those stitches.

Her chest was covered with scars from central lines—and she had "three" belly buttons. Or so we had teased her about the incisions from her G-tubes. I looked at the birthmark on her left forearm and her bushy, dark eyebrows.

God! What had happened to her shining blue eyes?

We had placed pictures of Jenny on the machines over her bed. There she was with her brother and new sister looking down at me. Happy. Full of spice and life.

Jenny's two favorite songs came to mind. "Victory in Jesus" and one Kelly Connor sang called "I Just Want Jesus." How could I bear to lose her? But was this fair to Jenny? Was this living?

She wasn't afraid to die. The only thing she feared was living in constant pain, unable to function independently.

She had touched Heaven when she saw Heather. She said you could not dream of going to a more beautiful place. There were many there to welcome her...Grandma Epley, Heather Lyle, Chris Barga, Judy Rose, Mrs. Johnson and others. I had given Jenny life 21 years earlier. It was time to give her life again.

Between Mother and Daughter

Honesty was a big thing between Jenny and me. Sick or well, we talked. Our relationship—mother and daughter—had been uncommon. It was time to lose my best friend. Tears rolled down my face as I held Jenny and told her what I had to do and explained what was happening to her body. Sobbing, I told her I wanted to take her off the respirator. She wasn't brain dead, but how could she live like this?

I begged her to understand I wasn't giving up on her. When I pulled myself up from her chest, I looked at her and tears began rolling down Jenny's face. What was she telling me? Was she scared? Did she think I was quitting on her? Or was I granting her peace?

When she was only seven she was nervous about singing her first solo in church. She did a great job in spite of the fact that a cute freckle-faced boy in the front row kept making faces at her in an attempt to get her to laugh. She had sung, "I'm Something Special." That she was! That she was! Not just to me. Not just to her family. Everyone she met found her special.

Someone had told me, "If God would say to you, 'I can loan this child to you for 21 years only or not at all,' what would you say?" Well, Jenny's 21 years with us couldn't be traded for anything better.

Enough is Enough

I wiped her tears, kissed her cheek and called for the nurse. I told her to cancel the procedure to remove the central line and I asked her to get Dr. Adams on the phone for me. It was time to let Jenny go.

The nurse came back and tore up my signed order for the central line removal. She gave me a hug saying, "What a special mom you are. How much you must love Jenny." At that moment, I wondered, "What kind of mother am I? What were Jenny's tears telling me?" My heart told me it was right to let her go. I had to believe God was directing me.

The nurse asked if she should tell Dr. Adams about my decision. I took the phone, shaking and crying. It was 11:00 a.m. and I knew his office was swamped, but he always took time for us.

"Enough is enough," I told him. "It is time to stop." He understood and agreed, Jenny would not want to live like this.

"How do we stop this?" I asked.

He explained he would turn off the respirator. The only thing I requested was not to let her gasp or suffer. He said he would give her morphine before he turned off the machine, but he couldn't make any guarantee. After checking his schedule, he told me he would be at CCU at noon. Again, he assured me it was the right thing to do.

Tom's Tearful Good-bye

Tom was standing there when I turned around. I explained what I had decided was best for Jenny. Tom was hurting deeply, but he was also worried about me. He hugged me hard and made it clear, this was the best decision.

He said he knew Jenny wanted to be released from her pain and that he was proud of me. I suggested he go in and talk to Jenny and tell her everything he ever wanted to say to her.

While Tom was with Jenny, I called Jon. He said, "You know what is right to do," confirming my decision. I appreciated the fact that he always trusted me in a crisis. Then I called Fran. Jenny once said, "I'm really glad you have Fran." Jenny knew I did not freely express my feelings to just anyone.

I overheard the nurses talking about Tom. They had closed all the blinds in Jenny's room except the one facing the nurse's station. The staff stood there, watching Tom talk to Jenny.

"Look there. He is just pouring his heart out to his sister. You can tell how much he loves her. He is talking constantly and tears are rolling down his cheeks." When I turned to look at my kids, I knew Jenny was crying too. Tom had a tissue and was wiping tears from her face.

Tom talked and cried the whole time he was with her. Then he gave her a hug, kissed her forehead, touched the guardian angel pin on her chest and left.

He hugged Meagan, who had just walked up with Pastor Dave. I told Meagan to go in and say good-bye to Jenny. Meagan looked like her lifeline had been ripped out. Jenny represented her whole new world.

We all felt shattered, but I thought, "We are fortunate to be able to say good-bye." Pastor Dave took his turn, not only as Jenny's minister, but as a dear friend. He had listened, cared, helped, loved, prayed and encouraged her. Whatever the battle, he never deserted her.

Now, he sat on the side of her bed and released her by singing "I'll Fly Away." He told her, "In a few minutes you will be singing with the angels. Please don't compare my singing to theirs, Jenny."

35. A Mirror of God's Love

About 11:20 a.m. Dr. Adams and Pat came rushing in. Pat leaned against a wall, crying. I was thankful to see them so I could get away from a lady from the chapel who was smothering me with her chatter. It was obvious Dr. Adams was nervous as he told a nurse to get some morphine. He had a daughter Jenny's age, and I knew he could relate to our painful decision. And I never doubted he cared deeply for Jenny.

Everyone was out of Jenny's room. Everyone had said their good-byes. It was time.

Released with Love

I couldn't believe Dr. Adams had come over so fast. He took my hand, and said, "Come on, Mom." It was 11:30 a.m. Indiana time. The nurse closed the remaining blind and the door. Dr. Adams and the nurse were on Jenny's right, I was on her left, and a priest was in the corner. The chaplain stood next to me. I appreciated the chaplain's good will, but I truly needed silent prayer.

A torrent washed through me. I wanted Pastor Dave in Jenny's room at my side, but Tom and Meagan needed him more.

The nurse handed Dr. Adams the morphine syringe. I leaned over the bed rail, running my hands through Jenny's hair, telling her how sorry I was for doing this, begging her to please forgive me, telling her how much I loved her.

Dr. Adams put the morphine into the port in her chest with shaking hands. Suddenly, I was aware of falling tear drops. I looked up to discover Dr. Adams was weeping. What comfort his compassion brought to me. Jenny was allowed to die through the hands of a caring doctor who believed in her. She would die with dignity and love.

Dr. Adams and a few other special doctors had given her a longer life, a better life, precious years in which she had touched many people.

Jenny had showed us God's love through who she was and how she fought to live.

Dr. Adams lowered the bed rail for me and patted me on the back. I trembled with tears, trying to say good-bye to Jenny. Over and over I asked Dr. Adams to tell me the date. I had to know the date my daughter died. Dr. Adams had turned off the respirator after giving Jenny the morphine.

Jenny would take a breath, then stop, take a breath, then stop. Our eyes moved from Jenny to the monitors and back to her again.

The time between each labored breath got longer and longer. At 11:57 a.m. Indiana time, August 26, 1994, it was over. My girl was gone. Jenny was with her God. There would be no more special times with her.

All the tears in the world poured through me. I was numb and still I was glad her pain was over. What did Jenny's last tears mean? I prayed they were tears of peace.

After we left Jenny's room, Tom, Meagan, Pastor Dave and Connie went in. I walked over and hugged Pat. She sobbed and sobbed. Dr. Adams had asked her to come to give us support and she apologized for not being stronger. But just by being there she had helped us. She was always special to us—those people from a neighboring state.

Dr. Adams asked if we could talk. We went around the corner and he asked if an autopsy could be done. He said it might help someone else, and, by law, he needed to ask. Everything was a blur to me.

"For almost six years, Jenny has been an experimental case. I feel she has done enough for other people," I said. No one was going to cut on her again. They knew the name of this last infection. They knew her organs had failed. "Do you really have to do it? Is it mandatory? I don't want it done."

Once again, he understood, for which I was thankful. He hugged me, telling me he was sorry. I knew he had done everything humanly possible. Jenny had been in the hands of one of God's physicians.

Dr. Adams signed Jenny's chart, and told me the nurses would clean her up and then we could go to her. I felt a gentle hand on my shoulder as Dr. Adams and Pat left. His head hung low. I wanted to relieve him of any sense of failure. He had been Jenny's window of hope and comfort many times.

I called Jon to tell him Jenny's suffering was over. "I will leave for the hospital immediately," was his first response. After a little discussion, we agreed it would be better if he went directly home, so he would be there when we arrived.

Comforting Words

The phone rang at the nurse's station. It was Dr. Kane, our family doctor from home. He said he had been uneasy all day and knew something was wrong. I told him it was over. Dr. Kane really cared for Jenny too, and had gone the second mile for her in many ways. Because he picked up her care at home, we were able to continue going to Dr. Adams in Indiana.

"If there is anything I can do, just let me know," he said. I knew he was sincere.

Then Fran Dean called, offering to make some calls for me. We didn't talk much. It was a bad time. Among others, she called Dr. Gardner's office. She knew their concern.

Pastor Dave notified the church and I felt he needed some time alone. He, too, had lost one special to him. The CCU staff was wonderful. They did everything they could to make things easier. We didn't feel like strangers. There was nothing superficial about these nurses. The CCU secretary hugged me, saying Jenny was in a nicer place and pain free.

"You know, Mom, you gave your daughter life again," she said. God was reassuring me through people that letting Jenny go had been right.

One of Jenny's nurses told me that so many times people keep their loved ones living on machines because they think it's best for the patient. But it isn't. Rather, it is for the family that can't bear to give up. She told me my decision was unselfish.

Nurses went in and out of Jenny's room. Tom, Meagan and I leaned on each other, waiting until we could see Jenny again. I was proud of these two young people. We were going through the worst time of our life and they were as strong as they could be. Pastor Dave and others came back, and still the lady chaplain talked.

Finally, the nurse said we could go back in. Jenny's room looked empty. All the machines had been taken out. No IV bags hung at bedside. No monitors hummed and beeped. There was an overwhelming sense of silence.

Pastor Dave, Connie and her daughter, Gail, and I were on Jenny's right. Tom, Meagan, and two of their friends were on her left. Their tears were sincerely spent. Jenny had been special to each of them. From the back of the room I could hear the chaplain talking to the priest. She meant well, but I couldn't handle it.

Encompassed by Peace

Watching Jenny's lifeless body, I waited anxiously, expecting to see her take a breath. It wasn't going to happen, but I kept watching. I was drowning in sorrow and asked if Tom, Meagan and I could have sometime alone with her. When the others left, Jenny's peace encompassed us.

We couldn't stop touching her body. We kissed her again and again, pulling back the covers. We wanted to remember everything about her. We searched to see if tubes were still in her poor body. The catheter and all the wires were gone. All that remained were tubes that had been surgically attached.

She was freshly cleaned except for that awful mess from the EEG. I hated seeing that in her hair. Her body recorded the distress of her illness—face swollen and purple, neck burst open, eyes bulging out, and still in our eyes we saw her beauty. No scarred body could keep us from loving her and feeling her love shining through.

Tom took down the pictures over her head. We couldn't take Jenny home, but we could take the memories in those photos. Tom reached down and gently took the guardian angel pin off Jenny's gown, the one he had placed there. He asked if he could have it. Yes, this token of Tom's love for Jenny was his to keep. Meagan sobbed. I think she had known we might lose Jenny someday, but now she was face to face with the reality.

Before we left, there was one more thing I had to do. I wrapped Jenny's arms around me and we shared one last hug.

36. If You have been Loved by Jenny

We took leave of the compassionate hospital staff and loaded our things. After a little discussion, we figured out how we would get all the cars home. Everyone urged me to ride with someone, but I resisted. I needed time by myself. Pastor Dave and I each drove home alone.

I remembered morning awoke to a beautiful day and it was still lovely. The early afternoon sun was bright and the splendor of late summer surrounded us in shades of green under a bold blue sky. I asked God to take special care of our Jenny, and to give her just such a beautiful day for her funeral.

After rolling down the window, I put my foot on the gas pedal and set off. A soft, warm, comforting breeze came through the window. The entire trip I drove automatically, taking notice of only one distinct thing. As I drove eastward, the funeral hearse from our hometown traveled west to bring our Jenny home.

Jon was at the house with a friend from work when I pulled into our driveway and my folks were there. Dad was sitting on our front porch crying. It reminded me of the many times he had come over when Jenny was desperately ill and had peeked his nose in, asking, "How is she doing?"

Each time I had to respond, "About the same, Dad," he had retreated, saying, "It's a goddamn shame. Just a goddamn shame." Then he would sit out on the porch and cry.

The kids and I unloaded the cars. The house was already filled with plants and flowers and a great sense of emptiness. In such a short time, people had called or been down to visit Jon.

The room where Jenny spent most of the summer looked just like it had the day we left. Colorful balloons were still tied to the end of her bed. Every time someone had given Jenny a balloon her face lit up as her eyes followed its restricted floating flight. It had often seemed as if Jenny was tethered to her bed along with the balloons.

I looked at the inspirational daily calendar Jenny had kept near bedside. On the day of her death the message read:

> Treasure each other in the recognition that we
> do not know how long we shall have each other.
> Joshua Loth Liebman

A Mental Memory Book

Machines, IV bags, a commode, Jenny's wheelchair, medical supplies, a stuffed bunny and lovely flower arrangements filled the room. "Get Well" and "Thinking of You" cards lined the wall. Had we only been gone four days? Looking at Jenny's bed, I could still see her there.

As more and more people arrived, a gentle spirit seemed to whisper "hush, hush" through the house like the ringing of a tiny soothing bell. People in our small town had pulled together many times to make Jenny's life easier.

How had they learned so quickly about her death? Through the coming days we would learn more and more about the heartstrings Jenny had tugged in our community.

Pastor Dave rushed in to say they needed us at the funeral home so everything could be arranged in time for a Monday funeral. He felt badly bothering us, but paper work had to be done.

After the papers were signed, we agreed to return Saturday morning to pick out Jenny's casket. Pastor Dave took us home and told us how much he loved all of us.

When I went back into the house, Connie and Meagan were trying to help by clearing out medical equipment and supplies from Jenny's room. Part of me felt pushed—Jenny was being pushed out of the house. They meant well, but I wasn't ready for this. I couldn't rush. My loss was overwhelming and housekeeping tasks were invasive.

Jon called me to the front porch. There stood Eddie Simmons, a friend from a local Christian singing group—The Glory Bound Quartet. He told us he had heard about Jenny, and, without thinking, jumped into his truck and raced to the house.

He looked down at his feet, apologizing. He had come so quickly he had forgotten his shoes. Jenny had been touched by the musical ministry of this group, and Eddie said he wished they could have spent more time with her. They had enjoyed getting to know her. We made an agreement. The Glory Bound Quartet would sing for her funeral.

A nursing friend from Dr. Kane's office came by. She had always been willing to help. Dr. Kane had been unsettled all day, she said, and kept asking if anyone had heard from Indiana. We both knew he cared about Jenny and wanted the best for her.

It meant so much as friends poured into the house, expressing their love, offering help. Food overflowed from the fridge. People were kind, but I felt I would never have an appetite again. I pushed Tom to eat, but we suffered the same. We understood each other. Cathy and Connie tried to keep things organized.

Personal memories of Jenny bombarded each of us. "Your pain became her pain—your pleasure and happiness, her joy," Cathy remembered.

"How was it she always had time to listen to problems of others?"

For Connie, a pair of high top tennis shoes were mementos of Jenny's fight with Lyme disease. Jenny simply hated the high tops she had to wear to help support her for a while, so she wouldn't get "drop foot" again. Connie had feigned jealousy. "When you don't need them anymore, I'll take them," she had said.

When we had urged Jenny to put them on, she would tell Connie, "Take the dumb things." When Jenny didn't need to wear them anymore, she had given them to Connie with the greatest pleasure.

Acts of Love

Function, just keep functioning, I told myself as I walked in a dull haze from one thing to another. When I looked up and saw Jenny's friends, "the girls" from a local bank, gathered across the street from our house, I broke down. Even former employees were with them. What a thoughtful thing to do. To come, and to come together. They had given Jenny their personal time, their love and a lot of ornery teasing throughout our years of fighting Lyme disease.

They had stayed with her in the hospital (writing mean posters about a mean doctor). They had come to the house to be with her and sent me off to a track event to watch Tommy. They were all busy with homes, families and work, but they always took time for Jenny. It was a mutual admiration society. For the first time, tears replaced our laughter.

Kelly Connor was there. A former employee of the bank, she had been a "big sister" to Jenny in many ways. "Kelly, will you sing at Jenny's funeral?" I asked. She said she didn't think she could handle it. I knew it was a large request.

Jenny and Kelly had shared wonderful times together working on Kelly's musical ministry, with their last great adventure being the Dove awards trip and their frantic all-night drive to get Jenny home for emergency surgery. Kelly thought possibly she'd be able to play the piano.

Kelly knew Jenny had no fear of death. "The glimpse she had seen of Heaven when Heather came to her was so wonderful and peaceful, contentment with no sickness," Kelly remembered.

"If we could only get a glimpse like Jenny had—we would say, 'Gosh, what's the big problem?' After all the tubes that had gone into that girl—I would have said, 'Go ahead and take me Lord. I am ready. This is enough—is enough—is enough.'"

Another banking friend, JoNell, remembered Jenny as an eighth grader in the front row of the school choir. "She glowed like an angel even then," she said. Thinking of the joy her own two daughters brought to her life, JoNell rejoiced in Jenny's radiant smile, her sense of inner peace, her wit and spunk and love of life, and her genuine affection and honesty.

After things settled down, Jenny's girlfriends wanted to go to town to get something for her to wear. Tom wanted to pay for it. This was something he had to do. We decided, to make Jenny look peaceful, a pretty nightgown and robe would be the thing to get.

While they were gone I called old friends who lived out of town. When Angie answered, I asked her if her husband, Steve, would do something for us. She said yes.

"Will Steve be a pallbearer for Jenny?"

"You know he will," she said. Then, as natural as can be, she asked, "How *is* Jenny?"

Hadn't she understood my request?

All of a sudden, she began crying hysterically. Finally, we had to hang up the phone. We were more like family than friends, and Jenny had always hoped she could have a nice guy like Steve for a husband. Steve and Tom were both 10s on Jenny's list.

That evening, I felt like everyone was trying to tell me what needed to be done. My mind was a whirlwind of confusion. I had never had to make funeral arrangements for anyone, and I certainly had never considered making funeral arrangements for Jenny. All I knew was that the funeral would be what Jenny would like.

After dealing with a flat tire and getting a clerk to open a store already closed for the evening, the girls had found a lovely gown and robe for Jenny. The nightgown was white. The long sleeved robe was pink, mauve and white-striped silk with tiny flowers for trim. It was perfect, but even this last gift could not ease Tom's breaking heart.

That first night was hard. Exhaustion would not allow sleep. I attempted to rest on Jenny's sick bed, surrounded by her medical equipment and personal things.

Upstairs, in her bedroom, the shelves remained filled in military orderliness with her books and tapes and trinkets. She had kept a remembrance from the Dove Awards Silver Anniversary in April 1994. It read "Grand Ole Opry House, Nashville, Tenn., CD Special Edition Commemorative Ticket."

A picture of Jenny with Goofy celebrated her high school music trip to Disney World. These keepsakes were tokens of two really special trips of her life. Neither souvenir recorded any of the stress and worry and pain associated with those trips, or the emergency surgeries needed upon her return.

By morning, our household was busy again. Tom came down, carrying Jenny's cross necklace and her "Sung" perfume. It was important to us that she wear her cross and have her favorite perfume. Jenny's clothes, pictures of her, and other items were picked up by a friend from the funeral home.

Tom, Meagan, Jon and I went to the funeral home to pick out Jenny's casket. The kids and I talked openly and knew what we wanted before we got there. It was more difficult for Jon to express his personal feelings. The funeral directors began explaining prices, colors and quality. I couldn't stand it.

"White!" I said. "It has to be white," even though I didn't see any white caskets around us. The funeral directors looked at each other. The white casket was back in a corner. They had already picked that one for Jenny. Embroidered roses on the lining of the lid matched the trim on Tom's gift robe.

For My Comfort

As we were leaving, I stopped. I had to see Jenny. The funeral directors were friends, they were understanding, but I was told Jenny wasn't ready to be seen. Five hours work had been done on her face and there was still more work to do. They sensed my pain. I had to see her. Nothing could be any worse than the way she looked when I had left her. I had to know her body was there, that she was covered up, that she was okay. They finally agreed, but cautioned, "We have more work to do."

As they rolled Jenny in on a cart, my heart yearned to hold her in my arms. She looked angelic and peaceful. Her hair had been washed so that it was bright, light blonde again. And Jenny's face looked beautiful.

"Jenny, help us get through the rough times ahead," I prayed silently.

How would we continue our lives with this special piece missing? We needed to draw strength from God.

The weekend was filled with endless visits and calls, deeply shared prayers and unrestrained tears. Tokens of caring continued to bombard our doorways.

Two of Jenny's New Jersey doctors called. Dr. Paige was at the airport when she heard the news and called our home immediately. These two fine doctors, who had been the first to diagnose and treat her Lyme, were saddened by our loss.

They had helped Jenny fight for life during two long and difficult hospital stays. Jenny had fought hard time and time again. If she could have beaten this last onset of Lyme, it would have been a victory for them as much as for her.

As arrangements for the funeral were being made, it continued to be important to have what Jenny would want. "What songs do you prefer?" the musicians asked. "You will know the right songs," was my repeated reply.

We had a closed casket, except for visits by the immediate family. We spent as much time with Jenny as possible. Tom, especially, needed to be with her. He would go to the funeral home before each public visitation hour and the staff would open the casket just for him.

After visitations were over, they would open the casket again and he talked and cried his heart out to her. He kept putting perfume on her so she would "smell like Jenny."

A yellow rose rested in Jenny's hand. Tom had bought it and placed it there. Friends and family offered tokens for her coffin—pictures, nail polish, music tapes, hair ribbons, guardian angel pins and other little personal things important to them and Jenny.

The funeral home was filled with her favorite flower, yellow roses, and other floral arrangements. Pictures of Jenny, her angel collection, and graduation mementos were displayed among the flowers. While words of sympathy and compassion could not ease our pain or sense of loss, we appreciated the sincerity of each expression.

A card and note from Heather Lyle's mother, Chris, was one of the most meaningful. Along with a personal message, Chris also shared a grand experience from her work with the Hospice program.

...Jenny touched so many, many lives. She definitely left a lasting impression upon this community. I wanted to share this story with you:

Through the Hospice program we took care of a little girl. After she died, her family shared stories. The aunt told us that the little girl saw a beautiful sunset one evening and said, "That's what Heaven looks like." Her aunt asked her how she knew that and the little girl proceeded to tell her aunt that the angels had taken her there. [She had been critically ill for over a year.]

The little one said that she and her Grandpa [who had died the previous year] sat on the clouds and hung their legs down through them [because the clouds are soft and fluffy and you can do that] and they would watch Grandma. And there were no tears and no pain and it was a wonderful place and she was not afraid to go back.

I found that story to be very, very comforting. It does-
n't take away that empty aching loneliness, but I think
sometimes God gives us glimpses of where our girls
are...I continue to pray for you.   Chris

37. High Fivin' All Over Heaven

The morning of Jenny's funeral Connie called me for my brother, Scott. He was in a lot of pain and wanted to know if he could see Jenny. *IF* he hadn't moved his family to Georgia, we wouldn't have visited them the summer of 1988, and Jenny wouldn't have been bitten by the tick which gave her Lyme disease.

It was an irrational *IF*, thinking this way, but we all had our moments... IF ONLY... Jenny never wanted Scott to think twice about where she got Lyme. She felt everything happened for a reason and God would always take care of her.

I told Connie I would meet Scott at the funeral home. When I asked Tom, "What would Jenny want?" Tom agreed. Uncle Scott should be allowed to view her. By the time Scott came, he had changed his mind and that was okay. No one was to blame, and it was now time to say good-bye.

When we arrived at the church with our friends Angie and Steve, it didn't look like a church ready for a funeral service. Helium balloons clinging from the ceiling of the fellowship hall reminded me of all the "Get Well" balloons Jenny had enjoyed and of the excitement the whole family had shared just a few months earlier, preparing for the kids big graduation party—making posters and banners, and planning festive food.

Jenny's funeral service would be joyful, a triumphant celebration of her life. There would be no hollow, token words, no somber songs. The brightness of her life would not be overcast with dark and leaden pronouncements. We were saddened and grieving. Our hearts were broken. But this was a time to rejoice, a time to lift up with thanksgiving the exceptional gift we had been blessed with for 21 years.

Many of Jenny's musician friends wanted to participate in her service so we would not swiftly be on our way to the graveyard. They all shared thoughtfully selected songs.

Of course, Jim sang, and God Bless Kelly, she also lifted up her love for Jenny and their Lord in song. People who loved Jenny crowded the pews and the fragrance of yellow roses overflowed the sanctuary.

Pastor Dave gave a love-filled message. He shared some of the "thousand thoughts a second" he had while driving home from the hospital after Jenny died. "What a contrast between bringing the body home and taking the spirit home," he said.

He realized, "There would be no fans and no band playing and no *high fivin'* as the hearse drove empty streets returning with her body. At the same time, they were *high fivin' all over heaven.*" He explained Jenny's body was just a suit that God had given her for a certain time, place and season.

That she had touched hearts in ways others never could equal. Pastor Dave said he had been witness to her "sweet, gentle spirit," which seemed to carry a strength of its own, ordained by God for His work.

His heartfelt message was founded in one incredible truth. "If you have been loved by Jenny, you have been loved," he said.

"Her funeral service wasn't hard," he later said, "because I knew and loved her so much. The more you love someone, of course, the hurt is greater, but the message is easier—there is so much more to say."

The previous April, Jenny had given a talk in church. Pastor Dave explained that Jenny would share once more through a tape from that earlier service. It had been my request.

Jenny's Message of Thanksgiving

First thing I would like to thank you. It's been a real rough time lately.

I've had to deal with a lot of things. I don't know if some of you know I'm back on IVs again and my Lyme is flared up. And sometimes it seems it never stops. But for some reason I was a different person this time, not as strong or as willing to fight back and at one point my spirit was really depressed and Dave has been through so much with me, that I got really discouraged and I didn't realize why God didn't heal me.

I thought after five and one-half years, it had been long enough. I thought He really taught me a lesson and why does this have to continue?

And I wasn't sure and I really started questioning that. I was angry and when I asked Pastor Dave if that was wrong, he said no—that I was just being human. But everything happens in God's time and I know that and after a lot of prayers and time it soaked in. But still you can't help but get angry because you want things done in *your* time. That doesn't always happen. Those that wait upon the Lord shall renew their strength.

I believe Jesus allows a lot of things to happen. Especially when you're sick or down or lonely you don't think about the good things.

You think about all the hard times and you feel sorry for yourself. But, through this illness I have matured so much. I am a better person and have more faith in God and more love for people and I realize what's important.

You all have been so wonderful through the last five and one-half years. I've had this illness for a lifetime. I don't remember anything before and I don't know what I would have done without you and Pastor Dave. Without all the prayers and support and love. I wouldn't be here today.

Without my family, I wouldn't be here today. My mom is the most wonderful person in the entire world. [Jenny had started to cry.] She's not only my best friend, but I can trust and confide in her with everything.

You really know who your true friends are when they walk through the worst times of your life with you. But

Jesus is the most ultimate friend of all and I just hope what I say here today ministers to you.

I hope it soaks in, because this song [I am going to sing] really ministered to me. It's an example of my life. And I know every problem is different and I know you probably haven't gone through the sickness I've gone through, but your problems are just as important. And I hope you let God direct your life because He'll do it.

So many things have happened through this illness that I know exactly where my life is going to go...what direction it is going to go and I'm going to make the most of what I have. Because God has given me the most perfect gift. Thank you. This song is called "There is a Way" and after the first chorus, feel free to join in. You are more than welcomed.

In April, even though Jenny wasn't getting better, she hadn't been afraid. What a gift. To hear her voice once again, expressing thankfulness, acceptance and love.

"There Is A Way" shares this message—when there are troubles and doubt, when things go wrong, we can knock on the door of the Lord, trusting in Him. It is an energized, jiving, hoe-down kind of song and Jenny had managed to sing it that way. After that explosive song she had ended by softly saying, "Thank you all so much."

At the end of her funeral service, the congregation sang "I'll Fly Away" and a yellow rose was offered to each person so Jenny could give of herself one more time. People took the balloons outside, letting them go at different times. Floating upwards, the balloons seemed to cluster together before they disappeared. There were no complaints about the long service. Rather, people remarked it had been a special experience for them.

"The funeral was a glorious celebration of Jenny's life through music, a freeing of her spirit," Sandy Waggoner rejoiced. It touched people in specific ways. A lady who had lost her husband the previous April told me she had never accepted his death. When she released a balloon for Jenny she also released one for her husband. At last, she was able to set him free.

Jenny's cousin, Eric, understood Grandpa Epley's pain when he heard my father say to a childhood friend, "I'll never understand why the good Lord would take the young and beautiful and let us old folks hang around."

Days which Follow Death

As we tended to chores and our various duties in the days following Jenny's service, we found ourselves thinking of her constantly. Depending upon the state of her health, our daily routine had usually been dominated by responding to her needs. When we found ourselves still *needing to do for her*, things we had never thought about before suddenly became important.

We decided to keep balloons and lights at Jenny's grave even though we knew she was in Heaven. It was a small way to deal with our grief. Through the coming years Jenny's grave would become a place of solace for Jenny's family and friends.

One day my father came into the house and said, "I had lunch with Jenny."

"You did?"

Dad's white crowned head nodded yes. After picking up a fast food meal, he had gone out to the graveyard, sat on a bench and had lunch with Jenny. He said he does that a lot.

The first weeks after Jenny's funeral, Tom was at her grave more than not, sobbing out his sorrow. He couldn't let her go. Slowly, over time, he came to realize that Jenny's spirit is with him no matter when he needs her.

The first Thanksgiving after Jenny's death, Jon, Tom, Meagan and I went out to Jenny's grave as a family. Since then, I've gone out alone and with family or friends. The little kids I baby-sit enjoy our trips out there, especially when we take balloons. Jon always takes notice of the bright lights on her grave if he has occasion to drive down a nearby road at night.

Connie laughs about our poor attempts to plant flowers at Jenny's grave. "Jenny knew they were from the heart and not from *Better Homes and Gardens*," she said. Thinking of the times Connie and I had nursed Jenny, Connie laughed, "We aren't as stupid as everybody thinks. We could have really messed Jenny up and she turned out pretty good."

I had to challenge. "Maybe she was smarter than we were." After a moment, Connie nodded her head in agreement, "That could be true. That could be true."

Cathy and I and her daughter, Cindy, Jenny's friend, took a birthday cake out on Jenny's birthday, sharing the love and laughter that we omitted on her 21st birthday. Cindy remembers how as little girls they played *friends forever*. "I was Cathy. Jenny was Sue."

Jamie and Aaron and others have gone out when they have felt a need to chat with her, and another friend, Jamie Brown, has found Jenny's grave to be a happy place. "I go out there and think about things we did. I tell her I miss her. If I have a bad day or something I just go out there." Jamie Brown still remembers Jenny on special days in special ways.

As we thought about how much Jenny loved her angel collection, we got excited about the idea of making an angel tree and leaving it up all year. Many people responded to our family project, until the branches of a lovely artificial evergreen tree were suddenly filled with angels.

Amazingly, not one of the angels was just like another. Some were given from people we knew. Others were left at our door—anonymously—some with written notes like: "I wanted my angel to be part of Jenny's angel tree."

Jenny's friends from the bank had an evergreen tree planted near our front porch as a living memory. Each time we leave and each time we return home Jenny blesses our comings and our goings. A ceramic angel rests under the bottom branches of the tree.

Pat, from Doctor Adams' office, sent a card and an original poem. It had been so kind of her to come and be with us that last morning at the hospital. When problems arise in her life, Pat handles them by writing. Jenny's death had touched her more than she could imagine, so she put her feelings into a poem entitled "Jenny."

> ...No matter how sick or bad you felt
> Or whatever twist life had dealt,
> You handled it bravely, you didn't complain.
> Even on days when there was so much pain...

The high school counselor, Sandy Waggoner, came to the house with a card *from Jenny*. She said that Jenny had *worked on her* all that day until she sat down and wrote a message to each one of us.

We were touched that Sandy was sensitive to Jenny's true spirit and to our needs. "Jenny was an inspiration to all who knew her," Sandy said. "She touched lives, changed lives, through her innocence, peacefulness and tranquility." Sandy felt that Jenny taught others how to pass through life with a kind spirit.

During some of Jenny's most difficult times, Sandy had visited Jenny in her room, encouraging her through her struggles. "We discussed God's purpose—how many hearts she had touched with her faith as a result of her illness," Sandy said.

The local paper carried features about Jenny. The staff always gave space to the things that were special about her. After she died a front page article, "Jenny Challenged Us," carried this lead: "She wanted to live...She wanted to graduate from high school...She lived to graduate from high school..."

The paper also carried a letter to Jenny from Sandy Waggoner, expressing things Sandy had always wanted to tell

Jenny..."You shared your love with everyone and that love will live on. We will not forget your wisdom and maturity that allowed you to see beyond the horizon of life...You helped me look at each day as a welcomed challenge and to be thankful that I have that day. You taught me to treasure people above all things."

The fall after her death, Jenny's cousin, Eric, would write a college composition entitled "Remembrance of Jenny," explaining why people who live good lives for themselves and others don't need a monument.

The winter after we lost Jenny the *lyme disease reporter*, a publication of the Lyme Disease Association of Ohio, carried the story of her fight with Lyme.

On the six-month anniversary of her death, all her musician friends from the surrounding area graciously gave a memorial concert in her name, which the public generously supported.

In the years to come there would be endless occasions when Jenny's witness, seeking out the goodness in life— fighting the good fight—would continue to bear fruit.

People in our church wrote an inspirational piece in the form of a letter. It described the joy Jenny experienced as she entered through Heaven's gates.

> ...She saw children shouting and squealing,
> Jumping together on a pile
> Joyously rolling and laughing
> One was Heather Lyle.
> Now when Heather saw her
> She cried, "Don't go away."
> But Jenny just smiled and said,
> "Oh, this time, I get to stay"...

Probably one of the most unpredictable ways Jenny was remembered was Tom's presentation at a grief workshop called "The Invisible Kids." Along with another young person who had lost a sibling, Tom gave talks on two different days. One day teachers and school counselors came to the program and the other day ministers attended.

People who were there said everyone was touched by Tom's powerful and moving words. Speaking in little more than a whisper, he clutched a large picture of Jenny in his arms as he spoke of her life and her illness, and the impact her loss had on those close to her. Of Pastor Dave he said, "It was important that Pastor was always there—just to be there and accepted by him—not to tell me how to feel."

If there is a grandstand in Heaven, I have no doubts Jenny was proudly cheering "Go! Tom! Go!" for her meek Tommy Tiddle Mouse.

AFTERWARD

I found the tragic story of Jenny Umphress extremely painful to read. Painful because of the suffering Jenny and her family and friends endured, and painful because in my medical practice I see so many stories like Jenny's story. Luckily, most patients are not affected by Lyme disease as extremely as Jenny. But, many cases I have seen are alike in that—Lyme is not considered as a diagnosis because "there is no Lyme in this area" or "your Lyme test was negative" or "two weeks of treatment and Lyme is cured so whatever problems you are still having it isn't Lyme."

Sadly, in 1988, Lyme was not as well publicized as it is now and sadly, even ten years later, Lyme was still under-researched and under-funded and misunderstood. As a physician who treats Lyme disease, I well know the feeling my patients have when they are not taken seriously or have been mistreated by the medical community. Everyday I talk to people like Jenny's mother who are told they or their family member needs psychiatric help because their physician is unable to accept Lyme as a diagnosis.

Lyme disease is still a mystery illness. We have miles to go before we begin to fully understand its effects on the human body. Caught early and treated adequately, it is very curable. Let it progress into a chronic stage and the battle is, indeed, uphill with two steps back for every one forward. It becomes increasingly difficult to prescribe adequate treatment for late stage Lyme as we must fight insurance companies, the CDC and sadly, other members of the medical profession.

For everyone who has struggled with Lyme disease, for their families, for all the support groups and for the handful of physicians who continue to treat Lyme patients, this book should inspire them to rededicate themselves. Hopefully, working together, we will be able to prevent another tragedy like Jenny.

To Jenny's family, I would like to extend my deepest sympathy. Your ordeal should never have happened. Hopefully. you will be able to glean some small measure of peace in knowing that Jenny's story will impact Lyme treatment in this country.

Jenny lives in every success story, in every patient who has fought and won, and in our hearts and minds forever.

Joseph T. Joseph, M. D.
Hermitage, PA

AUTHOR'S NOTE

On December 12, 1996, Meagan died following an automobile accident near Ada, Ohio.

OTHER RESOURCES

ORGANIZATIONS

The Lyme Disease Foundation
One Financial Plaza, Hartford, CT 06103
(800) 886-LYME, Fax: 860-525-TICK
lymefind@aol.com

American Lyme Disease Foundation, Inc.
Mill Pond Offices
293 Route 100, Somers, N.Y. 10589
(914) 277-6970
Fax: (914) 277-6974
Inquire@aldf.com

National Institute of Allergy and Infectious Diseases (NIAID)
National Institute of Health (NIH)
Office of Communications
31 Center Drive MSC 2520 Building 31
Room 7A03 Bethesda, MD 20892-2520
http://www.aamc.org/research/adhocgp/niaid.htm
(301) 496-5717

Centers for Disease Control and Prevention (CDC)
Voice Information System
(404) 332-4555

or

(CDC) National Center for Infectious Diseases
Division of Vector-Borne Infectious Diseases
Atlanta, Georgia 30333
www.cdc.gov.ncidod/ncid.htm

INTERNET SITES

Lyme Disease Network
http://www.lymenet.org/
43 Winton Road
New Brunswick, NJ 08816

The Lyme Disease Network of New Jersey
www.lymenet.com

BOOKS

Coping with Lyme Disease
Denise Lang
Henry Holt and Company

Everything You Need to Know About Lyme Disease
Karen Vanderhoof-Forschner
John Wiley & Sons, Inc.

Protect Yourself from Lyme Disease
Diana Benzaia
Dell Publishing
Special Sales Department

The Widening Circle:
A Lyme Disease Pioneer Tells Her Story
Polly Murrary
St. Martins Press

STATE LYME DISEASE SUPPORT GROUPS

Contact your state health department for support groups.